W9-BSD-936

SUBURBAN GOSPEL

SUBURBAN GOSPEL

Mark Beaver

[A MEMOIR]

HUB CITY PRESS
SPARTANBURG, SC

Copyright © 2016
Mark Beaver

Chapters of this book have previously appeared, in slightly different form, in *Memoir* ("Boys and Sex"); *Gulf Coast* ("Addressee Unknown"); *Tampa Review* ("Lone Baritone"); *storySouth* ("0 & 8"); *Fugue* ("Hazzard County, GA"); *Southeast Review* ("Soul Patrol"); *Third Coast* ("Taxidermy"); *Ninth Letter* ("The Badmobile"); *Blood Orange Review* ("Roadkill"); and *Crazyhorse* ("Benediction").

Book Design: Meg Reid
Cover Illustration: Lily Knights
Proofreaders: Beth Ely, Deborah McAbee, Rachel Richardson
Printed in Dexter, MI by Thomson-Shore

Library of Congress Cataloging-in-Publication Data

Beaver, Mark, 1968-
Suburban gospel : a memoir / by Mark Beaver.
pages cm
ISBN 9781938235191 (alk. paper) —
ISBN 978-1-891885-79-2 (ebook)
1. Childhood and youth—Biography.
2. Baptists—United States—Biography.
1. Title.
  BX6495.B425 A3 2016
  286/.1092—dc23
LC record available at http://lccn.loc.gov/2015032748

186 West Main St.
Spartanburg, SC 29306
1.864.577.9349

www.hubcity.org
www.twitter.com/hubcitypress

IN MEMORY OF MY FATHER,
DEWEY L. BEAVER

CONTENTS

Hello, how are you? I'm fine, 'cause I know the Lord is coming soon.

—PRINCE

INVOCATION

When the deacons at our Bible Belt church cued up a horror flick aimed at dramatizing Hell according to the apocalyptic book of *Revelation*, I figured I'd better get right with God, and soon.

Somebody killed the lights, plunging the sanctuary into darkness. The reel-to-reel tapes commenced spinning; then came the rattle of the projector and the flicker of light and suddenly you could smell the sulfur oozing throughout the room, see the sparks raining down, feel the temperature rise when the Devil tossed another log on the blaze.

This was the Atlanta suburbs. This was 1975: the heyday of horror, the decade of *The Exorcist, Texas Chainsaw Massacre,* and *Carrie.* Saddled with a shoestring budget, the filmmakers had resorted to pilfering every eerie cast of light and blood-curdling soundtrack for a sacred purpose. It was October, the bewitching season, and the weather had begun to turn, a chill wind rustling the leaves on the trees. But the temperature inside our church seemed suddenly to spike, as though someone had helped ol' Lucifer stoke the furnace.

I was seven years old, a small boy with a big head, prone to cowlicks, chapped lips, and bruises of undetermined origin. My pockets bulged and sagged with all the luggage of boyhood—bubblegum, baseball cards, and rocks. Which is to say I had very little inkling I was a putrid sinner in desperate need of redemption and could die at any moment and spend forever roasting on a spit in Hades.

I vividly recall only one scene from the film: a man lying on his back, cinched in torment, crying out for water and for anyone within earshot to loose him from his suffering. All around him, other lost souls languished in various poses of misery. There was much moaning, mourning, and of course gnashing of teeth. The camera zoomed in on the man, lingering on a solitary tear rolling down his cheek. My own face went flush. My ears burned. Fidgeting in my pew, I wanted to help the man—to reach across that impassable gap from my world to his and offer a sliver of ice to soothe his parched tongue. But as the Voice of Doom narrator was quick to remind us viewers, it was too late. *This misery will endure forever*, the Voice explained. The victim had already sealed his fate. He'd made an irrevocable choice.

In order to convey the timelessness of eternity, the Voice asked us to draw upon our imaginations. "Picture a mosquito flying around the earth," he commanded, his tone guttural with Old Testament-style authority. "Picture him, that common pest, circling the globe, over and over. See him flap his wings and chip away at the dust till he whittles the crust to its very core—to a ball tiny enough to hold in the palm of your hand. Consider how many millions of years of human history such a task would take to complete." Then, after a pause long enough to allow us to ponder a timespan so incomprehensible, the hammer: "That, dear sinner, is one second in eternity."

Well.

After the service, we headed to the Long John Silver's. As we waited out the line in the drive-through, a preacher shouted through the static on the AM radio in Dad's Chevy Malibu. Then, on the ride home, the car reeking with the smell of deep-fried fish, I asked my parents how I could go about avoiding spending the rest of forever in such a dismal place as I'd glimpsed tonight.

"Gotta get Saved," they told me.

"Saved from what?" I asked.

"Why, eternal hellfire."

They each had their redemption stories. Children of the Great Depression, my parents knew tribulation. After a hardscrabble upbringing in the hills of north Georgia where his mama's chatter about Jesus must have seemed less pertinent than the next ear of corn waiting to be shucked, Dad met manhood by huddling in frozen foxholes in Korea, listening for enemy movement and ducking gunfire. He survived his tour of duty and returned home, where he settled in Atlanta, took a wife, and finally heeded his mama's longstanding advice to fear the Lord. One night, at the behest of a group of churchgoers conducting what they called *visitation* in local homes, he dropped to his knees in his own living room and recited 1 Corinthians 2:9 before rising to his feet, Born Again. With those words, he became a devout believer whose first act as a Christian was to give up cigarettes—cold turkey—when a deacon's wife took offense at the smell. Nicotine had not passed his lips since. And effective immediately, he meant to apply his new life philosophy. On his postal route, where he worked ten-hour days with a burlap sack of junk mail slung over his shoulder, he soon came upon a boy shoeless in wintertime. Inspired by his newfound faith, he bought a pair of sneakers and promptly delivered them to the boy and his family along with their regular mail.

Mom had her own catalog of woes. She had endured a nightmare childhood with an alcoholic father who drank paint thinner when he couldn't get a fix of the real stuff. She never invited friends to her shotgun house in the Cabbagetown neighborhood on Atlanta's east side for fear her father would burst through the front door loaded with bad liquor and worse intentions and contaminate the whole house with his rage. Which probably explains why she claimed the highlight of her academic career had been her election to the Safety Patrol—a post that circumstance forced her to vacate when her mother stepped into a hole in the yard and snapped her shinbone, requiring her to quit school to take care of her baby sister, Elaine. Mom might have graduated early, but she had failed algebra; so she returned to the school next fall and finally turned her tassel a year later than her classmates. By age twenty-two she had overcome poverty, neglect, and abuse in one fell swoop by marrying a teetotaler with a respectable job, officially diagnosing herself as Nervous, and finding a measure of peace in the arms of a more loving Heavenly Father.

So they knew their way to the cross, my parents, and the words to seal the deal. It was a matter of faith, they explained to me. No deeds could complete the transaction. Only accepting God's grace could wipe away the fundamental sinfulness that was every man's burden as a result of simply being born human.

That night in the car, they told me about what they called the Age of Accountability. "When a boy gets a certain number of years," they explained, "he knows the difference between right and wrong. It's clear as day—it's like black and white. Once he knows that difference, the boy's got a choice right there. He can do the right thing, or he can go the other way and do wrong. It's up to him, you see."

I was absorbing all this critical information from the back seat of the Malibu. Dad kept checking the rearview mirror to see whether their words were sinking in. Mom turned sideways and strained against her seat belt to connect with me face to face and emphasize the gravity of the moment.

"Once the boy's old enough to make that choice, then he's accountable. He's responsible, you understand. All the choices he makes, they're on him. He can't say he didn't know. And he can't make no bigger decision than between Heaven and Hell."

I asked if I was that age yet.

"There's not a definite age," they told me. "Nothing in God's Word about a cut-off point. It's different for different people. Some folks understand pretty quick-like, but others—well, they take a while. We reckon you've figured it out."

This much was clear: If I was old enough to be accountable, then I could die right now and start suffering for the choice I made. I thought about that mosquito flapping his wings. I thought about holding the earth's core in my hand. I thought about that man in the movie lying prone on his back among the coals hissing and spitting like bacon grease. Clearly I did not want to go anywhere near that forlorn destination. I asked my parents what I needed to do to be Saved.

That night in my dad's car, in that short journey of three miles from the Long John Silver's to our brick ranch on King Arthur Drive, they led me through what they called the Sinner's Prayer. "Jesus," I said, repeating their words, "I'm a sinner. I believe you died on the cross for my sins. I'm ready to accept your grace. I'm ready to be Born Again."

We finished the prayer and said amen. Opening my eyes, I asked my parents what else I needed to do. "That's all there is to it," Mom said. "That's everything," Dad said.

As I blinked the world into focus, it took on new character. Everything blazed with Glory. That strip of Highway 5, where we passed the Dunkin' Donuts, the K-Mart, the Gas-n-Go, and all the other signs of civilization shining in the grainy dusk of autumn, glows in my memory now as though we were traveling through a celestial city.

Soon I would learn that, according to our church's creed, I could not become an official member without getting baptized, too. But I was only seven, and a bashful boy, and the thought of standing in front of our whole congregation, even with their arms outspread to welcome me, was more than I could pony up to at the time. So I settled for salvation. My parents assured me that, baptism or no, if Jesus were to return tonight, he would claim me as one of his own. "He's written your name in the Book of Life," Mom told me that night at bedtime.

And once your name is etched on those pages, nothing— nothing on earth, nothing above or below—can ever erase it.

FOR THE NEXT SEVERAL YEARS, acting the part of a good Baptist boy took little effort. Contrary to all I'd heard about Adam, Eve, and their legacy of Original Sin, it came natural. I memorized the names of the sixty-six books of the Bible in order. Sang in the children's choir. Participated in what our Sunday school teachers called sword drills, where we raced through the gilded pages of our Good Book—our 'Sword of the Lord'— to locate verses ahead of our competitors. I attended Vacation Bible School. Ate the spaghetti dinners in the Fellowship Hall. Dropped the dollar my parents gave me for the purpose into the offering plate. I paid rapt attention to all the stories of plagues and floods and crumbling walls of Jericho, all the parables of mustard seeds, talents, and prodigal sons. In musty Sunday school classrooms I completed arts and crafts projects: with yarn and glue I made a cardboard sign proclaiming *The Lord is nigh unto all who call upon Him*; with clay I molded a book and used a nail to carve *Holy Bible* into it.

On Sunday mornings I joined Dad when he and his fellow deacons convened in the pastor's office, where under a painting of a honey-haired, blue-eyed Jesus wearing his bloody crown of thorns, Pastor Davis led us in prayer, asking God to bless this Sabbath Day for His glory and honor. These deacons were men who during the week wore uniforms with their names stitched across the breast pocket. Men who spent their Sunday mornings using Octagon soap to scrub away all the grime and grease that had accumulated under their fingernails during the week. A dozen men regarded as the disciples for this congregation. They called each other "brother." Even as a boy, seven-, eight-, and nine-years-old, I understood the privilege of standing among them. It was like sneaking behind a backstage curtain—seeing all these men responsible for our church's mission circled up and inviting God to dwell among them.

Inevitably two of them would slide over to allow me to nudge inside, my head grazing their belt buckles, as if they knew I belonged there. It would have been hard for me to imagine, then, a future in which I wouldn't be part of that circle.

A NEARBY BAPTIST CHURCH sponsored a Christian school whose sports teams called themselves the Crusaders. But my parents sent me the public route—not only because they didn't want tuition bills, but more so because we lived in the suburbs. How much of a foothold could the Devil claim in a community of brick ranches nestled among swaths of farmland twenty miles west of Atlanta, sixty miles east of Anniston, and right in the middle of nowhere? Our whole town was saturated in Christianity anyway, so much so that even high school football games on Friday nights didn't kick off until a local preacher delivered an invocation—a tradition that continued, by the way, until 1986 when a kid in the marching band refused to bow his head, his father protested a theocratic union of church and state, and together they sued the school district. The boy, as I recall, wore thick, tinted glasses. His sandy hair featured a birthmark, a splotch of white near the crown of his head. Neither he nor I would call us friends, but he had been inside my house when we were younger boys. Once, some of the neighborhood kids joined us for impromptu wrestling matches in the den. The boy, I remember now, had a vicious headlock. Maybe that maneuver foreshadowed the kind of tenacious fight he and his father would put up in the future. His protest stirred up a national story. It drew more attention to our town than anything we'd ever experienced. In an interview with the local newspaper, the boy claimed, "A couple of callers have threatened to burn down our house. Others have threatened to wrap my saxophone around my head." In its legal defense, the school district noted that local clergymen had been praying before games since 1947. This was tradition. This was who we were. Representatives defended the invocations by claiming they "satisfy the genuine, good faith wishes on the part of the majority of the citizens of [the county] to publicly express support for Protestant Christianity." The school district resisted the family doggedly, but finally in 1989, after the boy and I both graduated, the Supreme Court ruled the pre-game prayers unconstitutional.

Nowadays, there's just a moment of silence.

I WAS SO IMMERSED in this corner of Christendom that, even as my age crept into double digits, my rebellion consisted only of sins modest in scale. I stole a GI Joe doll from the local K-Mart. I puffed cigarettes amidst the skeletons of dead cornstalks bordering our subdivision. I adopted a vulgar vocabulary on par with the neighborhood boys'. In short: I stayed the straight and narrow. On Sundays Pastor Davis did a bang-up job of clarifying the difference between right and wrong, and the Christian Walk seemed mostly a matter of doing the one and avoiding the other.

Then a strange thing happened. A thing I knew was coming, all right, but had no idea how to navigate when it arrived. An event that would transform me, as it transforms us all—one that would change my body, mind, and this Baptist boy's understanding of everything he knew about his rightful place in the universe.

I turned thirteen.

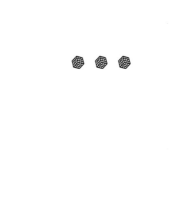

SUPER**WOW!**

S and, surf, and salvation: for months, the youth ministers at our church had been guaranteeing this holy trinity on our upcoming trip to an evangelical camp called SuperWOW! Brother Bill and Brother Dan promised sunshine, ocean waves, and blue, blue water. Bonfires and sing-alongs and heart-to-hearts under a crescent moon. They promised rock bands with light shows and a Christian message; speakers who could really *relate* to teenagers because they understood what we were going through; and fellowship with other believers from all across the Bible Belt. They promised us God.

Before hitting the road and commencing our journey to Jekyll Island on the Georgia coast, we posed for a group photo alongside the bus. It was the summer of 1981 so we were sporting Jams and OP shirts, Wayfarers and Swatches, Vans and

Chucks. As our parents played shutterbug with their Polaroid OneSteps, we slung our arms around each others' shoulders and squinted against the morning sun and said *Jesus* in unison when we smiled. Then we climbed aboard.

After we filled the seats, Brother Bill asked us to bow our heads. He stood in the bus aisle and said a prayer for our safe travels to SuperWOW! As he asked God to watch over us and help us grow in our Christian Walk, I was already imagining the setting. I pictured a veritable buffet of belles from places like Tallahassee, Chattanooga, and Birmingham with the Good News in their hearts and honey in their drawls. I saw myself cavorting under a glittering sky with girls who said their prayers at night and knew John 3:16 by heart. "Gracious Father, use us as soldiers in your service," Brother Bill was saying, "and let our lights shine into a dark world. We offer our hearts, our minds, and our bodies to your service."

On this last point—*our bodies*—he placed special emphasis, echoing the sentiments of Pastor Davis, whose Sunday morning sermon had included several direct appeals to the lot of us teenagers slumping in the back pew to resist the sins of the flesh. Pastor Davis had quoted the Apostle Paul: "Live by the Spirit," he implored us, "and do not gratify the desires of the flesh. For what the flesh desires is opposed to the Spirit, and what the Spirit desires is opposed to the flesh." He said our bodies would betray us every time. He said our flesh was weak, but our spirit strong. The body we needed to concern ourselves with was the body of Christ. "This," he said, his arms spreading wide enough to encompass everyone in the sanctuary, "*this* is the body of Christ!"

Now, Brother Bill was saying, "In Jesus' name we pray," which we knew was the signal for all of us to say amen aloud. He nodded to Terry, a middle-aged deacon who served as our bus driver. Terry tightened his grip on the steering wheel and checked his mirrors. He shifted into gear; the engine shuddered and roared to life as he gave it some gas. Our parents stood waving and blowing kisses as our bus pulled away with brimstone spewing from the tailpipe. Jekyll Island lay 300 miles to the southeast.

AFTER THE SIX-HOUR TRIP, we arrived to find a cluster of stubby redwood cabins, a cloudy swimming pool, a volleyball court, and a view of the Atlantic across a busy highway. We registered, claimed our bunks in the cabins, dumped our belongings. We hadn't even had time to get sand between our toes before we were filing into an auditorium the size of a gymnasium to see hundreds of other kids already assembled on pews. A glittering banner, wide as the stage, welcomed us to SuperWOW!

As we were finding our seats, a man strolled onstage and grabbed the microphone. He told us his name was Rick Stanley. "Reverend Rick, you can call me." He possessed cowboy boots, a tan straight out of a Coppertone commercial, and platinum-blonde hair that made him a dead-ringer for the wrestler Nature Boy Ric Flair, who I regularly saw back home on Ted Turner's Superstation. As if on cue, Reverend Rick acknowledged this resemblance in his opening remarks. "Me and the Nature Boy even share the same first name!" he said. "And you better believe I'd wrestle the Devil himself to see you come to Jesus this week."

But soon we discovered that this guy's real identity trumped even the famous wrestler angle: Reverend Rick was the stepbrother of Elvis Presley. "I'm kin to the King!" he declared. Elvis had been dead for several years now, but none of us had ever been in the company of somebody related to anybody so famous. Even my parents, whose musical tastes ran toward staid church hymns and cloying gospel groups like the Inspirations and the Florida Boys, owned an Elvis record—albeit a bland collection of syrupy ballads containing none of the sin and sensuality that had upended Western Civilization and made him the King in the first place.

It was becoming crystal clear how SuperWOW! got its exclamation point. It deserved it. This was no lame Christian camp. Reverend Rick was no blue-haired lady wearing saggy knee-stockings and heavy rouge, crooking fingers toward us and warning us that hell is hot. A current of spiritual energy was circulating through the crowd, tapping each of us on our ripe, red hearts, sweeping us up in a wave of raw emotion we'd not felt since, say, Couples Night at the skating rink.

Reverend Rick spent the next hour delivering his personal testimony—explaining how he had lived the fast life right alongside his famous brother, riding go-carts at Graceland and hop-scotching the globe to praise and adoration everywhere they went. He worked security for Elvis, which meant he was part of Elvis' *posse*. And the drugs—the drugs were everywhere. Women, too—all of Elvis' rejects or hand-me-downs. "I was the youngest member of the Memphis Mafia," he proudly claimed. "I was *it*, you hear what I'm saying?" Reverend Rick's voice pulsed with adrenaline—he was leaping from one escapade to another while hardly taking a breath—and we were mesmerized, as though all of this had happened just yesterday and he was going to escort Elvis from behind that *SuperWOW!* banner any moment now.

Reverend Rick's voice hit a crescendo when he summarized everything he had already told us about who he was at age seventeen: strung out, oversexed, under-supervised—in short, "I was flat-out *depraved*," he said. He paused for dramatic effect, letting us soak up all that beautiful debauchery.

But when he spoke again, we could hear the shame lurking in his tone. His body seemed to deflate; that golden mane took on a pallid hue. Elvis' life had spiraled out of control, yes sir, and Rick Stanley's right along with it. We now remembered where this tale had been headed all along. The climax was part of our national consciousness: the King, his bloodstream laced with barbiturates, slumped over on his toilet, gone.

The gist of Reverend Rick's message to us: "Young people, I've known two kings during my lifetime, but I'm here to tell you, only one of them is the King of Kings." It was Jesus who had helped him overcome the personal loss that everybody else experienced as global tragedy. It was Jesus who pulled him through the booze, the drugs, the meaninglessness in the aftermath of his stepbrother's demise. Reverend Rick pointed out that Elvis was a good Christian man—he insisted on playing a gospel song in every concert—but when surrounded by all the fame, well, he lost track of his priorities. It could happen to anybody. "It could happen to you," he told us.

Elvis' death was Reverend Rick's wake-up call. It became his catalyst for wanting to lead souls to Christ.

"It's only the grace of God that allows me to stand before you today," he said. "I'm a witness to Jesus' mercy, amen. And you want to know the coolest thing? You want to know what really *rocks* about Jesus? Folks, you can experience that grace too, if you're willing. If you'll just accept him into your heart."

Then Reverend Rick commenced an altar call. He invited everyone to make a commitment to Christ. "Don't wait till our last day on Friday," he warned, his voice tremulous. "Friday might never come. We aren't promised tomorrow, much less a whole week. Tomorrow, my friends, could be too late." An organist kick-started "Amazing Grace." The slow chord changes underscored Reverend Rick's plea. The houselights went down. The stage sat bathed in light, a heavenly life raft floating in a sea of darkness.

The invitation had barely been extended before SuperWOW!ers began filing out of the pews, making their way down the aisles in droves.

One of our own, a pretty girl named Angela Jacobs, her eyes glassy, tears welling, was the first of our group to head toward the altar. Soon enough, others joined her. Stacy, Jeffrey, Laura.

Kevin, Max, Elaine. Reverend Rick welcomed Angie, his arms outspread, his platinum-blonde hair now glowing again like a halo in the glare of the spotlights. Above all the lost assembled at the altar, the *SuperWOW!* banner rippled like a flag unfurled.

But singing yet another refrain of "Amazing Grace," I stood my ground, clutching the pew in front of me. I mouthed the words, but something akin to jealousy was simmering in my gut, because I could not join Angie Jacobs and all those other lost souls laying their burdens at the foot of the Old Rugged Cross. As the hymn played, I remembered that night when I was seven years old, the horror flick, the swelter inside that sanctuary—all sulfur and sparks and *Revelation.*

As much as I wanted to go, I was bound to stay right here, shifting anxiously from foot to foot.

I was already Saved.

BUT THERE'S THIS: Miracles were starting to happen. It was now Wednesday. It was everybody's favorite part of the day, Fun in the Son Time, which translated to a couple of unscripted hours outdoors. We were at the pool. And it was there, under the blazing sun of the Georgia coast, the Lord really began moving in mysterious ways. I had always been suspicious of chatter about Jesus raising Lazarus from the dead and all the other miracles until now, when another sort of supernatural event happened right here at SuperWOW!: a girl wanted to meet me.

My buddy Johnny and I were working on our sunburns when a vision on par with holy apparitions approached. Fine as one of Charlie's Angels, she was wearing mirrored sunglasses and a one-piece job with spaghetti straps and a little blue bow. But as it turned out, she was just a messenger. Without offering her name, she directed our attention across the pool.

"See that girl over there?" she said.

Across the way lay a blonde in a pink bikini. She was reclining on a chaise lounge, her bronze legs crossed at the ankles, and sporting mirrored sunglasses that made it utterly impossible to discern whether she was looking at us. She was a safe distance from the riot of the pool, bathing inside a fountain of sunshine belonging only to her.

"Her name's Tara," the messenger informed us. "Tara's from Tennessee." A sly grin broke across her features. "Tennessee Tara," she said, "would like to meet you."

"Me?" Johnny asked.

"Uh-uh," the messenger said. She pointed in my direction. "That one."

Johnny immediately began inquiring, in a rather shameless and desperate manner, whether this was a package deal.

Meanwhile, I was expending a great deal of psychic energy trying to decide how I might give the impression this was a regular occurrence. I couldn't summon any semblance of composure. And when this little Tennessee Tara smiled and sprinkled her fingers in a wave so cute it broke my heart, I lost all sense of decorum. I wasn't quite sure who I was. I felt dizzy, sick to my stomach—what my mother would call *a little peaked*. "Dude," Johnny said. "Check yourself." He was practically forced to carry me across the pool to meet this exquisite girl. The journey seemed to unfold in slow motion as I contemplated what on earth this rare species of female could have seen in me. Hard as I tried to vanquish the image, I couldn't help picturing what she was seeing as I approached: a scrawny boy whose naked torso resembled, as Johnny had jibed just moments ago, "a pirate's treasure. It's a...*sunken chest!*" Once he deposited me beside her, he paused only long enough to congratulate me before dismissing himself to pursue amorous adventures with the messenger.

SO WE WERE ALONE, this girl and I. She curled the strands of her hair around an index finger. She said hey.

I returned her greeting but pretended to be distracted by an ongoing game of Marco Polo in the pool.

We grew old together waiting for the next line of conversation. Finally, I said, "Your name's Tara?"

She nodded.

"Tennessee, right?"

"Uh-huh."

I could itemize the particulars: the honey-tinted skin; the mole on her cheek; the peach fuzz on the nape of her neck. But this Tennessee Tara was greater than the sum of her parts. She was the incarnation of all the lyrics on the radio—she was Jessie's girl, a Queen of Hearts, she had Bette Davis eyes. She was, in SuperWOW! vernacular, a *blessing*.

There, on matching chaise lounge chairs, a courtship transpired. I can only guess at what the breakthrough might have been, but somehow we made conversation. The highlight occurred as Tara and I stood amazed at the wonders of geography, realizing that Georgia and Tennessee are bordering states. We were astonished by how downright ordained this union seemed.

But SuperWOW! romances, we knew, had to take flight quickly. As Reverend Rick reminded us, God doesn't promise us tomorrow, much less a whole week. Our lives are conducted to the score of a ticking clock. It was Wednesday. We were already on borrowed time.

So Tara and I tried to hit the highlights of what would be a normal courtship and simply skipped all the red tape—such as getting to know each other. We climbed off those pool lounges and loitered beyond the watchful eyes of those charged with our supervision, down to the beach, where we took a lazy stroll as the surf spilled in and washed over our feet. In these few moments, as we made our way along the shoreline, we were burnished by the sun, glowing like ghosts, our very souls back-lit by recessed lighting—and the red burn that would scold us during the night was, in this flurry of moments, only a celestial shine. Tara glowed with sweat. Beyond her name and home state, this ethereal beauty was a stranger to me, but in her mystery she became precisely who I wanted her to be. She was Tara, she was from Tennessee, and she was a churchgoing girl: she was the summation of all my Baptist boy dreams.

We wandered down the shore, inhaling the pungent elixir of sand and salt, meandering toward an ancient pier that jutted into the ocean. Every step brought us nearer the bright and shining sun glowing in the distance and showering the horizon with spangles of golden light.

The tide rolled in, white foam coiling around our ankles. It rolled out, the sand shifting. Tennessee Tara seized this phenomenon of nature as an opportunity to stumble against my shoulder. An electrical current surged between us. Whatever was in her was now in me, transmitted through the first touch of our skins.

Somewhere along the way I reached out and took her hand.

When we arrived at the pier, we slipped under the boardwalk and into its shade. Our skin adjusted to the coolness, our eyes to the new grade of light. Overhead the wood creaked with the weight of footfalls. We knelt in the sand. There, we fell against one another. I felt my face drain of blood as Tennessee Tara split her lips with her pink tongue and leaned toward my mouth, and I barely had time to rehearse the logistics in my head, to arrange my technique, to game plan, before our lips collided and she probed my teeth with her tongue as though swiping off the tartar. It was a kiss, all right: my first. My heart fish-flopped and started ticking double-time. I was so paralyzed by the question of what to do next that I just sat there, a victim of lockjaw. My hands rested limply in my lap. My mouth slid feebly off hers.

But gradually I caught on, and we found something resembling a rhythm—until finally we slipped away from each other, a boy and a girl dumbstruck by the pure magnitude of the moment. God most definitely was good.

There was some small talk. An awkward, ill-timed joke or two. Eventually we climbed to our feet, wiped the sand from our swimsuits, and started back.

How long were we gone? The clock had lost all relevance. Time was something for mere mortals to trifle with. The sun had risen and fallen a thousand times, far as we knew or cared. My Tennessee Tara and I, we weren't subject to those rules anymore.

We returned well after Fun in the Son Time had ended. The pool now sat vacant, the surface placid and deep as the sky. Lights glowed inside the redwood cabins. The fraternizing between youth groups had ended and each church had split apart from the masses to experience Group Devotion Time alone and undistracted. Tara and I promised to see each other again tonight. But for now we had to scurry to rejoin our friends. I wanted to thank her—for the kiss under the pier, for the mole on her cheek, for that lilt in her accent when she said *Tennessee*.

But I was at SuperWOW!, and God was indeed good, so on the way to the cabin where my group waited, I found myself uttering aloud the same word over and over. It was a word teenage boys don't use unless their voices are dripping with sarcasm, but today mine was empty of all irony, all self-consciousness, and I was simply thankful for what had come to pass. "Hallelujah," I kept saying. "*Hallelujah.*"

INSIDE, I FOUND MY friends composing skits aimed at helping them make Christian decisions. I knew the drill: after rehearsing, groups of four would present their skits to the others, to be followed by intense discussion about peer pressure and what the Bible says about each situation. But when Brother Bill saw that I had arrived, he abruptly broke away from the group he was helping. He pulled me aside, wedged me into a corner of the room. I hadn't even had an opportunity to savor the idea that at this exact moment, in another of these redwood cabins, a girl named Tara was obsessing over me with the same single-minded fixation that I was experiencing, before he began telling me that Brother Dan, the other youth minister, was out there right now searching for me. "We've been *worried sick*," he said—a term I was used to hearing from my mother, not this twentysomething seminary guy, so devout *and* so cool, who strummed an acoustic guitar, wore a cross pendant around his neck, and popped the collar of his polo so that it stood straight up. During his chastising lecture Brother Bill said "man" a lot, wanting to maintain our informal camaraderie, but he made it clear that I'd disappointed him—the past hour of my life could be used as fodder for a skit about making Christian decisions.

And now here came Brother Dan, returning empty-handed of course, flustered enough to take the Lord's name in vain. He expelled a sigh of relief when he saw me, but he seemed even more agitated than Brother Bill. "We might as well have sent out an APB on you, man." How would he explain to my parents if I'd been hurt? If I'd disappeared altogether? "Not everybody at Jekyll Island is a Christian," Brother Dan said. "Where in the world were you?"

There was desperation in his voice—as though he sensed that SuperWOW! was not WOWing me appropriately. I didn't tell them I'd been with a girl named Tara. And I didn't tell them what I believed was the truth: *God* had been supervising us the whole time. He'd arranged our meeting and subsequent rendezvous. "I lost track of time," I said.

Still simmering, they stuck me into a group, where I sat guilt-ridden and offered only monosyllabic responses to my friends' appeals for me to participate. Ten minutes later I was half-heartedly playing the role of a boy offering to let his struggling classmate copy his answers to a test.

I would win no Oscars for this performance.

AFTER THE SKITS, BROTHER BILL cut the lights and struck a match. Cupping the flame, he lowered it to a candle in the middle of the room. He and Brother Dan grabbed their guitars and told us to circle up. They began strumming, segueing from song to song, all of them folksy and earnest, the lyrics freighted with utmost importance. On the wall the candle flame danced in mysterious, phantasmagorical patterns that seemed to possess more meaning that I could decipher.

This was SuperWOW! and I needed to do something dramatic—something that symbolized I was not the same boy who left home. Something, too, that could absolve me of caving in to the temptations of the flesh, at SuperWOW! of all places, when apparently I should have been *letting my light shine.* Though it was common for people to be Saved multiple times, as though the prior attempts just hadn't taken quite right, I knew I needed to do something else.

While the youth ministers plucked their guitars, the strings squeaking with every chord change, we passed the candle around the circle. When it came to each kid, you were expected to talk about your *feelings*—to reflect on what this time at SuperWOW! had meant to you so far in your Christian Walk. To tell the group what Jesus was saying to you in these quiet moments of revelation away from the distractions of the sinful world. "Lay it all out there," Brother Bill told us. "Set yourself free," Brother Dan advised. If you had a decision to make, you could start by expressing it here, in this safe space, where it was only you, your best friends, and the Holy Spirit.

The candle went around. Some pretty dark confessions came out. Some kids had strayed from the righteous path. Nobody spilled the details, but we could read the subtext. When Devin Pope said he had *drifted away* from Jesus, we knew he'd done the drifting on a cloud of reefer smoke. When Becca Castille said she'd *turned her back* on God, it was because she'd lain on her back with a boyfriend who (rumor had it) dumped her two days after the deflowering.

And when my buddy Johnny said he wasn't sure there was a God…well, we had no idea what he meant.

The cabin fell silent. The room suddenly grew stuffy, unbearably hot and claustrophobic. We looked at Brother Bill and Brother Dan. Surely somewhere in their seminary training they'd been taught how to deal with stubborn disbelief. They, however, glanced at each other with panic-stricken expressions before immediately launching into red alert. The next thirty minutes of Group Devotional Time consisted of trying to convince Johnny that God did in fact exist. "Look at the leaves on the trees, man," Brother Bill was suddenly suggesting. "How can we see all the beauty God created and deny His existence?"

All heads swiveled toward Johnny. He just shrugged.

"And what about love?" Brother Dan offered. "Where do you think love comes from?"

Johnny only stared at the candle flame, his grimace becoming ever more visible in the flickering light.

Some kids joined in then, offering their proof that God presided over everything—the Bible says so, they told Johnny—and what about babies—they're a gift from God, aren't they?—and one girl said "I just *know*, 'cause I feel it in my heart." Angie Jacobs, who had been the first of us to respond to Reverend Rick's altar call at the start of the week, scribbled away in her official Quiet Time devotional notebook, furiously filling the page with looping purple swirls.

Really, Johnny's announcement came as no surprise to me. After Tennessee Tara's friend, the lovely messenger, refused Johnny's overtures, he had slipped into a funk, the hangdog look on his face expressing very little WOW! All week he had been one of the few to resist Reverend Rick's magic—he seemed to possess some rare antidote to the platinum-haired evangelist's appeals that left the rest of us and anxious and repentant. When Reverend Rick told us we were all sinners in need of redemption, Johnny seemed unconcerned. When he told us no one knew the minute or the hour, Johnny fancied himself immortal. He'd always seemed to be *in it but not of it* anyway, drawn more to the chance just to hang out with other kids, do the car washes, sing the songs—everything the church folks called *fellowship*. Nobody had ever seen Johnny's parents, but rumors spread that his father was too much of a drunk to hold a job and that his mother suffered from some kind of debilitating mental illness. Johnny rode the bus to church with his sisters, two hideous girls with his same wiry hair and acne-ridden skin. The trio came for the conversation, for the occasional spaghetti dinners downstairs in the fellowship hall, for the chance to escape their house across the railroad tracks for a few hours on Sundays.

Brother Bill asked Johnny if he had ever talked to God.

Johnny looked around the room. He seemed to be daring anybody to meet his stare. "How many of y'all ever heard God's voice?"

Laura said she had, and Devin, and Karen too.

"Whatever," Johnny said.

I wanted to join the others, the defenders of the faith. I wanted to quote scripture, or cite miraculous interventions, or try to describe what I felt when Brother Bill and Brother Dan plucked those strings and harmonized with their matching tenors. I wanted to tell Johnny I knew these songs by heart, and that when I sang *I want to pass it on*, I believed what I was singing—I really did want to pass it on. I wanted to tell him I had kissed Tennessee Tara, and that on the way back from the pier she had lain her head against my shoulder, and that the surf had washed away every sin we'd ever committed.

I wanted to tell him God was alive and well. Right now, he was inside this very room.

But Johnny kept casting these furtive glances at me, as though he were gauging whether I was going to turn on him, too.

Eventually he grudgingly passed the candle along and various members of our youth group gave stirring descriptions of how the spirit had moved them this week.

When the candle finally came around to me, I just held it for a few moments, staring into the flame, feeling its warmth fan my heart. I searched for words to express some decision I'd made. I thought about Tennessee Tara, and Brother Bill and Brother Dan's scrutiny, and Johnny's contention that there was no God. I recalled Pastor Davis drawing a sharp line between flesh and spirit and encouraging us to crucify the one and live by the other. I remembered the movie I'd seen when I was seven, and the car ride home afterward, and reciting the Sinner's Prayer.

Now, all around me, my friends were swallowing deep gulps of air. The candlelight played on their faces. There were damp eyes, tear-streaked jaws, trembling chins. It came to me then—what I should do. It was so obvious, I wondered why I hadn't thought of it before. I looked up from the candle to find all eyes waiting expectantly for my revelation. I nodded my head to confirm to myself that I had indeed made a decision.

And in a tone of utter conviction I told them my plan: "I want to be baptized."

WHEN GROUP DEVOTION TIME ENDED I burst into the night a new boy with baptism now on my itinerary, but I found my Tennessee Tara had been transformed as well. She was suddenly, well, *distant*—indifferent and cold. She didn't greet me with the smile I expected. She avoided eye contact. Those glossy lips, which I had tasted just a couple of hours before, drooped pale and dry as though withering on the vine. I tried to rationalize her abrupt shift, because SuperWOW! did this to people. It changed us radically from moment to moment, testing our ability to recognize ourselves every time we glanced in the mirror. After all, I was not the same boy Tara last saw, was I?

All the youth groups had crossed the highway to gather on the beach. But down at the waterside Tara commenced a wide orbit away from me and seemed surprised and a little offended when I took her hand ready to pick up where we left off. I had vague plans in my head, sketchy, half-imagined images of us leaning toward each other to brush lips, to taste again that lip gloss that this afternoon blinded my eyes. I was still intoxicated by that illicit mixture of sand, salt, and sweat on her skin. The night was perfect for amorous pursuit. Above us, the stars were bright pinpoints in the night sky. The moon blanketed the sea in a gauzy film of light. Somewhere out there in the darkness waves crashed and churned toward the shore.

But Tara pulled away. She told me her group had been planning a shaving cream fight on the beach since before they left Tennessee. They had water balloons too, and marshmallows for their bonfire on the sand. Maybe tomorrow? she said. She *really* wanted to be with her friends. I said sure, whatever, no problem.

But I was certain she had not forgotten how time operates at SuperWOW! I didn't need to quote Reverend Rick. She knew what this meant. This was what they called *letting them down easy.*

Before climbing on separate buses to go home on Friday, Tara and I would hug and practice the Christian's infinite capacity for hope, exchanging addresses and promises to write. And I'd keep up my end of the bargain, sending a couple of letters that she answered in the most perfunctory of ways, a pen pal at best, signing simply *Tara* when I had written not only *Love* and my name but added *xoxo*. I must have been too earnest and insistent in my profession of love, because eventually she sent a particularly curt letter to suggest that maybe we should write as friends, given the distance between us. And when I wrote back to say I'd been listening to Hall and Oates' "Kiss on My List" over and over because it reminded me of her—had she heard it?—she stopped answering at all.

But tonight we were still at SuperWOW!, and she was romping through the waves with shaving cream smeared in her hair, and I was dawdling down the shoreline, trudging through the sand. The sky, now, looked Bible black. The bonfires glowed like match heads in the distance from where I stood, when I saw myself for what I was: a boy whose Tennessee Tara had decided she'd rather wear shaving cream and fling water balloons than study the ways of desire with him.

WHICH IS NOT TO SAY I abandoned my mission to indulge my carnal interests. On Thursday I found consolation in a strange phenomenon that has characterized romantic relations since biblical times: when a boy gets attention from one girl, others proceed to form a queue.

Freshly Saved, Angie Jacobs had been positively glowing all week, her face flushed with giddy godliness. She had spent the week writing prayers to God in her Quiet Time notebook. In purple ink she offered long, rambling reflections on her new life as a Christian, which she breathlessly shared during Group Devotional Time. She addressed all the letters to God, filling them with exclamation points and dotting the I's with hearts, and signed them *Yours, Angie*. Dark haired and green eyed, her skin tanned a rich brown by our week at Jekyll, Angie served as more than ample compensation. Brother Bill and Brother Dan had already declared that we would be baptized together as soon as we returned home—an announcement that Angie and I interpreted as the will of God. We had been raised on weekly doses of Red Seas' parting, a couple of fish feeding 5,000 hungry bellies, and water turning to wine—so God's orchestrating a little boy-girl action was simply all in a day's work.

When Friday came around, we sat together on the bus ride home, in the back row. With her purple pen, Angie wrote her name on my arm. She adorned the letters with elaborate swirls and elliptical flourishes to create a particularly intricate tattoo. Careful to avoid all appearance of indiscretion, we took turns averting eye contact with Brother Bill and Brother Dan whenever they turned to monitor our behavior. A little handholding, though, was hardly an offense, so she dropped the pen and we clung tightly together, our fingers intertwined, as the miles passed under us and we moved farther and farther away from SuperWOW!

ON SUNDAY MORNING CONGREGANTS packed the pews shoulder-to-shoulder. The organist was playing the prelude. A controlled chatter spread throughout the crowd. In some of the nicer churches I'd visited, the parishioners rolled in a pastel mural featuring the River Jordan for baptismal services. But in ours, the same cross as usual hung above the proceedings, its arms spotlighted by dull, jaundiced bulbs. The pool sat directly below it, behind the choir loft, the blue paint around the drain flecking and peeling. This time in the service had been reserved for weeks, because there was the general understanding that the bus would not return from SuperWOW! without a pack of kids awaiting baptism. Backstage, Angie and I wore paper-thin white robes similar to hospital smocks. Trying to cut the tension, I cracked a lame joke, something about our pastor's performing a hernia check on me. Obligingly, she laughed.

In the Baptist tradition, salvation and baptism usually happen simultaneously. You get Saved, typically in some public fashion where you make your way to the altar, tell the pastor you've made a decision, and face the congregation as he shares with them the good news that you've chosen to join their ranks. Then within days, or maybe a couple of weeks at most, you're baptized and thereby become a full-fledged member of the church. You can take the Lord's Supper, vote on church matters, see your birthday announced in the weekly bulletin. But when I was Saved at age seven, I had been too shy to go public with my decision, and all that mattered at the time was that my eternal salvation had been secured. If Jesus returned that night, he would count me among his number. My parents seemed content to allow God to move me to baptism in his time, which he had done, finally, at SuperWOW!

Now, after the call to worship and a couple of opening songs from the red hymnals with gilded gold lettering on the cover, the baptisms began. Pastor Davis led us one-by-one into the pool. Angie waited right in front of me in line. Soon it was her turn. She descended the steps into the water. Pastor Davis lifted his left hand toward the heavens. *Professing your sins*, he said, *believing in the sacrifice of our Lord and Savior Jesus Christ upon the cross at Calvary, and asking Him to enter your heart, Angela Jacobs, I baptize you in the name of the Father, of the Son, and of the Holy Spirit.* As Angie pinched her nose, Pastor Davis' left hand swooped in to touch her forehead while his right steadied her between the shoulder blades, and he leaned her back until she slipped beneath. The water closed around Angie. Her sheer paper robe billowed under the surface. Her hair haloed out around her.

A moment later she was raised a new girl.

A child of God.

The preacher held Angie's hand as she climbed out of the pool. When she reached the top step I witnessed something that would not only distract me from the sacred task at hand, but seal itself inside the deepest recesses of my memory for the rest of my life: Angie's wet baptismal robe was clinging to her body like a second skin. The water cleaved to her hips in such a way that I could detect the perfect contoured outline of her panties. They were white, with tiny red hearts.

Amen, the congregation uttered.

Out of sight of the onlookers, someone welcomed Angie with a wide beach towel. Angie wrapped the towel tightly around her body and tucked it between her breasts. She ran her fingers through her hair and commenced wringing water from the strands.

Praise God, Pastor Davis said.

Then he turned toward me, and smiled. He rested one hand on my shoulder. "Your turn," he whispered. He invited me toward the pool and I stepped down into the water. It felt as warm as the baths my mother had drawn for me as a boy, and a whiff of chlorine filled my nose. Pastor Davis began telling the congregation my story—that I'd been Saved sometime back, but it was this morning, after such a blessed week at SuperWOW!, that I was choosing to follow Jesus' example and make my decision to follow him public for all to bear witness. Somewhere out there in the crowd my mom and dad were watching me, but I kept my stare fixed straight ahead.

After the service ended, Angie and I, and the rest of the baptizees, would stand at the foot of the altar while the congregation filed by offering the right hand of fellowship, welcoming us to the body of Christ. They congratulated us. They said they were so proud. When they took my hand, they called me their brother. "Brother Mark," they said, and the name sounded right and true. They told me I had done well—that tonight there was rejoicing and celebration in Heaven.

But that was all to come. Still in the pool, now Pastor Davis was lifting his left hand, channeling the power of God. He again began reciting the words. *Professing your sins, believing in the sacrifice of our Lord and Savior Jesus Christ*...He placed his right hand between my shoulder blades. He nodded his head, gesturing for me to pinch my nose.

Maybe Jesus was entertaining other thoughts when John the Baptist welcomed him into the River Jordan. I imagine he was preoccupied with the spirit descending from heaven like a dove and alighting on him, and with listening for the voice of God to tell him that he was his son, the Beloved, with whom he was well pleased.

But there she was—Angela Jacobs, in all her glory, her glistening body tucked inside a terrycloth towel, a sun-kissed thigh splitting the fabric, water puddling around her toes.

In that moment I was confused about a lot of things but absolutely certain of one: Jesus, if he really was human, if the blood pulsed red inside him, surely he understood.

I couldn't look away.

BOYS & SEX

S oon the new school year began, and I came home one day
with a permission form requiring a parent's signature. Our
school's science department was announcing its upcoming Sex Education unit. According to this paperwork, teachers
would separate students by gender and present *an age-appropri-
ate overview of the process of human reproduction.* But the form
offered two boxes—consent or decline. Parents whose belief
systems conflicted with the proposed subject matter could opt
out, and the school would provide their kids with an *alternative
enriching educational experience.* Which I knew likely consisted
of watching the Chief Joseph *I Will Fight No More Forever* video
for maybe the seventh time. Instead of telling my parents about
the form, I simply left it on the kitchen table with the wish that

they would see it, give their consent, sign it, and shove it in my notebook to return to school without any conversation.

None of us wanted conversation.

My father was a Baptist deacon, my mother a Sunday school teacher. They had broached nothing resembling The Talk, and already I understood that one would not be forthcoming. They'd left instruction in all matters related to sex to Pastor Davis, who from the pulpit condemned adultery and fornication with equal disdain. Marriage was the only permissible place for sex, so without a ring and a license we didn't need to know anything about it. Which left me with foul armpits, a series of wet dreams, and absolutely no idea how any of these changes affected my standing with Jesus Christ.

This was 1981. America had just booted Jimmy Carter out of Washington, along with his peanuts, sweaters, and accent. Though Carter was our fellow Georgian and the first professed evangelical to hold the office, even Dad had voted against him—because he believed Carter had betrayed his Born Again brethren by refusing to stand up for family values. Jimmy was a sellout, Dad said. He hemmed and hawed about abortion. He interfered with the tax-exempt status for Christian schools. He seemed more interested in pleasing his party than acting on his convictions. And of course he confessed to *Playboy* that he lusted after women and committed adultery in his heart. So now Ronnie Reagan was making himself at home in the Oval Office, Jerry Falwell's face was everywhere in the media, and his Moral Majority was busily redeeming the nation's soul. Which meant that parents like mine were getting in the habit of saying NO with gusto.

Our church found all manner of ways to practice dissent. An example: As Jimmy's presidency was sinking, word got around the evangelical world that ABC was set to pilot a new sitcom called *Soap* that showcased perverse sexuality, including one of TV's first openly gay characters. Pastor Davis urged congregants to write letters protesting *Soap*, which they did dutifully, flooding ABC's offices despite the fact that none of us had actually seen the show. Of course, this firestorm of controversy created the predictable result—the show immediately swept its time slot and became the season's debut success story. Undeterred, we interpreted this turn of events as yet another sign that God's people needed to get busy. Time was of the essence. If we didn't draw our line in the sand this very second, we'd soon be resigned to posting fish symbols on the doors of our brick ranches to covertly identify ourselves to other believers.

So when Mom saw the permission form sitting on the kitchen table, she did not rush to sign her name and allow her son's head to be filled with sundry varieties of licentiousness. Like so many conservatives in pre-AIDS America, she suspected that learning about sex in a classroom was akin to eating the fruit of the Tree of Knowledge in Eden.

And we knew how that turned out.

No, this Sex Ed stuff was something to be mulled over. They'd firstly take it to the Lord in prayer, and wait for an answer. He'd move on their hearts in His time.

For my part, I couldn't help feeling like He'd already spoken on the matter, and would not be siding with me.

But here's what happened. The next morning, after I crawled out of bed, showered, and dressed for school, I trudged into the kitchen for a bowl of Frosted Flakes. As it had the night before, the form for the Sex Ed class was sitting on the table. I picked it up and took a glance. There, at the bottom, rested a little miracle of biblical proportions: someone had checked the box giving consent and scribbled a signature. And though signing school paperwork for absences, field trips, sports tryouts, report cards, and club participation always fell to Mom, this time I saw, in his crude, nearly illegible handwriting, my father's name.

OUR SCIENCE TEACHER, the dubious Mr. Harding, began his Sex Ed unit by declaring, "The purpose of all biological life is reproduction," and ended it with this ominous remark: "In the long history of mankind, the penis has been the cause of more wars than religion." In between these pronouncements he nattered on about chromosomes, fertilization, genetics. We smirked, sighed, rolled our eyes. We were, of course, duty-bound to pretend we already knew every fact; to act like this remedial stuff was a grand insult to us experts in human sexuality. After all, we were eighth-grade boys. We had strutted into Mr. Harding's classroom as though we owned this material. To confess any ignorance, expose our heretofore private fears, or betray even the slightest hint of vulnerability would have been downright girly, and would have reserved you a spot next door with the ladies, where you rightly belonged, you *wuss*.

What Mr. Harding's curriculum had done anyway was reduce sex to science, to X and Y, to sperm and egg—to multiple-choice questions that could be marked right or wrong on a test mandated by the state of Georgia. But we weren't impressed by terminology. We especially couldn't abide all these buzz-killing references to *intercourse*. We instead wanted the dirt, man, the low-down, the gist. All the forbidden knowledge our dads had withheld from us because they refused to sit us down, man to man, and deliver The Talk—the one our teachers promised we'd have, eventually. We were imploding with questions that nobody had the testicular endowment to ask. We wanted to know when we'd get hair under our arms. We wanted to know why one ball hung lower than the other. We wanted to know if we'd always feel everything, all at once. Above all, we wanted to know if what we suspected—that we really were ugly, deformed, and weird—was true.

And, please: What *formula* could possibly account for what happened to us when Kelly Bradford sashayed by, all blonde feathery wings, full-blown titties, and Jordache jeans? Mr. Harding felt it too. He possessed the same plumbing, we presumed. He was ridiculously old, probably in his forties, with a potbelly, a sad comb-over, and a framed picture of his homely wife on his desk, but surely once upon a time he had been thirteen. We'd seen his eyes inspect Kelly's Lacoste polo as he leaned over her desk to answer her question about cloud formations, or at least Joey McFarland said *he* had. What I'm saying is this: It was primitive, y'all, all impulse, blood lust, and mystery—not something to be dissected under a microscope, only ogled through a pair of binoculars, or a telescope, maybe.

WHICH WAS CONVENIENT because it was around this same time that one of the neighborhood kids, Leon Puckett, scored a brand new telescope. Leon was fourteen. He was merely the first of our crowd officially to enter high school, and still as virgin as any of us, but he had a habit of taunting us, leveraging that extra year of experience against us, saying, "Boys, you poor losers ain't had nookie since nookie had you." No budding astronomer, Leon was instead interested in all manner of juvenile delinquency—stealing baseball cards from the Stop-n-Go, bashing mailboxes with baseball bats, whizzing on Ms. Rebel's daffodils. He had visited the North last summer and claimed to have sampled Yankee culture courtesy of a Jersey girl. "Them chicks up there are *wild*," he informed us. He had a tricked-out bicycle, Steve Bartkowski's autograph, a poster of Farrah Fawcett, and a wicked curveball. He wore Adidas sneakers and informed us, with an air of unassailable authority, that Adidas stood for "All Day I Dream About Sex."

What I'm trying to say: He was an influence.

Word got around that Leon had woke one morning to find the telescope mounted on a tripod in his bedroom. It was a present from his father. Leon's old man was divorcing Leon's mom and moving out, but not without leaving behind this parting gift. Mr. Puckett must have felt compelled to give Leon something educational, something more academic than a skateboard, a BB gun, or a first baseman's mitt.

Instead of aiming his new gift at the stars, however, Leon aimed it a little more southerly, directly across the street, actually—where a young couple named Max and Janie lived. Max and Janie were my next-door neighbors. They were renters, twentysomethings, newlyweds. By our estimation, Max's most admirable possession was his souped-up '68 Firebird; Janie's was her ample breasts. Max spent most of his free time tinkering on his Firebird under the carport. Janie spent hers sunbathing on a chaise lounge in the backyard. She lay flat on her back in a bikini, one leg cocked up, or on her belly, her top undone. I killed countless hours throwing a tennis ball against the side of our house, fielding ground balls, gunning down imaginary base runners, and conjecturing what all went on inside the walls of Max and Janie's house. *Of course* I was jealous. I often fantasized about Janie. I didn't picture the two of us in any sort of sweaty entanglement; I simply imagined myself holding her, hearing her say my name, feeling the electric sheen of her string bikini as it passed through my fingers.

When my turn came for Leon to invite me over to marvel at his new telescope, he greeted me at the door with a startling announcement: "I saw Janie's knockers last night," he proudly declared. "No shirt, no bra, no *nothing*." He hurriedly led me into his room, where he had rigged up his new gift. There it was: a long, slender tube poking through the venetian blinds, toward Max and Janie's house across the street.

It really was an impressive arrangement.

"You should see 'em," Leon continued. "Nipples big as saucers, I shit you not." I did not doubt Leon's testimony. After all, having witnessed her tanning in her backyard, I knew, even from a considerable distance, Janie did in fact possess a bountiful bosom. "You're a lucky sumbitch that I don't charge you a dollar a glimpse," Leon said. And indeed I was lucky, all things considered, because I would have forked over whatever requested sum of my allowance for a chance to study Janie's generous endowment. Fortunately, though, Leon's entrepreneurial skills paled in comparison to his voyeuristic instincts. "Come here, boy," he finally said. He grabbed me by the arm and yanked me toward the window. He parted the blinds. Together, we peered across the street.

Same as always, Max and Janie's low-slung brick ranch sat glinting in the sun. The grass needed mowing. The ditch beside the yard churned with last night's rainwater. Grease spots scarred the driveway.

But then, upon closer investigation, I made a miraculous discovery: The windows were, in fact, curtainless. No blinds, shades, or screens. It was impossible to know precisely why this was the case, but Leon and I wasted no time forming our interpretation: Max and his bodacious bride seemed to be offering invitations to boys like us to witness their private lives. It was indeed a chance to view an unrehearsed and unrated slice of suburban life, circa 1981.

It would take several minutes for me to digest the significance of this opportunity. To Leon, voyeurism was only adventure, an opportunity to entertain himself for a little while at Janie's expense—because if his stories were to be believed, he had seen nude females before, not only through a telescopic lens but also in that faraway land known as New Jersey. But if this sudden twist of good fortune panned out, it would represent for me something else entirely.

Janie would be this Baptist boy's first real live naked woman.

"They ain't home from work yet," Leon explained. "If you can keep your pecker still for another hour or so, they'll come rolling in." He breathed on the lens of the telescope, wiped it clean with his shirttail. "You'll be able to see what I'm talking about. You'll see what all you've been missing."

IN THE MEANTIME, WHILE WE waited for Janie's imminent arrival, Leon acquainted me with his porn collection. Technically it belonged to his father, who had stacked the magazines in a milk crate, wedged them between two towers of cardboard boxes in the living room, and earmarked them for transport to wherever he now lived. But Leon had claimed it. "My damn inheritance," he called it. And rightfully so: the fact that his father had left the magazines available for Leon's perusal suggested that this was, school bureaucracy aside, his chosen method of educating his son about sex. A kind of trial subscription until he and his residue were gone completely. Whatever his intent, this much we understood: It was a glorious stash, a majestic pile, a veritable pornucopia of *Playboy, Penthouse, Hustler* and *Oui.*

Surely Leon's father, we reasoned, would not miss a magazine or two, or twenty. "Pick out one for yourself," Leon told me.

It was reassuring to know that, even according to Leon's skewed moral compass, he could not justify possessing every scrap of porn in the universe. His offer was a mere pittance. A crumb from his banquet. Nevertheless I felt humbled by the extremes of his generosity.

As a Baptist boy, I knew well that, of all the threats to civilization, pornography ranked near the top. But it was hard to summon the courage to reject Leon's offer, and even harder still when he started insisting I wasn't man enough to sample his mother lode. So Leon and I killed the next couple of hours rummaging through the pile while his mother slept through the afternoon. Every hour or so she would climb out of bed long enough to shuffle into the kitchen. We'd detect the swish of her bedroom slippers on the linoleum and quickly throw our stash back in the milk crate. Act as though she'd interrupted nothing more than another boring afternoon of Australian Rules football on ESPN. She'd fix a cup of instant decaf, light a Pall Mall, smoke it down to the nub while sitting at a dining room table stacked high with boxes of aftershave, hunting camo, and neckties. She'd stare at framed pictures of her soon-to-be ex that apparently she couldn't put away. The house was overrun with photos of Mr. Puckett—vacation snapshots and candids, most of them—always alone, usually shirtless, holding a beer, a string of fish, a golf club. Then she'd initiate small talk, ask me how my parents were doing, tell us to let her know if we needed anything. "Y'all are good boys," she'd say. "Fine young men." Sometimes she'd throw her arms around Leon, hugging him and patting him and mussing his hair until he cringed with embarrassment. Then she'd wander away again to her bedroom.

Inevitably, there would be an awkward silence in the space she'd left behind.

"Sunlight hurts Mom's eyes," I remember Leon explaining.

I remember, too, poring through those pages, thumbing through the centerfolds, the sticky pages clinging to my fingertips. The cumulative effect was nothing short of breathtaking. There were more naked women than I had known this world could hold. They all of course possessed the same general anatomy, but I recall being struck by how unique each individual seemed. Something as generic as a belly button could distinguish one from all the others. Eventually I made my selection of a recent issue of *Playboy*. It's difficult now to recollect exactly why I chose this particular magazine, but certainly the centerfold contributed. I believe it was a Miss September that captivated me most. Her bio said she was a Southern girl, from Alabama, or maybe Louisiana, and as I zeroed in on her glossy mouth I could almost taste the honey in her drawl. She had hair like Farrah Fawcett and fat wet lips, but I was certain she favored peanut butter-and-banana sandwiches and rooted for the Braves. Best of all, she was willing to stand still as I surveyed the topography of her body, the gentle swells, the flat plains, the contoured curves. The triangle of hair where her impossibly long legs merged seemed to whisper a secret I couldn't quite hear.

I was reeling with tumescence by the time Leon interrupted my carnal fantasy. He had to punch me in the shoulder to get my attention. "Hey, peckerhead," he said. "Max and Janie just got home."

WE HUSTLED TO THE WINDOW and began jostling for position. Sure enough, Leon had spoken the truth: Max's Firebird was now in the driveway. Leon immediately elbowed me out of his space and commenced spinning the telescope's knobs, adjusting its dials, squinting toward whatever vista revealed itself. It was a bulky, unwieldy contraption, that telescope, but he obviously had spent considerable time tinkering with its mechanisms and learning its capabilities. We fell silent, as though convinced any sound would blow our cover and doom our plot. We listened with our whole selves, each of us understanding in his own way that this was a moment of great weight and importance. I fought against blinking until my eyes felt like they'd dried into two marbles.

It was late afternoon, and in this slant of light it was tough to distinguish with my naked eye what lay beyond those window frames. Occasionally the black smudge in the background moved slightly, or at least I imagined it so, but really it was impossible to discern much of anything. If Leon was glimpsing greater detail with his telescope, he was keeping annoyingly silent about it.

But then, after a few minutes, just as our rapt attention had begun to wane, Janie appeared. She walked onto the carport. She was still wearing a dress, which allowed us quickly to deduce—smart boys that we were—that she had not yet changed out of her work clothes. She was toting a basket of wash. She kicked open the laundry room door and disappeared inside for what seemed a terribly long time. I swallowed. My pulse was ticking in my neck. With meticulous expertise, Leon continued focusing the lenses of the telescope.

Eventually Janie emerged from the laundry room, visible for only a few fleeting seconds before again entering the house. "She's fixing to change clothes," Leon assured me. "Get ready for the show." He spoke with certainty, as though he'd witnessed this routine countless times and knew the script. I imagined the next few moments of my thirteen-year-old existence: Janie standing in the open window, somehow sensing our presence, gazing directly across the street toward us until satisfied she held our attention, then without breaking eye contact removing every item of clothing in a slow, languorous unveiling.

We waited. There was no sign of intelligent life for a very long time.

How long did we linger there, holding our breaths, our voices only whispers, excitedly anticipating a glimpse of Janie's celestial body? It's hard to say. All I know is that eventually we exhaled. We started chatting. The subject strayed from the female anatomy; shifted toward baseball cards, likely, or maybe Leon's stereo system. The illicit thrill that had been surging through our veins began to dwindle until, finally, barely a drip registered in our bloodstreams. To summarize: we got bored.

Soon enough, with a sigh and more than a little frustration, Leon left me in charge of peering through the telescope. "Tell me when you see some action," he grumbled. With that, he departed the room—to excavate even greater depths of his monumental stash, I presumed.

As directed I took my turn with the instrument, experimenting through trial and error, testing the eyepiece as much out of curiosity as naked desire. Did anything reveal itself? Of course

not. Leon's new telescope might be a fine instrument for viewing the far-flung reaches of the universe, but it was useless for
glimpsing buxom Janie. I persisted, pursuing my goal much longer than I should have, probably beyond all reasonable hope, but
eventually I gave up.

As I was leaving Leon's house that evening, he set in again
about Jersey girls, holding forth on the pleasures of their exquisite flesh, dishing sordid details that, had I been in a different
frame of mind, would have spiked my blood and made me a pru-
rient audience. But I wasn't interested. Tonight Leon Puckett
had lost serious credibility. He was winding up as if to go on at
length, but I told him I had to go home. We were going to be
eating dinner soon. I had homework, or chores, maybe, or *something* to do. I was wearing a football jersey that sans shoulder
pads fit me about two sizes too big, so I rolled up the *Playboy*
he'd consented to let me keep, tucked it under my jersey, and
jammed it into my Levis.

Eventually I trudged across the street toward home.
Throughout the neighborhood, the lawns sat quiet. Living
rooms glowed with the blue light of TV screens. Somewhere
down the street a lone dog was lamenting the sorry state of the
world. Once inside my house, I fled past the family Bible in the
living room, straight to my room, and locked the door behind
me. After wiping my hands on my bed sheets, I extracted the
magazine from my shorts; I pinched the edges with my thumb
and forefinger, as though afraid of corrupting them with my
dingy flesh. I read the interview on back of the centerfold,
acquainted myself with Miss September's proclivities; I discovered her turn-ons and turn-offs, her favorite foods, what she
does to indicate she wants a guy to make the first move.

Mom called to me from the kitchen. She said dinner would
be ready in a few minutes. I told her I was doing homework.

Then I stretched Miss September out across my bed. Other
women seemed to teeter on stiletto heels, as though scared of

heights, but this Southern beauty wore them with assurance and grace. She also sported a matching diamond earring and necklace set with a golden cross pendant—and nothing else. She looked at me with confidence as though she possessed knowledge I'd been dying to learn—as though somewhere deep inside she contained information Leon Puckett, my Sunday school teacher, and the dubious Mr. Harding didn't even know existed. She seemed prepared to teach me some advanced curriculum, to share a few textbook tricks.

She smiled without showing her teeth, which undoubtedly were as perfect as a row of new piano keys, and stared directly at me, her eyes pools of tawny brown. She held my name on her tongue. She looked at me as though she understood, as though she cared about my story and wanted to hear every word. With her I could lay my burden down for a little while—it was okay, she seemed to say; she was a good listener, and willing.

If I heard her right, Miss September was telling me that she and I would try to figure it all out together.

ADDRESSEE UNKNOWN

That autumn, Atlanta police charged Wayne Williams with the murders of two black males, and my father announced he was going to be on TV. It was 1981; I was 13, a white kid, in a lily white suburban neighborhood of brick ranches with flower beds in the yards and bluebirds on the telephone lines—a world away from Atlanta's city limits where in the past two years 28 people with skin darker than mine, children mostly, had been counted among the dead. From the safe confines of our living room I'd witnessed nightly news images of helicopters hovering over parks, dogs searching wooded ravines, and Frank Sinatra and Sammy Davis Jr. performing a benefit concert to raise money for the financially strapped police department. Through what felt like only rumors, I'd heard about the reward signs and confidential hotlines, psychic predictions and green ribbons. But Wayne Williams' arrest meant I finally could play outside again.

The previous May, police had been staking out the Jackson Parkway Bridge when an officer heard a splash in the brown and sludgy waters of the Chattahoochee River below and spied a white station wagon disappearing into the night. Less than a mile down the road, they pulled the driver over. Williams, a twenty-three-year-old black man, told them he was a music promoter; he said he was on his way to audition a singer named Cheryl Johnson. Though Williams claimed she lived in the nearby town of Smyrna, in Cobb County, and that their appointment had been longstanding, police found no record of any Cheryl Johnson.

Within a couple of days, two boys fishing south of the bridge found the naked body of Nathaniel Cater, 27, a homosexual prostitute and drug dealer, floating downriver. Using primarily fiber evidence gathered from Williams' house and car, authorities would link Williams to Cater's death, and later to Jimmy Ray Payne's, 21—both of whom had been labeled "retarded" and were thereby perceived as children, which meant they qualified as victims of the Atlanta Child Murders. Williams was now behind bars, awaiting trial. It was November.

Even in the dim wattage of my eighth-grade brain, I found it strange that a music promoter who lived with his parents in Dixie Hills and a non-existent woman named Cheryl Johnson, a singer with no voice, somehow could manage to gain more fame and notoriety than anyone I personally knew. But tonight, at eleven o'clock, my father would be changing all that.

When Dad told us he'd be on the late news, Mom and I knew the murders and Dad's appearance held no relation. But he was secretive about exactly why he was newsworthy. What was the story? Unless they turned violent, unless they'd gone *postal*, postmen did not appear on the evening news. Still, I imagined whatever acts of heroism a boy raised on *Starsky and*

Hutch, Six Million Dollar Man, Kung Fu, and biblical miracles could conjure. I pictured Dad coming upon a house afire on his route, dropping his burlap mail sack to the sidewalk, and sprinting through a blazing door to rescue a baby from rising flames. I saw him wrestling a thief to the ground. I envisioned him pulling a woman from the wreckage of her car right before it exploded. For a few fleeting moments I reveled in the possibility that Dad had performed some variety of miracle, too—maybe even something on the biblical scale—and that tomorrow everyone at school would know about it, and by association mine would be the name on everyone's tongue.

But when asked which of these scenarios involved him, Dad was not forthcoming. He seemed to relish the suspense. That night, standing in our kitchen in his standard-issue uniform, he only grinned and propped his fists on his hips and stood with his shoes wide apart. "You'll just have to wait to find out," he said. "Thousands of people across the whole state of Georgia are gonna see me. I'm gonna steal the show from Mister Wayne Williams."

Dad was six-two and over two hundred pounds, with broad shoulders and hands big as catcher's mitts, but on this particular evening he seemed to assume even greater dimensions. His body seemed too big to be contained by the tight walls and low ceilings of our brick ranch on King Arthur Drive. He projected an aura of confidence suggesting he had long been expecting this crowning moment to arrive, and now history was merely unfolding in the manner it had always been fated to occur. He had that look in his eyes possessed by all people convinced their lives are about to experience a seismic shift in importance. As he started unbuttoning his blue uniform shirt with the eagle patch on the shoulder and pulling its tails from his trousers with the blue stripe running down the leg, he seemed certain, already, that tonight would represent a line of demarcation in his life.

He crossed the den and patted our nineteen-inch Samsung black-and-white on its plastic side panel and fine-tuned its rabbit ears. "It's a school night," he told me—and for a moment my heart sank at the possibility of missing my dad's burst into fame. Then he grinned teasingly, and gave me a big slow wink. "But I reckon you can stay up and watch."

IT IS A VERIFIABLE FACT THAT my father once paid good folding money to a company whose advertisement in a magazine claimed to research your family tree and—if you act now, while supplies last—provide an absolutely free special bonus gift: a genuine coat of arms. Being that my father spawned from stock wherein the only coats were second-hand, it is safe to say this offer of heraldry was as close as he would ever come to blue-blood ancestry. He did indeed receive the genealogical research in the mail. The family tree, as I recall, included vague and dubious references to both the French and the Eastern Band of Cherokee Indians. But Dad's main interest was in the family crest anyway. It seemed positively regal. Mom displayed it for a time on the coffee table in our living room, right next to the family Bible, which accorded it as lofty a status as any secular object could possess, but today its whereabouts are unknown. It has been lost somewhere among the slag of our family's history. I recall little about it, but I can attest to its central, unmistakable feature: a beaver with an enormous tail.

About my father: despite his conviction that tonight would mark the turning point in his life's story, he was not destined for notoriety. Instead his upbringing portended absolute anonymity. He was raised hardscrabble on a hundred acres of red Georgia clay during the Depression, the youngest of three boys who stuffed rags inside mittens to make boxing gloves, and then proceeded to beat each other senseless. There was a fourth child, too—the baby, a girl named Lucille—who completed the blurry family portrait that sat atop the upright piano in their living room for many years: the boys in overalls, the girl in a frilly dress, shoulder-to-shoulder, oldest to youngest, like steps in a staircase. Their mother satisfied her artistic inclinations by crocheting blankets, playing piano for the Baptist church, and baking perfect cathead biscuits; their father pawed the dirt and grew enough corn and beans to fend off starvation. He needed farmhands more than sons, and so he treated them as such. A Jehovah in overalls, he ruled with utmost authority, and his word was law. Paw-Paw Beaver, for example, forbade his bloodthirsty boys to kill a blacksnake in the corncrib, because it would eat mice—a commandment they unquestioningly obeyed, because their daddy owned a volatile temper and a belt as long as that vermin-eating serpent.

Dad's first employment was cutting pulp in a sawmill, a mere boy grunting alongside grown men missing appendages—fingers, hands, or even entire arms—so he likely felt more than slight relief when the U.S. Army drafted him—even though Uncle Sam promptly sent him to Fort Bragg, North Carolina for basic training before shipping him much farther: Korea.

It was there, in a strange and ominous land, he took up cigarettes, crouched in frozen foxholes, and became a Master Sergeant at age twenty-two. Somewhere there is a picture of him in his uniform, all cornpone and teeth. He looks as though he is incapable of seeing anything beyond the camera's eye and the next fifteen seconds of his life.

Of his experience in Korea, Dad told only one story for posterity. He claimed that, during the war, he once crawled miles with a dagger in his side. He never told how, exactly, the dagger had ended up piercing his body, or toward where, specifically, he was crawling. There was no context; the story's only image was a man bellydragging through arctic tundra on the other side of the world, a dagger protruding from his abdomen, blood trailing in his wake. Bright red against the stark whiteness of the snow. The number of miles he crawled always changed with the telling. Usually he claimed to have wriggled two or three miles, but sometimes the number inflated to preposterous distances, eleven miles, thirteen miles, and on one occasion I distinctly remember Dad claiming to have covered *twenty miles* of snow-blasted terrain with a dagger in his side.

The story was of course apocryphal—though Dad, with a high school diploma so tentative that it was practically on loan, wouldn't have possessed the vocabulary to call it such. He was missing any semblance of a scar. His gut bore no sign of violence. But I—unlike Thomas, who insisted on seeing Jesus' side before he would believe he was in the Savior's presence—I bought Dad's story. It was an altogether satisfactory tale for a boy like me to hear. It seems significant to me that the only narrative he ever told about his war experiences was complete and utter bunk. But it is a testament to Dad's fundamental pluck, grit, and spine that my age was into double digits before I ever doubted the veracity of his claim.

And in truth, it is quite possible that on the night I'm speaking of—the night toward which Dad believed his life had always been heading—I believed it, still.

EVENTUALLY HE RETURNED to U.S. soil with a nicotine addiction, a head full of gruesome images of death and destruction, and a yearbook of sorts—a leather-bound volume documenting the experience of his 24th infantry, with glossy pages and pictures black and white. Along with his furlough to Japan, Korea would turn out to be the extent of his international travels for the rest of his life.

Although Dad could hardly be called ambitious, he must have harbored dreams that he believed lay beyond the shadows of the north Georgia mountains, dreams informed by what he now had witnessed. It would be hard to keep the boy down on the farm after he'd drunk Japanese sake. So when he finally made it home safely from war, he hugged his mama and then promptly kissed her goodbye again. After spending so much time in that forsaken Asian countryside, unsure whether it would be the last landscape his eyes ever beheld, he decided that Fannin County in north Georgia was too small for his vision of things. He picked the cockleburs from his overalls and headed to Atlanta.

He got hired on at Sears and Roebuck on Ponce de Leon where he stocked inventory and met a fellow employee from the Cabbagetown neighborhood named Norma Fay who would become his wife and, eventually, my mother. He proposed thusly: "I'm thinking we oughta get married." She waited to hear what came next, but he'd clearly said all he had to say. "Well," she finally told him, "I'm thinking we should too." They married before the justice of the peace, on a date nobody knows, in a ceremony likely quicker than getting a driver's license. No photographer, best man, or cake. Only a couple of signatures on the paperwork to make it all legal.

And the timeline here has always been cloudy and suspicious, but suffice it to say that the Beaver clan met his new bride and firstborn son, my big brother David—whom Dad named after the Old Testament king—on the same evening. Now officially a family man, he started taking his to worship services at a Baptist church. He got Saved. He quit cigarettes, cold turkey, when a church member complained of their smell. He hung a sign in the living room that read: *As for me and my house, we will serve the Lord.*

Then one night, while he and Mom were still employees of Sears and Roebuck, Dad attended a union meeting—just out of curiosity, he said—but when he showed up for work the next morning they gave him a pink slip. He vowed never to purchase a solitary item from Sears for the rest of his life. Unemployed, with a wife and child depending on him, he studied for the Civil Service exam, and buoyed by his wife's fervent and desperate prayers, scored high enough to merit an offer from the Post Office.

Dad never called himself a postman. He told people he worked for the U.S. Postal Service. His preferred term held authority. Rain, sleet, snow, and dark of night, a man who worked for the U.S. Postal Service delivered the mail. He drove a truck through all Atlanta's one-way streets and then let his shoe leather take him where his truck couldn't go. The rest of us depended upon him to do his job. Doctors, lawyers, and Indian chiefs could not go about their business unless employees of the U.S. Postal Service took care of theirs.

All of which is to say: Once, I stood in the leaves at the base of a giant oak in our backyard and took a Polaroid of my father in the highest limbs of the tree. The oak had died. Its limbs overhung our house; so rather than fell the tree all at once, Dad had to cut it down one withered branch at a time. In the photo, Dad must be three stories in the air. He is so far up, he seems to fuse with the sunlight splitting the branches. He is raising his hands over his head as though he's just been crowned heavyweight champion—like Rocky Marciano, maybe, who according to Dad could have beaten that Ali character to a pulp.

When I was about to go away to college—to a gnat-infested south Georgia campus where the only ivy would be the poison variety sprouting on the edge of the intramural softball fields—Dad rescued the photo from the dregs of some murky neglected drawer. With something resembling pomp and circumstance, he presented it to me. Along the bottom edge, in a scrawl reminiscent of a grade school boy's, he had provided a handwritten caption: *We Beavers set our goals high.*

WATCHING THE ELEVEN O'CLOCK NEWS meant Dad was staying up long past his own bedtime, which also meant that since nine o'clock he had been intermittently dozing off. "Four-thirty comes early," he was fond of saying, and when he woke the next morning he would be following his usual routine, devouring two fried eggs and a plate of grits, downing a cup of coffee with cream—"just enough to turn the color"—while he watched some obscure preacher on the religious channel or studied his upcoming Sunday school lesson; then he would polish his shoes to a glossy spit-shine, scrub his dentures, and spend a good five minutes combing his wavy hair and admiring his reflection in the mirror. Now in his early fifties, Dad still possessed a full head of hair, and he intended to relish that fact until the good Lord chose to steal it away. Before church on Sunday mornings he would run a comb through his waves and ask anybody within earshot, "Have you ever seen a prettier man in all your life?" Dad was a vain man, all right, and a proud one, too—he would stop off at home before he came to my Little League games so he could change out of his uniform and comb his hair, even if he missed my first strikeout of the night, because he didn't want people thinking he was just another stiff in a uniform with messy hair.

As the night moved slowly, slowly toward eleven o'clock, I woke him every twenty minutes or so. "I'm just resting my eyes," he responded whenever I nudged him. Finally, it was time for the news.

Dad sat on his recliner; Mom and I took our places on the sofa. On the shelves surrounding us was a veritable library of books, hundreds of them, virtually all pertaining to a single subject: Christianity. Concordances, study guides, and of course every English translation of the Good Book imaginable. There were automotive manuals, too, and maybe a dust-laden home maintenance text, but only one novel: *Gone with the Wind.*

Dad had never read it. Indeed he never would. But he owned it because somewhere he had absorbed the notion that unless his house contained a hardback copy, he would have to forfeit his Southern citizenship. He lived a life in letters, all right, but the kind that meant tomorrow he'd spend ten hours delivering a truck full of them.

Anyway, as it had been for months, the lead story that night was Wayne Williams. There must have been other stories, too—apartment fires, maybe, or bank robberies. Local politics, or traffic accidents. And of course the requisite weather and sports. But the ongoing run-up to Wayne Williams' trial is all I remember from that night's edition. Though Williams had been charged with the first-degree murders of only two men, all deaths officially associated with the Atlanta child murders had ceased with his arrest. The prosecution was still reviewing evidence for the trial that would commence the next winter, in early 1982. Jury selection would likely begin in December. But the fact that new information was scarce did not stop the newscasts from focusing on the upcoming trial.

The thirty-minute show moved toward its conclusion. The clock hanging in the den now read 11:25. In five minutes everything would be over. But there had been no story about Dad. The news anchors told viewers they'd be right back after a commercial break. I don't recall which advertisers filled the commercials during that break, but I do remember spending that time in a panic, fretting the possibility that though Dad had performed some heroic feat, pulled off a miracle, WSB TV Channel 2 had chosen to cut it, because in comparison with child murders and vehicle recalls it was unimportant, routine, expendable. No one cared.

As the commercials ran, I found myself thinking about Cheryl Johnson, the singer whom Wayne Williams said he planned to audition the night he was arrested. Williams had claimed that Johnson gave him her phone number and address; that he drove around nearby Smyrna looking for Spanish Trace Apartments but found nothing; that he had stopped at a liquor store and called her number but it was busy. He claimed that he had called her again later, but no one answered; and a third time, when someone picked up the phone but told him he had the wrong number. Months had passed since the night of Williams' arrest, and still Cheryl Johnson was missing. Dad would have stamped her *Addressee Unknown*. I was thirteen, and not prone to recognizing irony in my textbooks, much less in the world around me—but it did not escape me that Cheryl Johnson, who did not exist, was more famous than my postman father. By all appearances, this fact was not going to change.

When the newscast resumed, the two anchors engaged in a little banter. They thanked viewers for watching, bid us goodnight, and signed off. The closing credits began to roll. A brisk and perky tune started playing. The names of the producers, the reporters, the writers, and the camera operators began to fill the screen. Still nothing about Dad.

On the screen, in the background behind the names, images of everyday Atlantans began flashing by. Little clips of footage, three to five seconds long. In each the subject is waving. There's a child, maybe three- or four years old, sprinkling her fingers as she careens down a playground slide toward the viewer. The next shot is a man exiting a barbershop with a fresh buzz cut. Then comes a waitress on her cigarette break; two gray-headed men playing checkers in a park; a MARTA bus driver squeezing the steering wheel; two black boys, their arms slung around each other's shoulders. Still another is clearly a homeless man, his grin a gaping hole of missing teeth. He waves clumsily at the camera as though swatting flies.

And then, just as the signoff is complete and another commercial break is about to begin, there is my father. He's wearing his postal uniform. He's smiling and waving at the camera with those hands that years ago ripped the husks from a million ears of corn and squeezed the udders of as many milking cows. On his right hand he's wearing a rubber thumb sleeve that, now, helps him sort through a million pieces of junk mail.

I glanced at the real thing—at Dad, flesh, blood, and bone, watching with me. I expected him to be slumping in his seat, as disappointed as I was. I expected this turn of events to show him how little his life had added up to.

But he was sitting on the edge of his recliner in his brown brick on King Arthur Drive, starstruck. His face was bathed in the glow of the TV screen; his eyes blazed with glory. Instead of lamenting how far he had to go, how much distance still lay between him and wherever he was headed, he seemed to be celebrating how close he had already come to that nameless destination—how many snow-laden miles he'd already crawled with that dagger in his side.

WSB Channel 2 News was ending their broadcast with clips of stray Atlantans waving goodbye, and one of them was a postman, a burlap strap over his shoulder, the sunlight spotlighting his full head of wavy hair, as though he's on stage cleaning up the set after everyone else has gone home but nevertheless occupying—for three seconds, maybe four—the center of the universe. He is a man who in this moment believes for all the world that he's witnessing the birth of his very own star.

LONE BARITONE

On the second day of middle school band class, I came to the regrettable discovery that my lips were too small to play trumpet. This was eighth grade. This was Beginning Band. And despite a crash-course introduction to trumpet during the summer, I was showing no skill or aptitude—nothing resembling what the director, Mr. Price, kept calling a "relationship" with my instrument. The trumpet felt heavy in my hands. The oil left a noxious stench in my nose. And my mouth never quite seemed to fit the mouthpiece as precisely as the other players' fit theirs—especially Joel Grantham's, whose lips blossomed like two ripe plums and whose finesse with his trumpet I attributed to the technique acquired from all the girls he allegedly had kissed. So on that second day of class, after Mr. Price's keen ear detected my inability to master the finer points of our school's rousing fight song, he responded with a simple but firm request: "Give us a solo," he said.

To the entertainment of my forty bandmates sitting in officious judgment, I licked my lips, took a deep breath, and proceeded to fill the room with a shameful array of burps, fizzles, squirts, and sour toots—all of which seemed to result directly from the sad but irrepressible fact that I could not maneuver my thin lips around the mouthpiece in such a manner that would fill the horn with just the right amount of air to produce *music*. I played two bars, stalled. Started again, from the top. Derailed again, inhaled, picked up where I had left off. Wincing at every bitter sound, I stumbled toward the crescendo. When I finally reached the last bar and its dramatic four-count note—the note that punctuated the triumph of being a Fairplay Middle School Pioneer—I gulped air until my ears clogged and my head swam, pursed my lips, and spat my lungs into the silver mouthpiece containing an opening the size of a grape—only to produce a sound resembling a foul bodily function.

This was not what I had planned.

I had joined grudgingly in the first place, against my better instincts, suckered by promises of summer camp, shiny trophies, spotlighted solos, and standing Os, all the while secretly hoarding my jealousy of those chorus kids down the hall who wore matching pastel shirts with rainbows and sang anthems from *Up With People*. They possessed voices of crystalline purity, those chorus kids, and golden hair swept back in feathered wings; and so it was that, bereft of both, I had signed up for band, fully aware of its reputation as the worldwide repository of geeks and nerds.

Anyway, when my performance mercifully ended, the room fell eerily quiet. Someone coughed. The tuba shifted his instrument from one beefy thigh to the other. Then one of the flutes giggled, a little bubble of sound, which forced Mr. Price to rap his baton against his stand and shoot a surly frown in their general direction. "It's not funny," he muttered. "It's pitiful. Pitiful's the word for it. Utter cacophony."

If I had encountered *cacophony* on a vocabulary quiz, I would have been mystified. But right now, at age thirteen, as I slumped in my chair with my instrument, I was in no need of a dictionary. I knew exactly what the word meant.

AND THEN THERE'S THIS: After class, Mr. Price called me into his office. He sank into his chair, propped his feet on his desktop. He steepled his fingers under his chin. Mired in silence, he seemed to be spending a few desperate moments in contemplation of how to address my particular set of failures.

Finally he shrugged. "It's just not that big a deal, man," he assured me. "It's not like you're the first kid born with little lips. Get what I'm, you know, saying?" Mr. Price spoke the way he played his alto sax—with a jazzy lilt—as though every conversation were set to rhythm and he were scatting. "You can play the baritone instead," he suggested. He leaned toward me conspiratorially, his voice only a hoarse whisper: "Here's a little secret between you and me, brother: it's hard to make a bad sound come out of a baritone!" Mr. Price was a bald guy, with a perpetual two-day beard. He sported ties slimmer than rulers. He snapped his fingers repeatedly during conversation, and bobbed his chin to the beat of some catchy melody tripping through his veins like heroin. He saw himself as a vestige of the fifties, of the Beat generation of musicians who defined the quintessence of cool. He cultivated a persona that suggested he'd been kidnapped from a piano bar in Frisco—where all the patrons quoted Kerouac and wore turtlenecks, berets, and dark shades at two in the morning—only to be turned loose to teach music to a bunch of tone-deaf pubescents. "No problem, no sweat at all, my friend. You can even play treble clef on the baritone so you don't have to learn the bass clef. How's that for a deal, man? Are you, like, with it?"

I nodded. Given band's standing in the social hierarchy of middle school, I knew he was making a pitch; this was nothing more than pure salesmanship. Recruitment was dicey, to be certain. Our band had no baritone player—I wasn't rightly sure what a baritone even looked like—but really I saw no other option than to be *with it*. At least he wasn't asking me to play tuba.

Mr. Price slapped his palms together. "I knew you were a real cool cat," he said. He wrote me a tardy pass for my next class. I turned on my heels, and as I was leaving his office, Mr. Price then offered some parting words. At the time, I thought he was only talking about the baritone; but if I'd been a little more on the uptake, a more shrewd observer of my own life, a boy who maybe knew himself a bit better, I might have applied those words to my life beyond the band room: "Now enjoy the ride, okay?" Mr. Price said. "*Just blow, daddy!*"

I BLEW THE BARITONE, ALL RIGHT, but mainly, I just blew. I had no innate talent, no gift. Synesthesia was not in my repertoire; I saw no colors or shapes or groovy psychedelic ghosts when I played, only the next ominous black note on the white page. I did not bop; I did not swing. I was not avant-garde. And genetics offered no hope for the future either. The only precedent of musicality in my ancestral tree was my grandfather who, according to family lore, strummed songs about lonely trains and cold women and dead dogs on an acoustic guitar—until one fateful night when he got drunk, fell asleep in a kudzu patch, and had his wallet—and his guitar—pilfered.

But I was the lone baritone. The tuba and trombone—they were loners too. (They were adolescent boys, so naturally they referred to themselves as the *tuber* and the *tromboner*). In our corner in the back of the room, there was no second-chair player—we were first, last, and only. To compensate, *we* arranged ourselves in chairs, determined by how long it had been since one of us provoked Mr. Price to stop play and rip his baton across his jugular as if committing hari-kari right there during second period. "Stop it!" he'd say. "Stop it! You're offending my ear!"

But I stuck with the baritone, probably because band seemed to attract a rather high percentage of our school's female population, many of whom spent countless hours sashaying through my imagination in various stages of undress. They were a mess of orthodontia, most of them, with thick glasses, acne blemishes, and flat chests. Nothing like those chorus girls down the hall. But they were female, and that counted for a lot in those days. The clarinet, in particular, seemed to draw several of the finer specimens—something about those lithe fingers clutching that tubular instrument made playing the school fight song for the twenty-third consecutive time somewhat bearable for me. Marooned in the back row between the skinny trombonist and the portly guy wearing his tuba like a life preserver around his waist, I gazed longingly at those lovely clarinetists and envisioned smooching them with my flimsy lips. Seeing them teasingly wet their reeds with the tips of their red tongues, then ever-so-seductively sliding the reeds inside their woodwinds: This was the stuff of my pubescent fantasies.

The baritone had its advantages, too. Because it was a midsized brass horn, somewhere between trombone and tuba in size, I wasn't required to lug it to and from school every day. I toted only a mouthpiece, small enough to slide in my front pocket. (Daily, the tuba and I shared the same pubescent joke: "Is that a mouthpiece in your pocket—or are you just glad to see me?") Upon arriving at class I had only to duck inside the instrument room—a long, slim alleyway shooting off from the main band room—to fetch the communal baritone. And Mr. Price did what he could to encourage me. On my report card he wrote the following in flowery script: *Fine baritone sound—will go far on this horn with normal effort.*

The curse of the lone baritone, however, was the fact that I had to play at all times. I couldn't fake it. Unlike the droves of trumpeters, clarinetists, and flutists, who could only pretend to blow whenever the fancy struck, I was obliged to play every note. Not even Mr. Price's trained ear could distinguish between thirteen and fourteen clarinetists, but my AWOL baritone would be easily detectable.

Occasionally the tuba or trombone would be absent. Neither of them possessed even an iota of ability, but nevertheless the band didn't seem quite whole without them. Even if I was currently last chair in our gang of three, I didn't value my promotion for the day; it felt instead like a vital piece had gone missing.

Once, though, I was sick for three straight days with strep throat. When I finally returned to school, still rife with congestion and a slight fever, I waited anxiously for anyone to comment on my absence. The tuba and trombone seemed oblivious. I coughed, blew my nose—theatrically. There was only the uncasing of instruments, the thumbing through sheet music. Furtively, I glanced toward each side of me, searching for any acknowledgment, but both my fellow loners seemed preoccupied with preparing their instruments. Finally, just as rehearsal was set to commence, the tuba leaned across me and called out, "Hey, tromboner, is that a mouthpiece in your pocket—or are you just glad to see me?"

AFTER CHRISTMAS BREAK, when we gathered for our first class meeting in January, I sensed a problem during warm-up.

The instrument felt unusually heavy. I dismissed my concerns because, well, it had been a couple of weeks since I had held a baritone. Maybe I'd just lost my feel for it. But when we began the first song the problem became too severe to ignore. It seemed that my baritone *gurgled* when I blew into it. Though the past four months had yielded slight but discernable progress, I apparently had lost any ability whatsoever to make the baritone produce a sound even vaguely resembling music. Nervously I pressed the valves, filled my lungs with air, and blew.

Mr. Price kept shooting surly looks in my direction and feverishly waving his baton, exhorting me to play louder. But the harder I blew, the more a trilled, liquid sound resulted—something akin to the noise a deep-sea diver makes when exhaling. This racket continued until Mr. Price called the tune to a grinding halt. He executed that suicidal gesture with his baton. Apparently some of us got the message later than others, because the group as a whole jack-knifed. An oboe kept honking for a full bar after everyone else had quit. "Stop, stop!" Mr. Price said. "I can't take it anymore! It's just too much!" The room went silent.

He seized this opportunity to deliver a brief but caustic lecture, the point of which was to chastise us for disrespecting the power, importance, and cultural significance of music. Music is the universal language, he reminded us. Music expresses the feelings for which there are no words. To underscore his point, he resorted to what I had often considered one of his disconcerting tactics: He referred to himself in the third-person. "Mr. Price is very unhappy with you right now," he announced. "You've got to give him more. You gotta blow, my friends. You know the Price is always Right, people!"

And then he again lifted his baton. We raised our instruments. "Posture," he reminded us. "Posture, my little friends!" He counted off the beat: on cue we resumed the tune. But our performance did not improve. And I was still perplexed by my instrument. The more I puckered and blew, the more it resisted.

Mr. Price aimed his baton toward me, demanding that I play louder. But when my baritone produced only a bloated sigh, like pipes churning in a Motel 6, I gave up. Disgusted, gasping for air, I dropped the horn to my lap and slumped in my chair.

Mr. Price again halted the song. He slapped his palm across his mouth as though struggling to stop himself from uttering words that could get him fired or, at the very least, censured. He turned his back on the group; the bald spot on his head shone like a wan bulb as he stared at the clock fixed on the wall. Nobody moved. Finally, after regaining his bearings, he spun on his heels with new resolve, crooked his finger in my direction, and summoned me to the front. He didn't call me by name, but by instrument—as in, "Baritone, come here, man." He was visibly unhappy with this opening performance of the new semester, and now he had a scapegoat. He began kneading his eyes. His weary countenance told the story. He should have been on stage in Frisco, but here he was surrounded by a bunch of no-talent losers who clearly did not see the creation of music as a sacred act capable of redeeming an entire civilization's soul. These next few minutes, consequently, should be an object lesson. As I headed toward the front of the room, winding my way through the serpentine obstacle course of instruments and music stands, Mr. Price commanded me to stop. "With your instrument," he said. "The baritone, please. Bring it with you, man."

I retreated to my seat and retrieved the baritone; hoisting it against my shoulder, I lugged it toward the front. Mr. Price tapped his foot. I briefly hoped that he was simply responding to that inner tune flowing through his blood, but the truth was, he was an impatient man.

Mr. Price decided that, if I wouldn't play my instrument with the group, I should play it *for* the group. He muttered something about being too old to suffer kids who aren't committed, who don't really want to play, who don't appreciate art. He stepped aside to allow me to occupy center stage and command the audience's attention. "So let's hear it," he said. "Let it rip. Solo, man!"

Head bowed, keenly aware of my classmates' eyes boring into me, I told him I couldn't.

"Go on," he said. "Play!"

"I can't," I said.

"Like, why, man?"

"There's a problem with my instrument," I whispered.

The lovely clarinetists near the front leaned closer, straining to hear me.

"What's wrong with it?" Mr. Price said. He was still tapping his feet at a staccato tempo.

"I don't know," I explained. "It just won't work."

"Well let me hear it," Mr. Price said. "Let *us* hear it."

When I lifted the instrument, a distinctly aquatic sound bubbled from inside.

A quizzical expression broke across Mr. Price's face. "Turn it upside down," he said.

I did as he commanded and wrestled the instrument over. Once the horn was flipped, its weight shifted internally, like a swelling tide, and sure enough here came a flood of water, an absolute gusher, a grand explosion pouring out of the bell onto my pants and shoes, and suddenly I found myself standing in a puddle, the ring around my sneakers spreading wide as a tractor tire. My band mates, all forty of them, exploded into laughter.

I looked around desperately. Out there, zeroing in on me in their crosshairs, was a grotesque array of faces, a disfigured and contorted panorama of bloodthirsty masks. I could hardly distinguish one kid from another. Somewhere among them was the culprit, I felt certain—the sadistic prankster whose garden-hose-in-the-baritone trick had worked to perfection. Surely he'd spent his whole Christmas break anticipating this very moment. Oh, the stories he'd tell. He must have been very proud right about now.

The flutists giggled; the clarinetists chuckled; the trumpeters snorted and crowed. Even my fellow loners, the tuba and the trombone, were clutching their bellies, their faces flush, their eyes swimming with giddy tears. The tuba was jabbing a pudgy finger toward my pants.

I surveyed my nether regions. To summarize: I looked as though I had wet myself.

The crowd roared.

I briefly calculated the odds of the Rapture occurring at this instant, of getting whisked out of this predicament by a divine wind and deposited safely into Heaven while this ruthless crowd stayed behind to endure however many years of tribulation we Baptists interpreted *Revelation* had assigned to them. According to scripture, no one knew the hour, but as the laughter echoed it was becoming apparent this was not it. So then I considered making a run for it, just plowing through the masses, overturning music stands and scattering sheet music, and barreling through the door in the back of the room. I pictured myself hitting the hallway full stride, sprinting out of the school and into the wider world where I could just keep running and running until I reached a place I'd never been and could become a kid I'd never seen before. But sheer flight was more than I could muster at that moment. So then I thought about just making a slow loop around the crowd, my face a pallid stone, excusing myself and gently pushing open the door and disappearing outside. Maybe locking myself inside a bathroom stall until I could comport myself enough to return to class. But it was already too late now for a graceful exit.

If it was true that band was the repository of geeks, then I was not merely a geek among geeks; I was the guy the other kids pointed to and said, "Man, look at him, what a *geek*." Standing there in front of all my peers, the bell of my baritone hanging upside down, my jeans soaking wet and a pool of water spreading around my shoes, I was not going to become the next cultural phenomenon. I would not be a star. I was not going to woo eighth-grade women with my musical prowess.

I was only the kid with wet jeans, soggy shoes, and a pair of very small lips.

THE NEXT MORNING, I didn't show up for band class. After such an embarrassing episode, I immediately set about repairing my reputation by getting out of band and into—anything. I badgered the academic registrar. Pickiness wasn't a problem, I assured her; I'd take whatever she could find. I contrived some kind of cockamamie excuse, something about wanting to "try new things," and maybe because it was the beginning of the new semester, the powers-that-be permitted me to drop band and pick up something called Industrial Arts.

I'd never even heard of Industrial Arts, but I was about to learn that IA, as they called it, was a gussied-up title for shop class. Soon I found myself surrounded by all the equipment of this brand new world—the jigsaw, the lathe, the mineral spirits, a pair of safety goggles plastered to my face—when I was summoned via intercom to report to the band room. The IA teacher, deeply absorbed in the *Atlanta Journal-Constitution*, set aside his sports section long enough to shoo me away.

Five minutes later I arrived at the band room. I nudged the door open. Dangling only my head inside, relying on the door's girth to shield me, I peeked at my former bandmates. They were warming up. They were wetting reeds, greasing instruments, emptying spit valves. They were shuffling sheet music, adjusting metal stands, running scales.

Probably anticipating my arrival, Mr. Price glanced up from his songbook and, spying me, began strolling in my direction with that distinctive gait of his. He let the door close behind him and joined me in the hallway. The school's mascot, a giant pioneer replete with coonskin hat and grizzly beard and ready musket, peered over us from a logo sketched on the cinderblock wall.

Mr. Price snapped his fingers, swiveled his head atop that thin stem of neck, and said, "Hey, man, why quit band?"

I plunged my hands into my pockets, stared at my shoelaces. I considered what words I could resort to in order to explain what I had felt yesterday. I wanted to say that I was too embarrassed to return to class; that I had only joined band in the first place because I wanted to belong somewhere, even among the cast-offs from elsewhere; that I had wanted to play trumpet, not baritone; and that I was ashamed to be too geeky even to fit in among the biggest geeks in our school. But I didn't say any of that. As I recall, I didn't say anything. I merely shrugged.

"You know you're the only baritone, right?" Mr. Price added as though he intended these words to trigger a revelation in me—as though I hadn't been living with the truth of this statement every day for the past several months. He laughed, incredulous. "I mean, you're it, man—you're the baritone!" He waited for me to respond, that foot again tapping out a frenetic tempo. He shook his head, tsked his tongue. "That's too bad, man," he finally said. "The thing is, my friend, you could really blow."

And with that, he turned on his heels and went back inside the band room.

I didn't immediately head back to shop class. I lingered outside the door. Soon enough the warm-up concluded. From the hallway, I could hear Mr. Price rap his baton against his metal stand and begin counting off. The rehearsal commenced. The school fight song began reverberating through the door and echoing into the hallway.

I cracked open the door and looked inside.

Band was proceeding along quite nicely without me. In unison, the woodwinds were chiming in on cue. The trumpeters were sitting up straight. The snare drummers were striking their licks. The chair between the tuba and the trombone, of course, was vacant.

Mr. Price was conducting the group as always, but at one point he set the baton on his music stand. As the band kept going he reached down out of sight. It was only when he rose again that I saw he was now clutching my old baritone.

A clarinet screeched. A trumpet came in a full measure too early.

But Mr. Price pursed his lips. Head bobbing, he shut his eyes, probably imagining himself gigging in some dive in Frisco, thirty years ago and thousands of miles away, the tinkling of piano keys, the rattle of ice cubes in a glass, a tip jar...

His fingers working the valves, Mr. Price swelled his cheeks and breathed into the horn. He was doing his best to lose himself in the music, to save his soul one note at a time; but it was clear that simultaneously directing the band and playing the baritone was too much, more than he'd bargained for, beyond all reasonable expectation.

It was a peculiar sensation, listening to the band play for the first time without my being part of it. I was gaining a new objectivity, hearing with new ears the same progression of notes I'd heard so many times before. I had one obvious response: They were terrible. This was noise. It was a racket bearing very little resemblance, I'm sure, to what Mr. Price heard in his head when he listened to *music*. And I saw, too, who was responsible for all this wreckage, the culprits throwing together all these bleats and honks and squawks: all the misfits, the kids like me, the porkers and grease-heads and zit-kings. All the kids who didn't belong in chorus, where the pretty kids wearing sunlight in their hair and matching pastel shirts sang Debbie Boone's "You Light Up My Life" with perfect timbre. The band geeks were in there, and I was out here, and my ears were ringing with their dissonance.

But it was too late to do anything about it. My choice was made. The deed was done.

I don't remember returning to class. I don't remember much at all, really, about the rest of that day, or that year, for that matter. Surely I went back to Industrial Arts, that morning and every one after, for the rest of my eighth-grade year. But I don't recall anything I made with those saws, planes, and drills, or who my classmates were, or even my teacher's name. If memory is all I have to go by, then I'm still outside the band room, alone in that hallway, listening to all that sweet cacophony coming from the other side of the door.

0 & 8

On Sundays, Dad worshipped the risen Savior, but on Saturdays our black and white Samsung TV became the altar for his worship of the South's unofficial religion: college football. He'd spend the morning mowing the lawn or tinkering under the hood of yet another deadbeat car, his jeans soiled with grass stains or his knuckles smudged with blood. Then he'd kill the afternoon watching Bear Bryant stroll the sideline in his houndstooth hat or Herschel Walker tuck the ball under his arm and plow through some poor free safety possessing the unmitigated gall to stand between him and the end zone. If Dad had his druthers, I would have been prepping for imminent stardom with Bryant's Alabama Crimson Tide or Walker's Georgia Bulldogs.

But by the time I turned thirteen, this fantasy had no grounding whatsoever in reality. All anyone had to do was take a gander at my scrawny chest and pipe-cleaner legs to see that gridiron glory did not wait in my future. I was not going to run the triple option and maneuver my way through behemoth linemen to clinch yet another trip to the Sugar Bowl for the Bear. If left up to me, famed Georgia announcer Larry Munson would never again growl, "Hunker down one more time, you hairy Dogs!" as the defense lined up for one last stop that would preserve a slim victory over an opponent of the Red and Black.

But Dad rigged up a basketball goal outside our suburban brick ranch. A precarious feat of architecture at best, it featured a plywood backboard nailed to a post buried two feet deep in the red Georgia clay. When a big rain came, the ground grew soft and the post leaned to one side or the other. I remember Dad getting home from work one day and, still clad in his Post Office uniform with the eagle patch on the shoulder and the blue stripe running down his trouser leg, joining me for a game of H-O-R-S-E. I beat him easily. Dad blamed yesterday's downpour, which had resulted in the goal leaning like Pisa's tower. "I'm a precision shooter," Dad claimed. "Any little defect throws me off. You're lucky we're not in a regulation gym."

Awkward as it was, that goal and the surrounding driveway became the setting for my earnest attempt to salvage athletic glory from the dregs of futility. Through all kinds of weather, I hoisted hundreds of shots every day until the rain, wind, and occasional ice wore the ball to a slick orb and warped its trajectory to correspond to the goal's tilting stature. Hoops was a poor substitute for gridiron greatness, all right, but in the end I did what I could to follow the advice we'd learned in Sunday school: "*Having gifts that differ according to the grace given to us, let us use them.*"

I played middle school basketball.

AND SO OUR TEAM GOT off to a bit of a rough start—an 0-8 start if we're counting here, and yes, it seemed like the whole school was counting—but we were sure things were about to change. We were eighth-graders; everything was always in a constant state of flux—our voices, our armpits, our moods— so we fully expected to reverse our (mis)fortunes on the hard court. After our latest game, Coach Keegan must have felt it too, because he postered our locker room walls with construction paper signs exhorting us to adopt as our mantra every cliché imaginable, including the worst of all sporting maxims: *It's not the size of the dog in the fight, but the size of the fight in the dog.* And we believed it. We indeed were puny, but feisty. We'd only lost that game to Turner Middle by 11 points, our slimmest margin of defeat to date, and we'd shown tangible signs of improvement. We'd reduced turnovers. Narrowed the rebounding deficit. Increased our free-throw percentage. Made our opponents wait until the fourth quarter before emptying the end of their bench and playing the kids with goggles, the ones who couldn't keep their socks from puddling around their ankles, the ones whose mothers made them wear mouthpieces. Listen: We were thirteen. We were, by definition, a work in progress.

Now we were lined up in the hallway, the dozen of us, caged by cinderblock walls, awaiting the signal to burst into the gym for a pep rally. And there was a salient fact, which these many years later, seems worthy of mention: I was first. I would lead my teammates onto the floor, pumping my fists, exhorting them to *Get hyped, guys, c'mon, let's go!* I'd never before had the honor of charging first into a pep rally; I'd always been one of the last stragglers, or, in one regrettable instance, the caboose. Adding to that visceral thrum filling my insides, tonight the schedule pitted us against our archrival, Chatham Hill. I took it as a vote of confidence that, on this special occasion, with those hated Wildcats next on our ledger, Coach Keegan chose me to tear through the blue and orange banner created by the spirit club.

My adrenaline was pulsing. I had entered that elusive realm of readiness—I was shuffling from foot to foot, on the verge of a sweat. *I was in the zone.* Chatham Hill should count themselves lucky we weren't tipping off right now. Jostling against those walls and each other, the stench of pubescence fogging toward the ceiling tiles, we seemed to be growing too big for that hallway to contain us.

But, first, the girls' team: 8-0, winners of every game by double digits, a ponytailed, trash-talking, Bubble Yum-blowing roster of assassins. They ran into the gym amidst wild applause from peers and faculty alike. Even the pariahs joined in, the dregs and the derelicts, the punks who, already, were killing most of their waking hours strung out on AC/DC and Space Invaders. And the veteran teachers too, the ones who had outgrown their need to redeem their own wretched memories of adolescence by becoming middle school cool twenty years too late. Look: Respect must be paid. Everyone understood the protocol here. And we all did our due diligence. The band played the school fight song. The cheerleaders smiled with cherry-gloss lips and shook pom-poms and yelled *Go! Fight! Win!* The girls' team gathered under the near basket and exchanged high-fives with an ease and finesse bordering on pure artistry.

As of late, our inverse records had become popular knowledge, and the collective student body had taken to making comparisons between the girls' run at perfection and our string of futility. And yes, quickly and decisively, a general consensus arose: The girls were better. If ever we scrimmaged, they would proceed to strike a blow for sisterhood everywhere by pummeling us into submission. And so this sentiment had been repeated so many times and with such certainty that, like all gossip in middle school, everybody soon accepted it as irrefutable fact. We boys did not dispute it. Somewhere inside our thirteen year old hearts, we too suspected the girls could beat us; and we hoped with all faith in the goodness of humanity that Coach Keegan—who surely had been a boy once—and the girls' coach would recognize the obvious and ignore the girls' standing request to arrange a scrimmage. We, however, did not trust the coaches in this matter. It seemed to us that the only way to avoid such an event coming to pass would be to win a game. Among our team there seemed to be the biding conviction that, if we could simply break through and win a single contest—even by a solitary point, even on a referee's blown call, even if Chatham Hill's best player took ill with a stomach virus at halftime—we could save face. We could put to rest all those comparisons of our records. Everybody would forget the scrimmage idea.

It was with these high hopes that we ran out of that hallway and into the gym. Again the band struck up the fight song and the cheerleaders shook their pom-poms and chanted. But then, unfortunately, there's this: Just as I exploded through the banner and sprinted ahead of my trailing teammates toward midcourt, something unexpected happened. Something very different from what we'd just witnessed when the girls took the court.

Jeers and heckles, hisses and hollers.

What I'm trying to say, y'all: They were booing us.

IT BEGAN AS A COUPLE OF CATCALLS, a stray whistle or two. Somebody shouted something unintelligible. But within moments the spark ignited, the bleachers rumbled with a deep, sonorous boom, and a single, unbroken roar of disgust filled the gym until it seemed the rafters shook, the band was drowned out, and even the cheerleaders were hushed by the unanimous sentiment of the crowd. Because I was first, I initially thought they were booing *me*. But by the time the last boy ran into the gym, the noise had swelled to such a din that there was plenty enough derision to go around. Every punitive aspect of middle school—the peer pressure, the conformity, the arbitrary judgment—seemed to converge in a perfect storm that united the entire student body against our ragtag assemblage of twelve boys.

But still: As we'd been instructed, we dutifully lined up, shoulder-to-shoulder, under the far basket. We thrust our chests before us. We jutted our chins forward. To no one's surprise, the boos only escalated. Standing there on the baseline, I searched the bleachers for any sign of consolation. A lone voice of compassion. An acne-scarred soul willing to declare solidarity with us losers and speak out against the masses. Alas—no one. Everywhere my peers were turning their thumbs upside down, pinching their noses, cupping their hands around their mouths to better amplify their opinion of us. Their faces became a blur of repugnant expressions, vile and lurid. At the other end of the court, the girls' team at first seemed dumbstruck, but promptly devolved into catty, well, *girls* whispering behind their hands.

In response, we did what teenage boys do—we acted as though we didn't care. If we didn't care, they couldn't hurt us; we could immunize ourselves against our own shame. Our collective body language suggested that we did not want to play basketball anyway—the school needed a team and, against our better judgment, we had consented to become one. We were taking one for the team, quite literally. We were martyrs here, people. Each of us turned to the teammate on either side, shrugged, grinned—tried our best to persevere with canned laughter. The kid next to me, Trey Flemings, and I glanced at each other a couple of times, recognized the primal fear dilating in the other's eyes and crouched to assume a posture of quick retreat if any foreign objects started flying from the bleachers. Anything seemed possible. We really didn't know what to expect.

Principal Sherburne climbed to her feet and strode toward the microphones assembled upfront for the standard remarks from the two coaches. Before she arrived at midcourt she was already employing her considerable girth and gesturing for the crowd to cease and desist this behavior right now, boys and girls, this very second—or else. She grabbed the mic, which immediately commenced whistling with shrill feedback. She said something, probably a few syllables of admonishment, and aimed a jagged finger at the crowd. But the boos only grew louder still. Nobody could hear a word she said.

When I again turned toward Trey, this time he was gone. He and the rest of my teammates had turned around and fled back toward the hallway through which we had entered.

There, Coach Keegan was standing at the door clapping and pointing toward the exit. He was pulling us out of the pep rally. He waved toward me as though conducting a fire drill, motioning for me to vacate the premises—immediately. My teammates were already attempting to squeeze through the door, each of them slipping through as the roar rained down from the rafters. I finally caught up to them, and a moment later I too was joining them in the silent hallway.

Coach Keegan was the last one through. He slammed the door shut behind us.

MY HOOPS OBSESSION HAD STARTED traditionally enough, when I was 10, with Bird and Magic's landmark national championship game in '79 (estimated viewing audience: 20 million). It had grown with the opportunity to toss up the jump ball for a Hawks-SuperSonics NBA game at the Omni in '80. It was Douglas County Night, and our rec league was sponsoring a contest in which the player who sold the most tickets to the game would toss up the jump ball and receive a ball signed by all the Hawks. My postman father sold over one hundred tickets to people on his mail route, thereby earning the prize for his son (who sold a grand total of two tickets—to his parents). I lobbed the ball toward the giant scoreboard above and then ran ducking for cover, because nobody informed me that this jump ball was only ceremonial—only NBA referees could officially commence a game. Two seven-footers, Tree Rollins and Jack Sikma, batted around my toss a couple of times before the ball bounded away and rolled to a stop near the scorer's table. A ball boy fetched it. Sikma shook my hand. Rollins offered a soul-shake. The hometown Hawks lost by 20.

But the watershed event confirming my love of the game came with the innocuous purchase of a single item from the toy section at the local Kmart: a Nerf hoop and ball. With this plastic rim, gossamer-thin net, and foam ball, I now found a toy commensurate with the capacity of my vast imagination. Listen: I became an All-American. I conjured a fictitious roster of teammates replete with positions, heights, and hometowns. I played a full 35-game schedule. I kept statistics. Example: It is a little known fact that in 1980 a fearless gunner bearing my name burst onto the national scene by scoring 37 points per game. After yet another victory, I imagined a gaggle of reporters crowding around my locker in search of a quote. I fancied myself good copy. I pilfered a broomstick from mom's kitchen and transformed it into a microphone. *Yessir,* I said. *It was a good win. My teammates were setting some great screens. I got some good looks and fortunately knocked down the open shots. I want to thank my Lord and Savior Jesus Christ.*

But real roundball proved more of a challenge. I desperately wanted to be a jock, a tough guy, ice in my veins, a kid who could step to the foul line with the game in the balance and drain two free throws without fear. It seems a flimsy mold for masculinity now, but in the early '80s, for me to be any other kind of boy would have resulted in a full-blown existential crisis.

I'd already explored other avenues—4-H club, beginning-level band, CO_2 cars. But sport was the vernacular in my family. I learned my seven-times tables by watching football games and counting touchdowns and extra points. I collected the entire first edition of Fleer baseball cards. I experimented, with unremarkable results, with Little League baseball and football. As a youngster I had shot up taller than most kids, sometimes a head higher, and gravitated toward hoops. I made the school team the previous year as a seventh-grader, but I didn't merit enough playing time such that my real hoop experience interfered with my imaginary one. We won a few games. We lost more. But now I was an eighth-grader on a slow ride through puberty, and those shorter boys had caught up or even surpassed me, and I still shot the ball with two hands because I wasn't strong enough to follow through with one. I played guard. I began the season in the starting lineup. But as the losses mounted, some personnel changes took place in the depth chart—what Coach Keegan called "a little shake-up in the line-up"—and I found myself demoted to the bench on a team that was riding an O-fer…and counting.

Consequently, I did not like Coach Keegan. To my mind, he was not a basketball coach. For evidence, I regularly recited to myself the facts. He taught Social Studies, not P.E. He was stocky, flat-footed, balding, with a wreath of curly brown hair. He wore a pastel blue tracksuit to every practice. He never talked about his own playing career, which served to make me suspicious of whether he'd ever had one. He never berated the referees either, which left me wondering whether he even knew the rules. He assigned positions in the most capricious manner, often changing them within a practice or game without any explanation of why. He provided no framework for attack; we ran no patterns, abided by no understood principles of play. He stuck us in a 2-3 zone and instructed us to box out when a shot was launched. "Play hard!" he insisted, but his commandment sounded trite and meaningless. Practices consisted of shooting a lot of free throws and scrimmaging half-court without any clear idea of what we were trying to accomplish. Occasionally, if our effort or execution did not seem to please him, Coach Keegan assigned what he called "gut sprints." We set the balls aside and ran, ran, ran.

The season began inauspiciously. On the first play of the first game, I passed to the wing and cut through the lane. We were running a give-n-go, the oldest play in the game, probably the first play Naismith conjured when he hung peach baskets. The ball struck my heel and bounced feebly away. It was an omen. The season quickly degenerated into a series of physical shortcomings, mental oversights, and outright travesties. Mike Eubanks fouled out in the first half of a game. Tyler Rogan raced the ball up court, aimed his pass at a teammate running the side-line, and proceeded to peg Coach Keegan between the shoulder blades. Sam Yeager grabbed a rebound in heavy traffic, swung his elbows wildly, and became so disoriented that he shot the ball at the other team's basket. (He missed. He always missed.)

Indeed, we thought our losses reflected Coach Keegan's inabilities as coach. As we moved inexorably toward a sea-son-long O-fer—and the girls kept humiliating their opponents by more points than we scored in an average game—our masculinity was at stake here. Surely we couldn't be to blame for why we weren't winning.

We orchestrated minor mutinies. When Coach Keegan commanded us to run laps around the school building, we'd jog around to the far side and slow to a rebellious trudge. We started wearing green sweatbands—despite the fact green wasn't a school color and didn't coordinate particularly well with blue or orange. Whenever somebody made a mistake in practice, under our breath we'd sarcastically invoke one of those ridiculous cli-chés from the locker room wall. *The measure of who we are*, we'd remind each other, *is what we do with what we have*—a phrase that takes on a whole new meaning when it's tinged with irony, and infused with sexual innuendo. Did I say we were eighth-grade boys? We might not have been good at hoops, but we were All-Stars at sexual innuendo.

AND SO WE HAD BEEN BOOED out of our own pep rally. We fled from the gym, down empty hallways that seemed so much bigger than usual; past bulletin boards declaring *Reading is Fundamental*; past the Lost and Found, the infirmary, the custodial closet, the cafeteria with the tables folded and rolled against the windows; past the wall of lockers where the cheerleaders had taped construction-paper basketballs with our names and uniform numbers etched in glitter—*Score that Basket!* and *Shoot for the Stars!*—until finally we arrived at Coach Keegan's classroom. We loped in. We filled the desks. There, stranded on the most distant wing of the school away from the rest of the student body, the other teachers, and the administrators—our whole community—we could hardly help but ascertain that all the rejects had been rounded up and quarantined in one tight space. Silently, we waited to see what came next.

Coach Keegan took his place in front of the chalkboard and stared at his shoes as though contemplating what kind of impromptu speech he could craft. He lifted his chin and surveyed the crowd. He searched our faces with the same kind of desperate expression we'd witnessed during time outs when our opponents put together another patented 14-2 run. We weren't expecting sympathy. After all, just as we had blamed him, he probably blamed us. He seemed poised to remind us that, after all, *we* were the ones who had missed all the shots, committed all the turnovers, lost all the games. *It's hard to make chicken salad out of chicken shit*, he must have been thinking. But then, surprisingly, came this: "Sorry, fellas," he told us. "I'm real sorry you go to school with a bunch of knuckleheads." He paused as if giving his brain ample time to come up with something more. We waited patiently, hopeful. But apparently he'd said all he had to say. He shook his head; he shrugged. He clapped his hands together once, sharply. Finally: "We got some time," he said. "The next class doesn't start for a half-hour. Make yourselves busy."

And with that Coach Keegan declined the opportunity to teach some kind of lesson. To impart wisdom. To tell us again about the size of the fight in the dog. He did not refer to any of those clichés. He didn't attempt to torque this catastrophe into a Teachable Moment that we would remember years from now.

We waited for him to reconsider. We studied him in utter silence and with a kind of attentiveness that, on another day, under routine classroom circumstances with study of, say, Aztec and Incan civilizations on the schedule, he probably would have appreciated.

But he would not be persuaded. "While you puzzle over how to kill some time," he said, "I got work to do," and collapsed into his own chair. He rummaged through his desk drawer until he located a red pen and began dutifully grading a stack of quizzes.

The only sound in the room was the squeak of Coach Keegan's swivel chair and the shuffle of papers as he finished one quiz and moved on to the next—until another teacher appeared in the doorway. It was Ms. McCleskey, a comely young Math teacher who had inspired among us plenty of lascivious locker room chatter. "Bill," she said. Coach Keegan lifted his head, set his red pen aside. Ms. McCleskey entered and crossed the room toward his desk, her steps delicate, an expression of grave concern spreading over her features. "I'm so sorry," she said. She began offering sympathy. She apologized on behalf of the entire school. She wished there was something she could have done. It was all just so—unexpected. "I admire what you did," she told him. "Real courage and leadership—that's what you showed." She patted his hand. They chatted for another brief moment before she apologized once more and disappeared out the door.

Then it was again just us—the Fairplay Middle School Pioneers basketball team.

After a couple more minutes of quiet, I think it was Darnell Nichols and Shane Woodson who folded a piece of notebook paper into a tight triangle and started up a game of paper football. Almost immediately others began pairing up and following suit. Jeff Rutherford and I squared off. We debated the heavier topics—we argued over whether our opponents' flick of the football was actually overhanging the edge of the desk, and we ran our fingers along the edge to confirm the results. We made goal posts of our fingers and thumbs and flicked extra points. Trey Flemings drew a hangman's noose on the chalkboard and proceeded to solicit letters from teammates. Donnie Gibson and Lee Isakson started thumb wrestling. Ronald Sinclair and Jason Tatum engaged in a cutthroat battle of Break the Pencil. And to our surprise, it wasn't long before a little miracle happened: We became so absorbed in quelling boredom inside our little foxhole that we forgot why we'd retreated to it in the first place.

Listen: We didn't beat our rival Chatham Hill that night. In fact, we didn't win a game all season. And yes—one day, at the very end of practice, Coach Keegan and the girls' coach confirmed our worst fears and arranged a scrimmage. With every tick of the scoreboard clock, the outcome seemed to matter much more to us than to the girls, who bypassed their trash talking and wore stoic expressions as they passed the ball around the perimeter in search of a good shot. After ten minutes of mostly ugly basketball, with the score tied 6-6, Coach Keegan called the game. In May, at the end of the school year, one of the girls, a point guard with a jheri curl and eyes in the back of her head, signed my yearbook.

She can sue me for plagiarism, but here's what she wrote, word for word:

You're a very nice person that I like a lot. I enjoyed watching you play hoops. You know, you can really handle a basketball. Keep up the good work.

> *Seriki Riley*
>
> *# 33*
>
> *81–82 Champs*

But all that was still to come. Right now, only minutes away from the end of the pep rally and kids spilling out of the bleachers and heading our way, we were still alone, twelve boys and their coach. Here, in the safe confines of Coach Keegan's classroom, we could flick paper footballs end over end through the uprights of our fingers. We could still picture our story ending the way sports stories are supposed to end. A victory over our archrivals. The final buzzer sounding and a chorus of dramatic music swelling as our chastened classmates swamp the floor in slow motion and pat us on the backs and tell us they knew we could do it. High-fives and smiles and hugs all around. In those stories, we were still capable of winning a game and becoming whoever our imaginations could conjure.

We were thirteen. The season wasn't over. We didn't yet know there was any other kind of story to tell.

ROCK EAGLE

In the summer of 1982, when my father began fretting that his suburban boy was spending too much time squeezing his joystick and shooting Asteroids on his Atari game system, he toted me to visit my grandparents in the foothills of the north Georgia mountains. Here, in the rural setting of his own boyhood, Dad took me for a winding afternoon stroll past the sun-bleached gray barns to the pastureland. I was fourteen. I'd just finished eighth grade. Along the way Dad did his best to acquaint me with the features of the rustic lifestyle. He let me feed a gelding that Paw-Paw was boarding for a neighbor. He pointed out the abandoned slaughterhouse, a stack of bricks so decrepit it looked as though it had been dropped from the sky. He rattled off the names of trees—poplar, dogwood, oak, and pine—pronouncing them with a reverence perhaps as close to poetry as he would ever venture outside the book of Psalms and his Baptist church. He noted the subtle differences in the veins running through their leaves and referred to the bark as *skin*.

Already this jaunt represented something of a compromise of Dad's vision of things, because we were traversing not the hundred acres of stubborn red clay where he'd undergone his raising, but instead the mere eleven acres where his mama and daddy moved when they sold their souls and up and decided to move to *town*. Which is to say: a place resembling civilization. A place with only a gravel driveway, unpasteurized milk in the fridge, and well water—but a wood burning furnace and indoor plumbing, too. Though Dad had spent his adulthood in Atlanta, where he'd been domesticated by marriage, fatherhood, and his job carrying mail through a hundred streets named Peachtree, he evinced a palpable longing for the feral days of his youth, and intended to impress upon me a proper respect for the land, and my own wild places, before my callow days were exhausted.

We were heading toward the creek that severed the pasture and divided what Dad called the upper and lower fields. It was July, the sun a pulsing ball of fire and the air thick and filmy with humidity. Already I was feeling withered by the heat. My skin—blanched by so many afternoons in the dim recesses of the local arcade or my murky bedroom—was leaking sweat in a slow burn. So upon sight of cool bubbling water, I sprinted ahead. But just as I was about to take a running leap across the creek, Dad called out from behind me, his voice guttural, raw, and desperate in a way I was unaccustomed to hearing from him. "Get back!" he commanded.

I stopped in my tracks. Dad commenced taking up rocks— big, fist-sized ones that seemed to materialize out of nowhere— and hurling them—*thunk, thunk, ka-thunk*—into the velvety moss sparkling emerald and gold on the bank's yonder side. I searched for whatever Dad was aiming for. But only after his throws had found their target did I realize he had just spared me from plunging directly atop the triangular head of a particularly agitated and venomous snake.

It was a moccasin, about three feet long and thicker than my wrist. Faded cross-bands ran the length of its body. Though it was now indisputably dead, I kept my distance and took a wide berth. I'd possessed a healthy fear of snakes as long as I could recall, probably dating back to Sunday school where in our notch of the Bible Belt the serpent of course carried the most sinister of reputations. Probably because he was a Baptist deacon, Dad seemed to take special pleasure in slaying this foe and no doubt saw symbolic import in the whole ordeal. He was already telling me how it was the stark white of its cottonmouth that had drawn his experienced eye—just as I was about to take flight across that stream. But lying there motionless, laid bare for my examination, this viper seemed bereft of all capacity to inflict harm.

Soon Dad employed a dead oak branch to pluck the snake from the bank. He held it aloft for my inspection, the corpse hanging limp as a piece of tired rope. As we followed the path back to the house, Dad took time to explain the gravity of the incident. "Nearest hospital is ten miles away," he told me. "You liked to leap right into those fangs of his." Once we made it to the house, Dad climbed the porch, jabbing the stick toward family members like a mischievous kid poking dogshit at the neighborhood boys. But these boys were my uncles—Dad's two brothers—and they had seen their share of dogshit and dead snakes, too. They didn't flinch. They instead marveled at its color. They were impressed by its girth. "That's a purty snake," Roy declared. Allen nodded in agreement. Paw-Paw spat tobacco juice into a JFG can. With a glass of buttermilk at her side, Maw-Maw sat fashioning old egg cartons and yarn into a decorative wastebasket. "Well," she said.

Dad set the moccasin in the yard and stretched it to its full extension. He stood back to admire it. Then, while I recounted the story to the others in a tone rich with gallantry, he disappeared into the kitchen for a few minutes before emerging again with a jug of vinegar and an empty, gallon-size pickle jar. He slid the stick under the snake, hoisting it, and dropped it inside, coiling it from tail to head. When he poured the vinegar into the jar, the snake buoyed and seemed animated for a frightful moment before Dad secured the lid.

AS DAD DROVE US HOME that evening, the pickle jar sat in the floorboard between my sneakers, and I felt as though I were transporting the wilderness of north Georgia to the sterile suburbs of Atlanta. During that two-hour ride I fancied myself a fearless adventurer returning from a lawless land with tangible proof of the dangers lurking therein. A snake of any type was a rare discovery in our subdivision of brick ranches, and a poisonous viper practically unheard of; and so it was that upon our arrival home, much discussion and debate ensued among my neighbors as to what this occasion meant with respect to my young life. Randall Clayton's dad, who sold used cars for a living and served as a lay preacher in his Methodist church, inspected the snake and told us, in a tone of utter certitude, that Dad had saved my life. "That snake had bit you," he said, "you'd be a goner, boy." He sounded convincing. But whatever it meant in the universe's cosmic scheme, this snake's demise seemed timely and fortuitous indeed, because it just so happened that the next week I was scheduled to attend 4-H camp, where I would be presenting a project based on Georgia wildlife.

Now that I was a teenager, this impending trip to summer camp carried a tacit importance that neither my parents nor I ever named but surely felt. By this time I had come to be known as a disappointment. I seemed indifferent to the spiritual greatness that Mom, in particular, believed I'd been "called" to attain. She had named me after the writer of one of the four gospels, and believed I was destined to work as a missionary among the natives in some faraway jungle, spreading the Good News, my eyes lit with God's love. My teachers, though, labeled me an underachiever, a tough sell. Parent-teacher conferences consisted of them telling my mother, over and over, I had *potential*. Finally, one of them, a mercurial woman named Ms. Gonzalez, suggested 4-H club. We'd had a few run-ins, Ms. Gonzalez and I. She found me unmotivated; I saw her as overbearing. As a result, during this particular conference there seemed to be tension between Ms. Gonzalez and my mother, and perhaps she was beginning to doubt her justification for treating me as she had. She began citing her pending divorce as the reason for her irritability, taking my mother into confidence perhaps simply because she, too, was a woman. After rambling on about how stressful her life had become, the rigor of balancing her personal sorrow with her professional expectations, Ms. Gonzalez seemed to remember the occasion of our meeting in the first place, and returned the conversation to me. As if to apologize for burdening my mother with her own troubles, Ms. Gonzalez began praising me. She said I was a smart apple. A little grit and determination would take me a long way. She patted my hand. She eyed me with a compassion that I'd never before received from her. "You have so many talents," she told me. "All you need is an opportunity to showcase them." She curled her fingers into a fist and pumped it once, hard, apparently attempting to inspire in me a go get 'em attitude. She told my mother that a weekend at an upcoming 4-H camp called Rock Eagle would "allow your son to shine. You know, he possesses so many gifts that people need to know about!" The unfamiliar warmth in her voice made me suspicious. I considered whether to press her for details, for an enumeration of the talents the world and I were ignorant of. Ultimately I spared her the trouble of naming them.

But I did my due diligence. Weeks of preparation went into my project. I completed at least some cursory research in the *Encyclopedia Britannica* in my school library, and I remember sprawling out on my bedroom floor and sketching a full-color picture of the wild—a slice-of-life tableau of some wooded locale where I had never been. I rehearsed my spiel repeatedly, and presented it to my parents, who gave me high marks. Even Ms. Gonzalez offered a few pointers. The school year ended. As July and my departure drew closer, I felt ready. And now, in a turn of good fortune that seemed to suggest the universe's approval, I had secured this reptile as the ideal visual aid.

On the appointed Friday morning, my parents drove me to the county 4-H office, where I boarded a school bus containing a crowd of kids from the various middle schools. We were soon puttering east on I-20 toward a town called Eatonton. The fact that my parents were not accompanying me contributed to the mythology I busily created during the bus ride: to my mind this camp represented my striking out on my own, unencumbered by background or familial obligation. When I joined 4-H the leaders had told me that the club itself had no birthplace and no individual creator—it had been simply called into being by necessity. The world needed emphasis on Head, Heart, Hands, and Health and, thus, 4-H was born. And so: somewhere between my hometown and Rock Eagle, I invented the boy I planned to use this weekend to become. He was, above all, an outdoorsman. Undaunted by extreme temperatures, pestilence, or hostile terrain, he was the kind of boy who could feel perfectly at home in the wilderness setting I had drawn for my project. If you dropped him into that place, he would employ only his wits, instinct, and bare hands to survive. I saw the faceless strangers at Rock Eagle accepting me unquestioningly as that boy, because after all they had no knowledge of any other. I could be whoever I said I was. I imagined accumulating a pile of ribbons, badges, and sashes over the weekend—and a story to accompany each one. I pictured myself sporting them proudly as I disembarked the bus.

When my parents saw me next, I would be shining like tinsel.

UPON OUR ARRIVAL AT ROCK EAGLE, the counselors introduced themselves, split the males and females into groups, and promptly led us on separate tours of the premises. The male counselors went by unisex names, Riley, Austin, or maybe Blaine; they were boys in their early twenties, college kids with stringy unwashed hair and splotchy beards. They asked how the bus ride had been, and seemed to take our grunted replies into careful consideration, into pensive reflection, and to shake their heads and say, *That's very cool, man.* Whatever our mumbled answer to their sincere questions, they declared it *awesome* or *amazing* and nodded their heads approvingly. They had hairy legs, scrawny shoulders, and virtually identical wardrobes: they wore arrowhead pendants, flip-flops, and T-shirts with Native American dream catchers emblazoned on the front.

Their tour climaxed with a visit to the camp's main selling point: a stone effigy sculpted in the shape of a giant bird. According to our hosts, Native Americans built Rock Eagle for religious purposes over 2,000 years ago. It was a quartz rock formation—over 100 feet long and 100 feet wide, and taller than eight feet at the breast. What did we think about *that*? Did we have questions?

We did not give it much thought at all. We did not pose questions. As a general consensus, our crowd was underwhelmed. From our ground-level vantage point, Rock Eagle looked very much like a big pile of rocks. We did not feel sacred in its presence. We did not feel an electric current connecting us to these

Indians who long ago, in this very spot, had built a monument to their gods.

But our interest did register a slight change when, as we resumed our tour, Riley, Austin, and Blaine began talking about the upcoming event that would conclude our weekend at Rock Eagle: a dance. It would be tomorrow, Saturday night, after the competitions had ended. There'd be a deejay. Music, food, and fun. The girls would join us.

That Friday night, while the other boys wallowed in their escape from their parents' supervision, I climbed onto a top bunk and prepared to inherit my fate. I silently rehearsed my presentation, whispering the words to myself. I took satisfaction in knowing I could visualize my outline in my head—I could picture the words as I'd written them on the page. I considered which body language might best accompany my words—whether a few dramatic hand gestures would help win over the judges. I distinctly remember praying to God that I would win over the judges. Down below, though, in the bottom bunks, this gang of kids away from home for the first time reveled in the freedom of the night. They were rowdy, these boys. They were disturbing the peace. They were so unruly, they kept the counselors awake in the next room.

One of the counselors threw open the door. "Guys, hey guys!" Blaine said. He summoned our attention. "Hey, I've got an idea!" he said. "Be very quiet. Close your eyes and listen to nature outside. Listen, listen. What do you hear?"

A hush fell over the group. There was a pause. Everybody looked at each other.

"What sounds do y'all hear Mother Nature making tonight?" Blaine asked.

General befuddlement pervaded the cabin. A long, awkward silence. Finally, someone said maybe he heard the wind.

"Good, good!" Blaine said. "What else do you guys hear?"

A second kid said he heard crickets.

A third one said he heard a bird flying.

"That's great!" Blaine said. "That's what I'm talking about. You're cooking with gas now, boys! What else?"

The moon, someone else said.

"Beautiful," Blaine said. "That's really beautiful. Poetry, man." He was a good guy, that Blaine. He meant well. "Did you hear him, fellas? This kid's a poet and didn't even know it. He heard the *moon*! Awesome. Rock Eagle is an awesome place, y'all. Anything else you guys hear out there?"

One kid, a portly stump of a boy from Rockdale County, shushed everybody to silence. "Shh, shh, what's that?" the boy said.

"What's what?" Blaine asked. He cocked his ear to tune in whatever music would flow next from the blanket of night outside. Everybody leaned closer, as if synchronizing their heartbeat with the cadence of the woods at nighttime.

Then, with timing even I had to admire, this fine young scholar from Rockdale raised one butt cheek and cut a vicious fart. The noxious stench wafted toward the ceiling, where it lingered till morning.

AT PROMPTLY 8:30 A.M., with two bowls of Frosted Flakes still sloshing in my belly, I joined a trio of boys in a room vast enough to contain an echo. Our competition would soon begin. Each of us killed time by sizing up the others. One of the boys drew my particular interest. He was clad in blue jeans, hi-top canvas sneakers, and a horizontally striped T-shirt. Originally I suspected his homespun persona was all affectation, a contrived act, but then he introduced himself. "Lionel Pierre Lewis," he said, priming my hand like a water pump. "What's yours?" His accent was backwater. His drawl called to mind stray dogs, Vienna sausages, and BB guns.

I had dressed in what I thought was appropriate attire for the occasion: a starched polo, green polyester pants, patent leather shoes. I meant to make an impression. Poise and confidence: that's what the judges would see in me. Before ever speaking a word, I would have this crowd convinced they were in the presence of an authority.

Initially my preparation paid off. Once my presentation began, I had my act together. I was employing impeccable hand gestures as I alluded to my poster-board and detailed the delicate network of ecological balance. I was speaking with fluency beyond my years and backing it up with facts. I was educating the masses, all the while keeping my ace in the hole—my water moccasin—under wraps in a paper bag until just the right moment, when the fluorescent lights above would serve as a spotlight for my grand crescendo. The way I had it figured, this whole competition was nothing less than my coronation, and that night at the dance I would officially be crowned. To put it humbly: I was dishing an erudite presentation.

Which, unfortunately, turned out to be the problem. It sailed over the judges' heads. I was on an intellectual rampage—holding forth on biodiversity and wetlands and deforestation—but they were still a cup of coffee short of awake. One judge kept patting his shirt pocket as though he really needed a cigarette. The other seemed lost in a daydream as he stared at the floor.

Nevertheless, I was still detached enough from reality to think I actually had a chance of winning—until near the end of my presentation.

That's when my poster fell.

Even in that draftless room, the poster-board featuring my hand-drawn wilderness setting slid off the easel and skidded across the floor like a windblown piece of trash before coming to rest facedown on the tile. I remember smirking, or exhaling with disgust—some indication that *this was not my fault*. Some larger forces in the universe were conspiring against me. I could have seen this occurrence as random: in 1982, at a 4-H camp called Rock Eagle in Eatonton, Georgia, a poster-board fell off an easel. But prior to this moment, I had been so convinced that this weekend would mark some kind of turning point in my life, I now couldn't shake the thought that the turn had been a proverbial wrong one, which had taken me in a very bad direction. I remembered praying to God the night before that I would win, and now I felt utterly abandoned. I tried my best to compose myself, to perhaps win some pity-points by summoning a climactic resolution despite the odds. But by the time I broke out my pickled snake, and thoroughly underwhelmed the judges with my piece de resistance, my body language must have been such that simply surviving this ordeal would in itself constitute a kind of victory. When I resumed my seat I did so with all the aplomb of an abject failure. I slumped in my chair. Those Frosted Flakes commenced curdling in my gut.

Lionel Pierre Lewis presented last. He toted a green aluminum tackle box to the podium. It was beat-to-hell. Clearly it had sat in dank garages, languished in the bed of pickup trucks, been pinged by steady rain, falling acorns, tobacco juice. I saw this sorry excuse for a visual aid and formulated a single thought: This kid needs to hitch the first ride back to Mayberry.

Lionel commenced his presentation by setting the tackle box on the table, popping the clasp, and raising the lid to reveal (not one, not two, but...) *three* tiers of tackle: flies, lures, sinkers, floaters, spinners, line, reels, and plastic worms. And this much was clear immediately: Lionel knew his jargon. He knew pike, carp, bass, trout, and what he called "flatheads," which through a process of shrewd deduction I gradually interpreted to mean catfish. In his vernacular, he did not frequent ponds or lakes—he called them "fishin' holes." These bodies of water were hidden in secret locations, their whereabouts far removed from the recreational hacks. Only the genuine article could drop his line in a fishin' hole.

When I heard Lionel couple *tackle box* with the word *grandpa*, I knew I was in trouble. But my death knell was the phrase *passed away*, as in: *My grandpa give me this tackle box a coupla days before he passed away.* Things were amiss. Here I'd been informing the general public about conserving our natural resources, and this huckster was trotting out his dead granddaddy's ghost to tug at the heartstrings of these gullible louts calling themselves judges. It hardly seemed fair. Lionel was rummaging through his tackle box, plucking items at random with no discernible strategy, no evidence of rehearsal, simply reminiscing his way through a Show & Tell-style presentation. "Oh, here's a spinner," he was saying. "Grandpa used this one to catch a seven-pound big-mouth last summer. It was the last fish he ever caught…" He was stringing together anecdotes as they entered his simple mind one right after the other, and by the end of the presentation he had caught himself a veritable mess, including two impressionable judges who swallowed the bait, whole.

When the competition ended Lionel was wearing a blue ribbon and flashing the kind of cornpone grin that blinds you.

Did I win anything? I did indeed. I garnered Honorable Mention—which hardly seemed honorable at all when you consider this particular competition included a grand total of four contestants.

In our corner of the world, where four varieties of poisonous snakes lurk underfoot and we believe a particularly cagey one literally spoke to Eve, I should have known better than to think a serpent would bring good fortune.

Without calling us by name or even making eye contact, the judges shook our hands and thanked us for our participation. Then they dismissed us. Outside, somewhere near the pile of rubble they called Rock Eagle, I hoisted my pickled snake, summarily dumped it into an aluminum trashcan, and trudged away.

STILL, THERE WAS THE MATTER of the dance. The counselors held it outside in the evening air, under a pavilion with a tin roof. There were streamers and white-hot lights. A disco ball dangling from a wooden rafter overhead. An inviting spread of soft drinks, cheese balls, potato chips, and candy bars. A deejay playing "Le Freak." And though I showed up wounded and sensitive to the prevailing injustice of the universe, I found that Fate was not yet ready to grant me reprieve. To wit: Through some mysterious process I couldn't fathom, all my fellow 4-H-ers had already paired up. I'd like to claim I was stag only because I was late, but the truth is that the other kids possessed a code I was oblivious to. They understood the subtle rituals of mating season. They held some intrinsic knowledge of how to *connect*. And yes: Lionel Pierre Lewis, still wearing my blue ribbon, had reeled in a partner, a little *do si do* with pigtails, Wrangler jeans, and cowgirl shit-kickers. I scanned the periphery of the crowd for a lone wallflower. Every girl was spoken for.

It was then that a chaperone appeared, a plump Team Mom-type with oversized teeth and a little too much lipstick for my sour mood. She introduced herself as Mary Anne. Mary Anne said I looked thirsty. "A soda will do you some good," she said. And before I even had time to recognize I had been sucked into conversation, she was dragging me toward the refreshments and offering me a Mello Yello and chatting with me in a tone I suspected was filled with pity but maybe not. Our conversation was undoubtedly pedestrian, strained by the impossibility of finding any common ground; so before my drink was half gone she relieved me of it and set it on the table and grabbed my hand and started escorting me toward the crowd. "May I have this dance?" Mary Anne shouted before turning her head and ignoring my reply. She pulled me toward the middle of the action. There, amidst all the legitimate couples, I found myself paired up with this woman—culottes skirt, varicose veins branching across one of her calves, somebody's *mom*.

Too absorbed in their own budding romances to dither with a fortysomething woman and her choice of dancing partners, the rest of the kids seemed oblivious to us. Which was helpful, because it did not take long for Mary Anne to reveal her deficiencies as a dancer. She began trying to synchronize her steps with the music. She began clapping her hands awkwardly, as though trying to pound two fish together. Meanwhile, I just slumped with my fists plunged in my pockets. "Come on," she implored me. "Let's see what you've got!" The best I could manage was shifting my feet around without any particular regard for the beat. Hoping to satisfy her, get her off my case, I tapped my foot restlessly. Snapped my fingers. Bobbed my chin a couple of times. Finally she reached out and snatched my hand again and commenced twisting me around in a circle.

I remember "If I Can't Have You." I remember "Staying Alive," "Ring My Bell," "She's a Bad Mama Jama"—and a particularly awkward slow dance to Peaches and Herb's "Reunited." And I remember shuffling around that cement floor, slick with oil stains, the lights aswarm with the wings of a thousand moths, and the crickets singing in the pauses between the songs while the deejay changed records.

Though she possessed particularly fleshy triceps that waddled in contrast to the groove, Mary Anne thought she was tearing up the floor. She seemed to be working under the audacious assumption that kids were clearing the floor to open space for her physical artistry. She bathed in the glow of the disco ball orbiting above her head. At some point she opened her eyes and seemed stunned by the realization she hadn't awakened in some other dimension. Her body fell idle long enough to take in the movement of her partner—this boy who was, strangely, *me*—and she marveled aloud at what I hadn't known I was doing until that very moment: "You're a good dancer!" she yelled above the din.

I surveyed my feet and came to the startling discovery that I was, in fact, dancing. This revelation inexplicably inspired me to break into a spin clearly derivative of the line dances I'd seen on *Soul Train*.

"How did you *do* that?" she wanted to know. "Can you teach me?"

I performed a second spin.

"Let me try that!" she said.

And then Mary Anne launched into some kind of clumsy spin that knocked her hair from its tight bun and sent her stumbling headlong into a dizzy whirl that ended as ingloriously as it had begun—with her desperately pawing for dry land. "Is that how you do it!?" she asked.

I just nodded as though I knew what I was doing, and resumed strutting to the groove. It was one of those events in your life that, even as it's happening, takes on all the qualities of memory. You experience these moments through a hazy scrim of sensations, and later, when you recall them, they seem more dreamed than remembered. It's probably only then that you suddenly understand why all those ancient Indians would choose this very place to construct their giant bird, why they toted and stacked all those rocks, why they would have thought this site was sacred. You again see this woman with the varicose veins and too much lipstick who could have stayed by the punch bowl and off the dance floor instead of rescuing you from the sum of your failures. In these moments of memory, it's as though you've mounted the back of an eagle eight feet tall with wings spanning more than a hundred feet, and you're flying high enough above your past life to realize that what's going on down there looks maybe an awful lot like what the folks in our Baptist church meant when they used the word *grace*.

HAZZARD COUNTY, GEORGIA

W e neighborhood boys got in the habit of showcasing our evolving vocabulary when we gathered on Friday nights at Leon Puckett's house to watch *The Dukes of Hazzard* and talk dirty to Daisy Duke. We believed our language should reflect our new status as full-grown men. After all, we recently had passed the eighth-grade Sex Ed unit mandated by the state of Georgia. We'd perused the veritable library of smut circulating among our dingy fingers. We'd taken our respective turns with Leon's telescope, ogling my next-door neighbor Janie's open window for a glimpse of her celestial body. So: Friday night meant Waylon Jennings singing "Good Ol' Boys" and our suburban posse crowding around Leon's color TV to spend a primetime hour in Hazzard County, Georgia, which showed up nowhere on a map but most certainly occupied a vivid place in our imaginations. It meant one of us—usually our host, Leon himself, because he was officially a high schooler and therefore more worldly than the rest of us—crawling on his hands and knees close enough to fog the screen with his noxious breath and telling Daisy, in no uncertain terms, what he'd like to do to her. "Listen up, baby," he'd say. "Lemme lay you across the hood of the General Lee and make you do a Rebel Yell."

Of course Leon spoke for all of us. Though he had a poster of Farrah Fawcett on his wall—yes, *that* poster—it was Catherine Bach—aka Daisy Duke—who had become the latest celluloid vixen to stoke our fantasies and trigger a burning sensation in our loins. She seemed fit to maintain this status for a good long while. She was a Southern girl, after all, and could never seem to find a steady beau, bless her heart, which made our ignoble crowd believe we actually had a chance.

During the boring parts of an episode, when Bo and Luke Duke drove the General Lee like a bucking bronco through the red clay back roads of Hazzard, infuriating Boss Hogg and eluding Roscoe P. Coltrane yet again, we ignored the show entirely. Unless, of course, Cooter Davenport made an appearance. Cooter provided us ample opportunity to laud the show's writers for naming a character after a woman's private part. Otherwise, we killed time by raiding Leon's refrigerator or inflicting bodily injury on one another.

We had no acceptable and socially-approved outlet for this sexual energy tripping through our veins, so we waylaid each other with pillows, thumped each others' ears, and made lewd references to each others' moms, this time incorporating words from our Sex Ed unit like *hymen, vulva,* and *labia.* We could identify these features on a textbook diagram, but we didn't know anything about them otherwise. Only Leon Puckett even claimed firsthand knowledge. We compiled a spiral-bound notebook containing frank and lurid assessments of every girl in eighth-grade. We ranked each according to the criteria—all anatomical, of course—we thought constituted feminine pulchritude. We exhibited no interest in personality, disposition, or character, because the girls ignored us, generally, and stashed away their intangible qualities to themselves.

Among our questionable outfit, I was the designated poet. I would like to think this appointment had something to do with my facility with words; more likely, it resulted from the fact I was the only one passing Language Arts. Anyway, one Friday night Leon paid me a dollar to improvise some verse about Bobby Manning's mother. Her name was Joan. The finished product would win me no awards, but I do remember feeling particularly proud of the concluding couplet rhyming *Joan* and *moan*.

But when Daisy Duke graced the screen in those cut-off denim shorts and that plaid shirt tied to reveal her blessed navel, we put aside all distractions. We paid rapt attention. We each felt the strange stirring in our Fruit-of-the-Looms and hid our tender hearts and our sincere devotion from one another by vowing publicly to spoil Daisy's considerable virtue.

Here's the upshot: these were just the rules we played by. Everybody knew them tacitly. Daisy was there to be ogled, groped, and manhandled. But to profess any sort of love for her—or for any of the more pedestrian varieties of female such as the girls who actually occupied our same orbit—would have generated grave suspicion of whether your wood was wet, or if you had any wood at all.

Which meant I kept my love for Daisy a secret. I suspect I wasn't alone in my desire to put all bluster and bravado aside and just *talk* to Daisy. Surely the other boys also imagined themselves taking a window table at the Boar's Nest and asking Daisy to sing for them—because as dedicated viewers, we all knew what Daisy really wanted was to be a singer, and for somebody to listen to her song. But if there were others, we didn't commiserate. It was against the code. A violation of some kind of primal pact we'd made with each other.

So when Leon Puckett crawled toward Daisy with his tongue all adrip, I egged him on, too. I had no choice but to believe that I alone, of all the boys in the world, had begun to comprehend an insight burning hot within the dim wattage of my pubescent brain. An insight that, if I'd had words for it, would have gone something like this: Bodacious as she was, Daisy Duke possessed, right beneath that lovely swell of cleavage, something unlikely and wholly unexpected.

A beating heart.

IN JUNE, THE SCHOOL YEAR ENDED and *The Dukes of Hazzard* went into summer reruns. And by July, hoarding my love for Daisy had convinced me something was wrong with me—that I lacked the callousness essential to adolescent boyhood. This, along with hours spent alone in the bathroom inspecting my nether regions to determine whether I was developing in an *age-appropriat*e manner, persuaded me to journey to our local public library in search of all the answers to the questions I believed Mr. Harding's Sex Ed unit had deprived me of. In those days, they told us the public library was our ultimate resource, our portal to new worlds of information. Dewey Decimal was our friend. Reading was *fun*damental.

Once I began my search, the card catalog fulfilled my research needs, and almost instantly I was in possession of the call number for a book named, concisely enough, *Boys and Sex*. The mere title of this manual promised answers to all the questions I had failed to ask Mr. Harding during his drab lectures summarizing the procreative process. My questions would have borne little relation to the logistics, to what went where and how, because

Mr. Harding had done his pedagogical duty with the science of it all. What I really wanted to know resided nowhere in his glut of facts. Which led me to a conviction that, had I uttered it aloud, would have shamed my evangelical Christian parents—the selfsame parents who taught me better than to speak blasphemy and are hereby absolved of all responsibility for my reciting it here: Securing this book felt like a quest for salvation. It represented, at once, sacred text as well as ultimate self-help manual.

I scrawled the call number on a strip of paper and commenced my search. I followed Dewey Decimal to the 600s, where I made a troubling discovery: *Boys and Sex* was absent from the shelf. Hoping only to blame some careless misarranging, I scoured the section, running my index finger along the spine of each and every volume. Then I checked all surrounding shelves. Surely my book was somewhere among these towering stacks. I explored with the single-minded compulsion of a boy driven by his glands. If there was a stray piece of lint, I discovered it. But *Boys and Sex* was nowhere to be found. Which, of course, led me to the obvious conclusion: Some other sex-ignorant boy had pilfered it.

Consequently, here's where the ominous music starts to play.

I approached the librarian at the reference desk. She was filling out some paperwork. Her blue hair gave her a bearing of experience, of immeasurable knowledge, as though at some point in her distinguished career she had laid hands on every book ever written. She was a calm presence, with a patient, sincere manner about her. Clearly a credit to her profession, she seemed to take deep personal satisfaction in helping those seeking her assistance. The librarian could not know that the child skulking toward her desk was desperate to learn the methods of desire. She did not know that this boy before her, wearing a Braves cap, a knock-off Izod polo with the alligator replaced by an absurd looking *dragon*, and Trax sneakers, was willing to risk all claims to decency and his relationship with Jesus Christ in exchange for information regarding a missing book.

I cleared my throat. "Excuse me, ma'am."

The librarian glanced up from her paperwork, peered at me over the half-moons of her bifocals. She smiled pleasantly. "How are you today, young man?"

I told her I was good.

"How can I help you?"

I peered over my shoulder, performed a quick reconnaissance of the area. "Do you have a book called *Boys and Sex?*" I whispered.

"Have you checked the card catalog?" she asked. It's likely that her volume was neutral, but at the time it sounded a little too loud in my ears—something on the scale of a sonic boom.

"Yes ma'am. I checked the shelf. It's missing."

"Perhaps it's been checked out," she said.

As the librarian began sifting through her files, I considered that other boy for a moment—the one who now possessed the book. I imagined him sitting on the floor in his room, somewhere in the basement recesses of a nearby split-level, his legs crossed Indian style, his pulse skipping through his blood, *Boys and Sex* weighing heavily in his palms. I pictured the boy cocking his ear, listening for footsteps outside his closed door, ready to shove the book under his bed at even the slightest suggestion of another human being loitering near the top of the stairs. I felt a great comradeship with that boy. I wished that the two of us could lie side-by-side, shoulder-to-shoulder, on that bedroom floor, poring over the pages of *Boys and Sex*. I wished that we could compare notes; that we could ask each other all the questions we had been so very afraid to ask Mr. Harding; that we could fill in the missing facts in each other's understanding; that we could know, when I went home, that our secret would be between us. I wished we didn't have to go at this pursuit alone—that learning the mysteries of sex was not such lonely work.

While the librarian continued consulting her records, I again cased my surroundings, suspicious that someone who knew me might be lurking in the vicinity. The air conditioner hummed, a low pleasant drone—but a bead of sweat trickled down my ribcage. I pretended to investigate the periodical section. I skimmed the pages of *Sports Illustrated*, feigning to study it when in fact I wouldn't have been able to recall a single word just moments later. I even peeked outside the window to assure myself that my mother, who had agreed to wait in the car studying her upcoming Sunday school lesson while I picked up a *Hardy Boys* or two, was still preoccupied.

"Young man!" I heard. The librarian summoned me to the circulation desk. I approached her hopefully. "Yes, it's just as I thought," she reported. Her face held an expression of sorrow and regret. She seemed apologetic that she had to break such news to me. "It's been checked out, I'm afraid."

I could not raise my head. Something approximating despair was rising inside me, clogging my chest. I felt my face flush, my eyes go glassy. My lower lip might be trembling. "How long will it be out?" I asked. "When is it due?"

"It was just checked out," she responded. "It's not due for almost three weeks."

The world's axis seemed to be grinding to a halt, leaving me perpetually fourteen, ignorant, and confused. Three weeks seemed an eternity. She might as well be telling me to come back when I turned twenty-one. I tried not to blame the librarian, but who knew somebody's *grandmother* could be the bearer of such bad news?

"Would you like to put a hold on it?" she suggested. "Would you like to reserve it?"

I said yes. "*Yes*," I said. "I'd really appreciate it."

"Splendid," she said. She clasped her hands together. She swelled with satisfaction at having performed her job admirably. She was allowing information to reach the masses. Surely moments like these were why she had entered such a noble profession in the first place. She jotted a notation in her perfect librarian script. "Is this for school or for personal interest?" she asked.

With this question, her voice seemed to take on a new tone. It lost its melody and dropped an octave. I heard compassion, or maybe pity. Standing there—yes, in the *summer* of 1982—I felt like this old woman was able to see through me—she knew me in a way that maybe nobody else did. She seemed to understand something core and essential about me. Her eyes held me in such a way that convinced me she wanted to place a grandmotherly hand atop mine and assure me that everything was going to be okay—that she wanted to give me a chance to tell her what kind of boy I was. She maybe saw me as the kind of boy who next Friday night, instead of joining my ignoble crowd at Leon Puckett's house to watch *The Dukes of Hazzard*, would stay home, in my own bedroom, with my black and white TV tuned to the show. Maybe I would wait through the car chases, the schemes of Boss Hogg, the stuttering of Roscoe P. Coltrane for the welcome sight of Daisy Mae Duke on the screen. Maybe when she appeared, all made up in her short-shorts and high heels, with sheen in her hair and a smile on her lips, maybe I would pull my chair closer to the screen as though I were making myself at home at the Boar's Nest. Daisy would bring me a glass of milk, with a wink and a smile, before taking the stage to sing, and then I'd settle in and listen to her song.

But far as I knew, there was no room in this world for that kind of boy. I was fourteen. I'd passed Sex Ed. My dad was a Baptist deacon, my mom a Sunday school teacher. So when the librarian asked whether this book was for school or for personal interest, at first I stood there blinking stupidly, recognizing this moment as the logical culmination of my life so far, before finally I answered the only way I knew how.

"School," I said.

SOUL PATROL

So there they were: black kids, maybe twenty altogether, wearing matching black T-shirts with bright yellow letters that read **SOUL PATROL**. On the backs of their T-shirts, each wore a different nickname: **FRESH G, SMOOTH J, C-LOVER, H-TOWN**. Xavier, one of the few I'd ever actually spoken to, called himself **THE X-FACTOR**. They were mostly seniors. It was 1983, so the Soul Patrollers breakdanced, wore Jheri curls like Michael Jackson, and invented a whole series of five-minute handshakes that only they could memorize. Before school, in the student parking lot, they circled around souped-up Impalas and Oldsmobiles, blasting the Sugar Hill Gang, Kurtis Blow, and Grandmaster Flash and the Furious Five, and rapping along with the lyrics as though they'd composed every word themselves. They told the rest of us not to push them because they were close to the edge, and we obeyed. Between classes, they didn't just walk down the hallways; they strutted in their laceless Adidas—they glided, effortlessly, as though forever riding one of those moving sidewalks at the airport. They wore parachute pants, Kangol hats, mirrored shades, and diamond studs in their ears.

And here I was: quintessential ninth-grade. The kind that other freshmen saw in the hallway and said, "That kid is *so* ninth-grade." Oily brown hair swept back in wings. A pubescent shine that made my face glow like a halogen light bulb. An Adam's apple big as a wrecking ball.

But because I was a ninth-grader, the future suddenly required my attention. The previous eight years, teachers told us, were just rehearsal for this new stage of our lives. Now, what we did mattered. As an introduction to high school, the curriculum airdropped me into a class called *Career Planning*. There, I was instructed to think about who I was, where I wanted to go, how I intended to make it all happen. The results were predictable. The straight-A kids wanted to ace every class and become valedictorian. The jocks wanted to score touchdowns on Friday nights and win football scholarships to SEC schools. The potheads wanted to get high in their parents' basements and play guitar in death-metal bands. The Future Homemakers of America wanted to catch a husband and begin procreating.

I wanted to be in the Soul Patrol.

I wasn't a senior; I wasn't cool; but of course the biggest obstacle facing me was that I wasn't black. I was not going to let this minor detail stop me. I spent many hours dreaming of wearing one of those Soul Patrol T-shirts. The back of mine would say **KID BEAVE**. To hasten my transformation, I compiled all the accouterments of the hip hop lifestyle. I bought an Afrika Bambaataa tape. I became a devout follower of his Universal Zulu Nation. I incorporated *yo* into every sentence—as in "Yo, moms, how 'bout spotting me twenty bucks so I can buy this pair of Smurf-blue parachute pants with, yo, like a thousand zippers?" I scored a new pair of hi-top Adidas and started calling them "my kicks" to anybody with ears. I began breakdancing on Friday nights in the Kroger parking lot with my friends, including a handful of black kids who were too young, too uncool, or maybe too *white* to be recruited into the Soul Patrol. I started calling my group of friends *my boyz*. When my mother bought a new washing machine, I deconstructed the leftover cardboard box and created a flat surface perfect for practicing backspins until I grew sick to my stomach. I rented *Breakin' 2: Electric Boogaloo* and watched it till the tape started squealing, pausing frames to imitate the moves and rewinding to watch them again. During class I scribbled the lyrics to rap songs in the margins of my *Fundamentals of Algebra I* textbook while Mr. Wingfield rambled on about polynomials. In summary: over the course of maybe two months time, I began to see it as my bounden duty to bring soul to suburbia.

I was white—I was aware of that fact—so I knew that the best I could ever hope for in this life was to become an *honorary* member of the Soul Patrol. I was still just enough in touch with reality to understand that the Soul Patrollers were not going to award me a T-shirt. There was not going to be an induction ceremony in which they presented me a mix-tape of all the newest underground jams, taught me, step-by-step, all the cool handshakes, and christened me Kid Beave. All I wanted, really, was to penetrate the walls of the Soul Patrol. I wasn't quite sure how a white, ninth-grade wannabe could infiltrate such select society. But if just one Soul Patroller could somehow, in some way, acknowledge my *street-cred*, I could go to my grave knowing I was *phat*.

One of the Soul Patrollers—Montrez Haynes was his name—incorporated the moves he had learned in his Brown Belt karate classes into his dance steps. He fused breakdancing and martial arts into a weird, exotic, and utterly magical hybrid none of us had ever witnessed. His whole gig was so well-polished that every movement seemed natural, like Montrez was the first person to do it, but the rest of the world had been sitting around waiting for somebody to do it. Watching him do his thing, you felt like you were bearing witness to some kinetic moment sparking into existence, a moment so pure and undiluted that it was like watching somebody create a work of *art*. Right there in front of you. Historians would write about it one day. Kids would study it. It broke my heart, how cool it was. Pep rallies, I remember, showcased the football team, cheerleaders, and a crotchety old coach whose appeal for support at Friday night's game was invariably drowned out by feedback buzzing through the microphone. But the star of the show was Montrez: spinning, leaping, and kicking, all in perfect rhythm with the bass beat of the latest jam.

Montrez was rumored to hate white people, but I figured this was probably only because nobody had ever seen him actually talk to a white person. He always hung out in the circle of Soul Patrollers—in the hallways between classes; in the cafeteria at lunch; after school in the student parking lot. I heard whispers that Montrez had got into a fight with a white guy from our rival school and put the kid in the hospital with a couple of karate kicks to the neck.

Montrez had somehow managed to carve out a niche at our high school in suburbia, a place where it was easy to be anonymous. Over 2000 kids created gridlock in the hallways during every class change. Each lunch period incited a Darwinian scramble to secure the last slice of greasy pizza. The sheer size of the student body called for law enforcement to supervise every nook and cranny of campus during assemblies. To get attention, boys joined Future Homemakers of America, set off firecrackers in the hallways, swigged six-packs under the fluorescent lights of the Circle K, or spray painted graffiti on the football field. Girls threw massive parties when their parents went out of town, bummed cigarettes off the night manager at the Taco Bell, or crawled into too many back seats with too many boys. Every kid tried to distinguish himself, and most failed. But *everybody* knew the Soul Patrol.

Looking back, I realize now what I didn't see then: these kids were still very much the minority in a school that was overwhelmingly white—and their membership in the Soul Patrol was a recognition of a common experience. On the other hand, the impenetrable wall between the Soul Patrollers and the rest of the student body created a type of segregation. Those black shirts with the bright yellow letters sent an "Us and Them" message. A lot of the white kids downright *hated* the Soul Patrol. *They don't want to be part of us*, they said. *They want to do their own thing.* Our history teachers taught us that, just a scant fifteen years earlier—a month before I was born—a native Atlantan named Martin Luther King Jr. had given his life to break down barriers between black and white, to create a society where people could move seamlessly wherever they wanted to go. Eliminating separate water fountains, bus seats, and schools were just the first steps; the next would be breaking down the social barriers—the intangible lines sometimes symbolized by a T-shirt with bright yellow letters.

I understood my peers' suspicions, but I couldn't help feeling protective of the Soul Patrollers, even if I couldn't explain why. My desire to be part of them seemed to be the culmination of a long series of experiences that had made me feel as though these kids' identity was somehow intertwined with mine.

AT THE TIME I BEGAN first grade in 1974, my family lived in a tiny white pocket of east Atlanta surrounded by dozens of predominately black neighborhoods; and when I started first grade I found myself one of only three or four "ghosts," as the black kids called us, in a class of thirty students. In the aftermath of King's recent death, The City Too Busy To Hate did not live up to its official nickname. Despite his best intentions King was a polarizing figure, even in his hometown. I would like to report that my family had been on the fighting front of the Civil Rights Movement, but the only comment I ever recall my father making about King was that "he could've kept his behind out of jail if he'd have just obeyed the law"—a remark that, I would soon learn, sort of misses the whole point of King's philosophy.

But the hatred ran both ways, too. The most vivid memory I have of first grade was watching one of the black kids throw my box of crayons on the ground and grind his heels into it, over and over. Or maybe it's another kid pushing me out of the cafeteria line and kicking my Evil Knievel lunch box against the cinderblock wall. It's likely that these events happen everywhere, but what makes these memories resonate to this day is the certainty they happened because the color of my skin was different. My teacher, a young white woman named Ms. Zabel who wore butterfly collars and polyester bellbottoms, seemed sympathetic to my plight, but fundamentally unable to do anything about it. Chances are she considered herself progressive, a difference maker, because she was, after all, *here*. She was a first- or second-year teacher, probably, and already preoccupied with formulating her own plan for survival in this setting, and maybe an exit strategy too.

By the Olympics of '96, East Atlanta would become a model of successful gentrification, a place that considered itself edgy but only in the trendiest kind of way. There'd be a tattoo parlor, a dive bar, and a liquor store, but also a vegan restaurant, a high-end boutique, and a place to sip lattes on a sun-splashed patio. A warm, pastel green sign welcomed you to the neighborhood. Beautiful murals featuring a rainbow of multiracial faces adorned many of the buildings. New constructions ran in the three-hundred-thousand range. But in the early '70s my few white neighbors referred to East Atlanta simply as "Blacktown," even though they and we lived in it.

Blacktown had crawled all the way down Moreland Avenue, the main thoroughfare through East Atlanta; but it hadn't yet spread to all the side streets that split off like veins from Moreland. One of those veins, Black Oak Drive, contained the red brick ranch that had been the first house my parents ever built. Originally, it had only two bedrooms, but to a young couple who'd previously lived only in trailers or under someone else's roof, it was a mansion. Within their first year of marriage my brother was born. It took thirteen more years, but when I finally came along they had nowhere to put me; so they converted the carport to a third bedroom where my brother could play his Three Dog Night records as loud as he wanted. My mother hung fern baskets on the front porch. Stuck folding chairs in the yard. Dug a flowerbed around the trunk of a pine tree. Left breadcrumbs for the blue jays. In our world, this was called *putting down roots*.

On all sides, though, life was becoming precarious. Down the street, there lived a stringy-haired teenager named Rocky who cut all the sleeves out of his T-shirts, wore hip huggers with flare legs, and sported a wallet chain. He rode a Harley with an engine that sounded like a chainsaw, and I feared he'd run over me just for an afternoon's entertainment. Up the street, an old woman lived with six or eight snarling German shepherds whose very presence precluded anyone from snooping around. Around the way, over on Cavanaugh, a black man had raped a widow in her own house. "Meanness," my mother called it. My grandmother, who lived on Cavanaugh, agreed: "Pure meanness," she decided.

Soon my parents tried to rescue me from this predicament by doing what a working-class family could: they moved to the suburbs. At the time I had no clue that my puny, insignificant life was part of bigger, cultural movements in society. I didn't understand that history's zeitgeists are nothing more than the collective sum of nobodies like us doing things that, at the time, seemed as trivial as parking a U-Haul in the driveway and loading it with all the clutter our family had cobbled together in this lifetime. If the PhDs in the universities were now calling it *White Flight*, we hadn't heard anything about it. All we knew was that now my dad had a bigger yard, my mom had peace of mind, and I had thirty new classmates who looked like me.

The house we moved to possessed a third bedroom that had *not* been converted from a carport—and a front yard big and wide enough to roll with hills. Deeper in the neighborhood a couple of young women, splitting the rent, kept a jar of rabbit tobacco on their coffee table, and told me it was marijuana. Across the street, the father of one of my new friends had moved out and left behind a stack of *Playboy*s for us to peruse at our leisure. Otherwise, there were no signs of evil. No motorcycles, German shepherds, or rapists. No "meanness." And no black people.

For the first time in my young life, race did not affect me on a day-to-day basis. I continued through elementary and middle school. I collected baseball cards; I played Atari video games; I spent Saturdays at the skating rink; I attended church on Sunday mornings, Sunday evenings, and most Wednesday nights. It was easy to think that my little isolated and insular world was the only one there was.

But when I started high school I soon discovered that maybe a third of our student body was black. Across the tracks in neighborhoods called the Honeyhole and Kudzu Korner lived hundreds of black kids who poured out of federal and state housing projects and filtered into my high school. We weren't diverse in that there were people of all ethnic backgrounds mixing together—you were either black or white in our school—but suddenly the world seemed a lot bigger.

I would like to say that I embraced that wider world from the very beginning, but that would be a bigger lie than I can tell. There were many times when I stood idly by and became more a part of the problem than the solution. I laughed at my buddies' racist jokes. Engaged in teenage banter, I even called one of them a *niggerlover* while on a field trip to see the movie *Gandhi*, of all things. But one of the moments from that time brings me around again to the Soul Patrol. It's a moment that might have little to do with Dr. King, or White Flight, or where the South was headed in the aftermath of Civil Rights. But to my mind, it's worth mentioning these many years later.

ONE AFTERNOON DURING THAT ninth grade year, I left class to go to the bathroom. While the classmates I had left behind were busy conjugating verbs in their grammar workbooks, I was clutching my hall pass and aimlessly meandering the cavernous hallways. I sipped from every water fountain along the way. I aimlessly peeked into classrooms where my imprisoned peers sat stultified by integers and photosynthesis, adverbial clauses and European serfs; by teachers whose muffled voices sounded like the records we played backwards in search of Satanic messages.

Finally, out of destinations and feeling the effects of hitting all the water fountains in the school, I arrived at a bathroom on the other side of the building. I had just finished washing my hands, wadding the paper towel into a ball and shooting it at the wastebasket in the corner, and was headed toward the exit. Another kid was coming in as I was leaving. It was a tight space, that exit. I was turning sideways to squeeze through the door when I saw that it was Montrez Haynes.

He was wearing his black T-shirt with bright yellow letters. The diamond in his ear sparkled with brilliance; his Jheri curl glowed with a glossy sheen.

I nodded toward him. I tried to contain my reverence, as though we were just two fly guys acknowledging each other on neutral turf.

Then he did the unthinkable: He slipped out his hand toward me. Montrez Haynes, the Soul Patroller who was rumored to hate white people, who I'd heard had put a white kid in the hospital with one of his lethal brown-belt spinning kicks, was offering five to, of all people, *me*, a little ninth-grade wannabe who had spent the school year blowing every dime of his meager allowance on hip-hop and funky clothes in his relentless quest to become a member of the Soul Patrol.

To this day I have no idea why Montrez offered his hand. I'd like to think he had been cruising the Kroger parking lot with fellow members of the Soul Patrol—patrolling for soul, as it were—and saw me with all my *boyz* breakdancing under the streetlights while somebody's car stereo boomed my Bambaataa tape. I'd like to think he saw me busting a move under those streetlights and said to one of his fellow Soul Patrollers, "Man, look at that white kid. He's got *soul*."

But today I'm not picky about the reasons why. All I know is that Montrez Haynes stuck out his hand. It wasn't one of those funky handshakes that lasts five minutes and sends the tacit message that the two of you are in some special clique together. It was just a brief touch of skin, a fleeting grip of fingers. Not a word passed between us. And not a word ever would. Montrez continued into the bathroom. I entered the long wide hallway, and headed back to class.

TAXIDERMY

I t is a tribute to my adolescent ingenuity that I conceived a foolproof strategy for keeping my parents out of my room: I plastered my walls with Prince posters. These glossy images were a particular affront to my father. Because he was a Baptist deacon whose musical tastes ran toward the Florida Boys and The Inspirations—gospel groups who sang of Beulah Land and restricted their bodily movements to innocuous toe-tapping—Dad possessed no firsthand knowledge of Prince's raunchy oeuvre of tunes about incest, fellatio, and unfaithful girlfriends falling for other women. He didn't need the details. Prince's mere appearance was enough. In his worldview, no self-respecting man would dare broach a space enshrined to a prissy waif wearing bikini briefs, sky-high stiletto heels, and a pompadour.

Consequently, if Dad had something to tell me, it was shouted through the wall, and likely drowned out by the thump of my stereo blaring Prince's falsetto. Over time such obstacles led to a brittle silence between us. Most of what might have been said went unspoken altogether. But if what Dad wanted to say to me required saying, he sent Mom as an emissary to crack the door and deliver the message through the sliver.

One night in the fall of '83, she rapped on my door. I was lying in bed listening to *1999*, staring at the ceiling and contemplating a purple Armageddon in the supine posture that summarized my life philosophy at age 15. Because she had learned through experience not to open my door without invitation, Mom waited for me to lower the volume and tell her to come in. Then, in a voice that sounded vaguely apologetic, she informed me that Dad was calling a family meeting. "He says you better hurry up," she told me.

I was hardly surprised. Just days earlier, I had gotten my hair permed at the local salon—an audacious act likely aimed at provoking a response from Dad. I'd been anticipating his overreaction ever since. He had been circling me, stone-faced and silent, perhaps hoping that time would reduce his fury to a mere smolder. But apparently he had been stewing in his juices too long. He had clearly had enough. It was time for an intervention.

I wore mirrored sunglasses for the occasion, even though it was nighttime and the setting was our living room. I suppose I meant to reflect Dad's disappointment back at him. I sprawled on the couch, my shoulders slumped, a carefully rehearsed scowl on my face. Dad and Mom occupied separate recliners, their elbows propped on their knees in order to communicate the seriousness of their intent.

I've forgotten most of the details of our conversation, but I do recall Dad labeling me *timid*, which in his lexicon translated to girly, at best, and at worst, faggish. He went on at length, listing my transgressions, invoking the word *sin* more than once. He of course spent the obligatory amount of time condemning my hair, too. As his lecture progressed, his face flushing and his voice growing evermore plaintive, I sensed that an announcement was clearly in the offering. Dad was about to issue a decree. He seemed to be building toward some *statement* that would, to his mind, reverse the trajectory of my misdirected life.

Finally he arrived at his proposed solution: "You're fifteen," he said. "It's time you went hunting."

I was relieved. If he had been watching closely, he might have detected the fluid stream of pent-up air expelling through my nose. At least theoretically, I bought Dad's plan—though I wouldn't admit as much publicly. Like any boy, I embraced the prospect of rising early while lesser males slept, braving the bitter cold, shouldering a rifle. From the safe confines of my bedroom, rife with the funk of adolescent boyhood, I imagined Dad leading me into Faulkner's Big Woods, forging a path with his boot steps, parting the dense thicket. Through the hazy gauze of imagination, I pictured myself eventually making my way alongside him, two alpha dogs marching through the woods shoulder-to-shoulder, together cutting a broad swath through the world. I saw myself doing a lot of pissing and snoring and scratching and spitting. To summarize: I felt the testosterone dripping.

"There's a safety course," Dad was explaining. "A state requirement. Georgia says you have to pass that class before they'll give you a license." There was no equivocation in his tone. No indication that any of this was up for discussion or debate. It was clear that he was tired of watching his son—skinny, bookish, with a perm and an affection for effeminate musicians—stray progressively farther from the model of manhood that he embodied. "A new class is starting at the county firehouse in a couple of weeks. Two nights is all it is. Your mother will get you signed up."

From behind the veil of my mirrored lenses I did my best to act put out, put upon, belabored. I acted as though this whole scheme were a grand waste of my valuable time. But I had enough foresight to avoid making some kind of contrived argument against hunting, condemning the depravity of it, the bloodlust required to end a poor animal's life.

Dad probably would've taken his revenge by waking me a full hour earlier.

IN THE DEN WHERE MY FATHER regularly fell asleep watching *The Andy Griffith Show* in his recliner, he had mounted two deer heads on the wall. Though these heads had been part of the décor as long as I could remember, I'd never given much thought to what motivated Dad to stuff his prey. The heads seemed to belong in a roadside bar in, say, Tennessee—the kind of place with stale peanuts, six-dollar flatiron steaks, and Hank Williams on the jukebox. Over time grizzly beards of dust had sprouted around their muzzles. The antlers had become hat racks—at any given time eight or ten of Dad's baseball caps, stained with motor oil, WD-40, and his sweat, hung from the tips.

Whatever Dad's motives, I had to admit: These boys looked real. The one on the left was a modest six-pointer. He'd been Dad's first kill, which made stuffing him a matter of obligation. But his wall-mate was the kind of trophy buck that hunters dream of spying in their crosshairs—a ten-point rack big as a doll's rocking chair with antlers thick as corncobs. It was as though the process of taxidermy had somehow kept them alive—as though any moment now those eyes would ignite, their ears would twitch at the sound of a limb snapping a mile away, and those nostrils would flare and snort. They'd become skittish, feral and wild, and if someone wasn't watching they'd bound through the boxy rooms of our brick ranch in the suburbs and make a break for it.

Sometimes when I was alone with the two of them, I'd gaze into their eyes, at those unblinking black marbles. On first glance their glossy eyes seemed shallow and empty, devoid of meaning, but the longer I stared, the more I discovered they were in fact too deep to see the bottom of. They seemed to know things about my father I could only guess at.

But these two boys weren't talking.

Outside the woods Dad was not a man given to intimacy. He'd been born in 1928, raised hardscrabble during the Depression on a hundred acres of dirt by a farmer who needed workhands first and sons second, and by comparison he must have considered himself a genuine *dad*. But almost all expressions of physical intimacy ended by the time I was, say, eight or nine. There was little conversation either. Rarely did he attempt to impart wisdom or share advice. And the occasions when he did take me aside were fraught with awkwardness and false starts, as though a man who'd always driven automatic transmission was suddenly faced with the complexities of a stick shift. As a young man, he'd spent those nine months freezing in foxholes in Korea, where he became a Master Sergeant, but when I asked once with all the tact of a bloodthirsty nine year old boy whether he'd killed anybody, he'd said, "We're not going to talk about that." And indeed, we never did. Except for occasional outbursts of anger, he rarely expressed emotion and seemed generally suspicious of it. When his mother died I remember mourners filing by her coffin for a last look at Maw-Maw's face and my cousin Sharon sinking to her knees, too saddled with grief to carry her own weight. I remember Dad's long neck, his raised chin and set jaw. He loved his mother with something bordering on obsession, but his were the only dry eyes in the room. On that sultry afternoon in that old clapboard church he was stoic, all right, but the word that comes to mind is *beautiful*. I was a teenage boy then and not given to describing my old man as *beautiful*. It was not a word I would have used then—only one I feel the need to say now.

FIRST, THERE WAS THE MATTER of getting some hands-on experience with a gun. A few days before the safety course began, Dad escorted me out to the driveway with the kind of pomp and circumstance rightfully accompanying a rite of passage. There, in the grainy light of a fall afternoon, he first informed me that I was never to call it a gun. "What you're holding in your hands," he told me, "is a rifle. Only amateurs call it a gun." This issue settled, he moved on to the practical concerns of caring for and tending a weapon such as this one. He showed me how to clean it. "There's an art to it," he insisted—a proper sequence and method to breaking it down, oiling it, rubbing linseed into the stock, polishing the barrel. "Hold it up to the light," he said. "Take a look at the grain."

To demonstrate, he went to work cleaning his own rifle, a 30.06, but I proceeded to stalk prey with my unloaded weapon—a largely impotent .22 better suited to slaying rabbits than deer—from the terrain of our suburban driveway. To begin, I hefted it in my hands, feeling its weight in my palms. Then I moved on to hoisting it against my shoulder and peering through the sights. Aiming at the leaves on the oak trees, cocking the hammer, and fingering the trigger as I fixed each target in my gaze. Then, drawing a bead on squirrels in the trees, birds on wires, or cars on the highway, I puffed my cheeks and simulated shooting sounds as I pulled the trigger. I imagined the true report of the rifle, its kick against my shoulder.

Next Dad taught me how to load and cock. He taught me how to shoulder the rifle and take aim. He taught me when to pull the trigger, and how. As he led me step-by-step through the process, I clearly understood, even in the dim wattage of my fifteen year old brain, that this lesson was a matter of inheritance. He was *passing down* knowledge essential to our identity. Rituals like this one showed us who we are. A circle was spinning. His father had delivered this same lecture, and now he was delivering it to me—and one day, I would be teaching it to my son. When the lesson concluded, Dad extracted the bullets and slipped them into his jeans with the same nonchalance he would have pocketed a palmful of pennies. Here, Dad informed me, was where his lesson differed from the one he had received from my grandfather. "My daddy kept his rifles in a closet, always loaded."

"Why didn't Paw-Paw unload them?" I asked.

Dad paused to consider my question. Furrowing his brow, he seemed to be probing some new idea. "Probably for the same reason he didn't neuter his dogs," he finally said.

WITHIN MINUTES OF ARRIVING at the county firehouse for the first meeting of my safety class, I discovered a problem with my choice of footwear. I'd worn hunting boots, all right, but brand new ones. They weren't leather. They were suede. And they weren't brown or black, like the other boys' boots in my class. They were mustard yellow—a gourmet, Grey Poupon yellow. In the wrong light, they shone almost gold.

I'd worn them tonight because I wanted to dress the part of a genuine marksman. Without uttering a word, I wanted to establish my wilderness-cred. This very afternoon, perhaps against her better judgment, Mom had bought them for me. She wrote the check and passed it to the salesman without a word of protest at their cost. She had been the one to escort me to the salon where I got my hair permed, so maybe buying the boots would serve as a kind of redemption for us both.

Which might have worked with a different crowd. Maybe five minutes in, I was able to ascertain that, for these other boys, this class was a mere formality. They could have taught it themselves. Einsteins stuck in remedial math is what they were, enduring two evenings of firearm safety, wildlife management, and woodland conservation, when all they wanted was to see something die. At the end of the course, a test, which they could take right now and ace, would merely be the final step in officially becoming Southern Men.

By all appearances these boys' mamas had dressed them in camo in the crib. They were pioneers and survivalists. They had come down from the far-flung regions of the county, the rural zip, the pastureland. They showed up with sawdust sleeving their arms, sweat circling their armpits, grease caking their fingernails. They wore beards, some of them, and sideburns long as bowie knives. They smelled like manual labor—like sheetrock, engine sludge, and horseshit. Some of them, they made clear, had already killed their first buck; now they were just making the whole thing legal, satisfying the *guv'ment*. During breaks they splattered the dirt out back with tobacco juice. They critiqued the instructor's oversights. They said *shee-yut* and *I be damn*. Maybe what I'm trying to say is this: These boys didn't know Whitman, but they were intimately familiar with his barbaric yawp.

I recognized some of them from school, but only faintly, because they'd been assigned to the vocational track, where they spent their days on the outskirts of campus tinkering on carburetors or operating jigsaws, vague shadows visible only through garage doors or shop windows.

As they filed into the firehouse, their feet clomping over the floor, I gradually diagnosed the problem with my boots. The suede ran smooth as my cheeks, but these boys' boots were battered, beaten, bruised. Rimmed with grime, smeared with mud, creased with sweat. Splattered with oil, paint, and sawdust. They had trudged through leaves, these boots, waded moccasin-infested waters, stomped out forest fires. They had forded rivers, wrestled steer to the ground, rounded up all the little dogies.

Wearing these self-same boots, these boys had driven wagon trains, blazed trails, and caught spinning tomahawks with their bare hands.

All those afternoons I had wasted watching reruns of *Diff'rent Strokes* while the Great Outdoors beckoned outside my window—these fateful days, I saw now, had been my demise. Retribution was nigh. I'd been worrying over whether Mr. Drummond would make a good home for Arnold and Willis, when I should've been shooting squirrels with BB guns, poking roadkill with a stick, acquiring poison ivy.

I should've been practicing my barbaric yawp.

THE INSTRUCTOR, A MAN WHOSE DRAWL and demeanor suggested he loved his dog and could recite the lyrics to "Freebird," began his lecture with what he called the First Commandment of Firearm Safety: *Watch that muzzle!* This dictum seemed reasonable. Common sense was the only requirement for mastering this stuff. What kind of novice doesn't know that he should keep an eye on the business end of his gun? Call me Daniel Boone.

But the curriculum quickly took a more complicated direction. The instructor lectured about Remington and Winchester, distinguished between lever, bolt, and pump. I listened till my ears burned. I scribbled meticulous notes. But my head was spinning. It wasn't long before I got lost in a spiral of information, my brain clogged by facts, charts, and statistics. I had no idea there was so much to absorb. My fellow scholars, though, yawned with condescension. They doodled in the margins of their instructional manuals, assumed various slouches, scratched their groins with impunity. Where did these guys learn it? How had they come by it? What would become of me when this was over? Would they ship me north, tell me to forget about becoming a man because, sad as it seemed, the best I could ever hope for was to become something embarrassingly inferior: a *gentle*man? I might as well be a Yankee. Or God forbid: *French*.

As that first evening drew to a close, I gave up hope of mastering the course content and instead formulated an alternative. It had to do with my footwear. Surely these boys' boots had been new at some point. They had to break them in, somehow. So as the instructor concluded his lecture, I made a vow: Between now and the next class, I would break these suckers in. When tomorrow night rolled around, I would be the proud owner of a pair of honest-to-God shit-kickers.

WHEN I GOT OFF THE SCHOOL BUS the next day, I ran straight to the backyard in my mustard-colored boots. I pulled the garden hose to a bare, grassless spot, where I proceeded to soak the dirt until I engineered a patch of sheer slop—an oozy, slurping pigsty.

Then I commenced stomping around, goose-stepping, marching through the muck, savoring that sucking noise. Next, I was spitting on them. Beating them against the driveway. Throwing them against the wall of our brick ranch. Slathering them in mud, scuffing them with rocks, dunking them in a pail of water my mother used to mop the floors. I scouted out trees to fell, firewood to haul, calves to birth. I briefly considered where I might locate some cow pies or chickenshit. Maybe a tick or two would consent to attach to my boots. It seemed a good idea. But, alas, this was the suburbs.

The result? They were a bit squishy, a little waterlogged. They felt like concrete blocks on my feet. But by the time class started on that second and final night, I had achieved the desired effect. My boots looked as though they'd been dragged straight through Hades by a monster truck driven by a pack of rowdy yokels.

THAT NIGHT, AS THE INSTRUCTOR chattered on about woodland conservation, I jutted my feet into the aisle, offering my classmates ample opportunity to behold my boots. I tapped my foot vigorously. I strewed a trail of dirt crumbs over the floor. Anticipating the first bathroom break, I imagined a whole string of boys lining up to issue compliments, to envy my boots' rugged authenticity, to say *Shee-yut, wish I had me a pair of them, I be damn.* I soon became so preoccupied with showcasing my footwear that I missed a considerable chunk of the information that undoubtedly would be on the test at the conclusion of tonight's final class.

Midway through, the instructor finally called for a break. The herd headed for the bathroom. Behind me in line was a boy who clearly possessed all the signifiers of legitimacy. His shirt read *American by Birth...Southern by the Grace of God.* His back pocket was emblazoned with the circular outline of a Copenhagen can. And of course his boots looked as though he'd defended Atlanta against Sherman that very afternoon. "I gotta piss like a horse," he announced to no one in particular. As I passed through the door I held it open for him longer than simple courtesy required—apparently long enough for him to get a whiff of the suburbs on me. "You *better* hold that door for me," he said.

As I relieved myself inside a stall, I muttered under my breath, cursing this guy's arrogance. I concluded he was a son of a bitch. He was an asshole. He was a redneck dumb fuck.

If I had been a brighter boy, the kind who knew shit from Shinola, I would have taken this kid's words for a frank assessment of my identity and would have been grateful for the perspective. I would have accepted what he seemed to understand intuitively: I was not one of his kind. He seemed to know something about me that I didn't yet know about myself. I could have saved myself a lot of time and trouble if I'd been able to see myself with the same clarity with which this boy saw me. He'd done me a favor.

But I did not know shit from Shinola. I hadn't picked up on the foreshadowing in the books I read, much less in my own life. Shit and Shinola looked much the same in my dim view of the world.

So of course I hobbled out of the firehouse that night in my aching boots, license and certification in hand, as proud of my seventy-five as any test score I had earned in my life.

ON THE OPENING DAY of hunting season, October 1983, Dad rousted me out of bed at 3 a.m. Obsessing over the ungodliness of rising at such an hour, I wriggled into a pair of long-johns, overalls, three pairs of socks, a flannel shirt, a sweater, a bulky coat, a toboggan and, yes, my boots. Dad rolled me to the car. If we had been following the script, we'd have been driving a pickup truck with mud splashed high on the fenders, but instead we headed for Talbot County in Dad's Ford Fairlane.

We drove south, Dad's wrist draped over the steering wheel, his dashboard a faint light in contrast to the darkness outside. We followed the strip of black asphalt and barreled past fallow fields, gaping pastures, and a thousand miles of barbed wire until finally we stopped at a Waffle House. Inside: guys like us. Camo was the hue of choice. A bunch of unshaven good ol' boys shoving hash browns down their gullets and blinking sleep from their eyes. The waitress served me a waffle so burnt it appeared drizzled with gunpowder. My complaint went unspoken, but apparently Dad read the disappointment on my face. He wanted this inaugural hunting experience to be perfect. The stuff of unblemished fond memories. So without a word he swapped his waffle with mine and pretended to savor the artillery aftertaste.

Back in the car, he nursed a cup of coffee as he drove. The heater churned hot air into the floorboard. On reaching Talbotton, we exited near the brick remains of an old cotton mill, vacant and destitute for decades probably, kudzu snaking through its decaying windows and falling in a heavy net toward the rubble below. The moon was milky, a little less than split in half, its pale light spilling on the slow, stagnating turn of a creek running alongside the mill. The asphalt gave way to a dirt road wrinkled like a washboard, gravel spitting and popping under tire, shocks bouncing and springs squeaking as they found the groove between the ruts. We trundled past houses still cloaked in darkness, fields of skeletal corn scarcely visible in the moonlight, a diamond-lit blanket of night overhead. Against the backdrop of the sky, the only visible thing was the silhouette of a telephone line strung out like a banjo string.

Eventually Dad brought the car to a halt. He nudged the Fairlane against an embankment on the shoulder of the road. Within a few moments we were out of the vehicle and crouching beside the roadway, studying fresh tracks in the red dirt. "Been a lot of traffic through here," he said. I looked back with longing at the warm, snug car.

I didn't put a lot of forethought into my next remark: "If so many deer are crossing the road," I asked, "why don't we just sit in the car and wait for one to pass?"

My father could have called it quits on the whole endeavor right then. He would have been justified. But to his credit, he suffered my question and actually offered an explanation reasonably empty of sarcasm. "Gracious, boy," he said. "You ever play tennis without a net?"

THE WOODS CLOSED UP behind us. Whatever slip in the curtain through which we entered sealed shut. Inside, the darkness condensed, held its breath. The stars overhead disappeared as though erased from a blackboard. The brittle ground crunched under our boots. Dad was carrying his scoped 30.06

in the crook of his arm. I toted my .22 with both hands, the safety on. Without blinking I focused on his orange vest. Briars snagged at our pant legs; spider webs clung to our arms. We sidestepped puddles frozen solid. Soon we crested a ridge that plunged into a deep ravine and meandered through a thicket dense and impenetrable as night. When a covey of blackbirds exploded scattershot from their perch in a naked tree, my heart flew into my throat. But as we trudged onward, the darkness gradually thinned until, finally, daylight beckoned. Just as dawn was breaking Dad stopped and surveyed how far we'd come. He stood motionless, his ear cocked, frigid air pluming from his mouth. "Here," he said.

Day broke. Branches of trees just starting to take on definition, a bleak sun suffusing the woods with pallid light. The air brittle and crisp, the kind that fires your senses and sets you on alert. I had expected to climb a tree and take up residence in a stand high above the forest floor. But, responding to Dad's directive, instead I found myself *still-hunting*—sitting alongside him on the ground in the crotch of two thick roots at the base of a venerable oak tree. Dad pulled his pocket-sized New Testament from his coat and started reading, presumably until a big buck decided to make an appearance. Meanwhile, I pondered how long it would take for that OJ I had drunk at the Waffle House to make its way to my bladder.

Within minutes I wanted out of the woods. Inside my mustard-colored boots, my toes were going numb. My face flushed, my fingers stinging, I was already looking forward to returning to the car for lunch, when the sun would sparkle and we'd sit on the hood eating sandwiches sealed in Ziploc bags and drinking Cokes wrapped in aluminum foil and reveling in our status as men.

Maybe an hour of this misery passed. It must have been while I was slipping into semi-consciousness, convinced I was in the throes of hypothermia, when something drifted through the periphery of my vision. I squinted to take in whatever was moving in the distance.

They had simply appeared, materializing from the landscape, as though they'd always been here. They dipped their heads, snorted at the ground. They flicked their tails playfully. They wore sleek coats of tawny brown.

"Dad, over there," I whispered. "Look at those *dogs*."

He swung his head in the direction of my pointing finger. His eyes grew wide. He squeezed the barrel of his rifle. "Them ain't dogs, son," he said. "Them are deer."

UPON CLOSER INSPECTION I too saw that they indeed were deer, five of them, foraging on the forest floor, completely oblivious to our presence.

"They're all doe," Dad whispered. "But sit tight. Sometimes a big buck'll come trailing through after them."

In the safety class we had been told about doe days, when you could take aim on a female deer. This wasn't a doe day. You couldn't shoot. All you could do was watch them graze until finally something spooked them and they bounded into a stand of trees, white tails flagging, and vanished.

Nevertheless, to see a deer on my very first hunting trip was lucky. I knew Dad often endured a string of lost trips without seeing any tell-tale evidence of a deer's passing—the rubs on tree trunks, the droppings, the faint prints on the ground. I knew that mornings Dad woke in darkness and pulled on his camouflage; daybreaks he sat huddled under a poncho in a rickety stand thirty feet up, with only his pocket-sized New Testament, a Thermos of coffee, a can of Vienna sausages, and his rifle; evenings on the long empty-handed drive home he sipped the lukewarm dregs of coffee from his Thermos and fought to stay awake. As the miles passed, he thumbed the dial until he found hellfire-and-damnation preachers on the radio, their guttural voices fading in and out as the signal warbled on the country roads, until finally, as he neared I-285 and the perimeter that circled Atlanta, static filled the airwaves and stilled those smoldering tongues.

Yes: simply seeing deer was an event.

But then, within a few minutes after the doe had passed through, against whatever odds, a buck appeared. Dad saw him first. "There he is," he said now. "Over there. A spike."

It was hardly a buck at all. He possessed two stubs for antlers. He was skinny, his ribs two slats of bone. Except for the spikes, he looked virtually identical to the harem of doe that sauntered through earlier. If it had been a buck of any reputation, undoubtedly Dad would have shot it himself.

Which is why Dad instead told me to raise my rifle. My .22. My glorified BB gun. "Slow," he said. "Steady." His breath was hot in my ear, his voice a hoarse whisper laced with adrenaline. "Get him in your sights. Don't make any sudden movements. Don't jerk the muzzle, whatever you do. Quiet now. Steady."

I raised my rifle. Blood pulsed in my ears. I fingered the trigger, squinted down the barrel. I aimed directly at the buck's shoulder, where Dad had told me the heart lay. The buck raised his head, his jaw chewing vigorously. He snorted, his nostrils moist and gleaming. I envisioned the next few moments of my life, after I had pulled the trigger, when we would kick through the dry leaves in careful approach to find the buck lying on its side, its eye still blinking, its flank shaking, legs jerking and twitching as though still in full gait. Dad would slice his knife across the jugular to bring a stream of blood and catch a palmful of it and smear it across my face. He'd muss my hair and spike it with gore. *Wash me in the Blood.* He'd dress it right there in the woods, trimming away the fat as though performing religious ritual, demonstrating every technique as something holy, before dragging it to the car, where he would fetch his Polaroid from the trunk and snap a shot of his handprints on my cheeks as proof and evidence that his son was yet another in a long line of men. He'd soon be making an appointment with the taxidermist.

It was then that the spike heard something. He lifted his head for a split-second in perfect profile and then broke into a run. His tail flashed white. He scurried toward the edge of the clearing. He was headed for some underbrush.

"Shoot!" Dad said. "Now! *Now!*"

The deer was in my sights.

"Pull it!" Dad said.

But I just kept fingering the trigger.

WE STAYED IN THE WOODS maybe until noon, but the trip essentially finished the moment I refused to pull the trigger. Now we were walking toward the car. By this time the wind was stirring. Leaves rustled and skidded across the ground. Dad was still doing his duty: he was telling me how deer bedded down during the day, how you often could roust them out as you tromped through. Then he was pointing out where a buck had scraped his antlers against a tree trunk and stripped a bare spot in the bark. But all of it was perfunctory. His voice sounded dry—hollow and unconvincing.

Before we reached the roadway, we entered a clearing where Dad and his fellow club members kept an abandoned school bus. For overnight trips, they had equipped it with a heater and a portable stove and used it as a makeshift lodge. Dad pushed open the door and invited me inside. The dense air smelled of must and charred cans of Spam and Beanie-Weenies. A couple of sleeping bags lay strewn across the floor. Dad found a garbage sack sitting in the corner and started rummaging through it. Then, satisfied with its contents, he slung it over his shoulder.

Outside, in the clearing, Dad pulled out two- or three-dozen aluminum cans and a few glass bottles and began rigging up target practice, assembling a makeshift shooting range. He perched the cans and bottles atop stumps and fence posts and fallen trees. He set them at various distances. They glittered in the sunlight.

"Take a few shots," he told me.

I suppose Dad was offering a chance at redemption. If I wouldn't kill a deer, maybe I could at least prove I possessed the marksmanship to do it, which in itself would constitute a minor victory. But my heart wasn't in it, and it took me a while to summon enough grit even to lift my weapon to a shooting position. But eventually I aimed, I fired. At first I missed the cans and bottles entirely, the bullets flying into some vacuous hole where wasted ammunition disappeared. Soon, though, I began to make better use of the sights. The cans began to fall. They pinwheeled through the air in miraculous arcs of beautiful death. The bottles shattered into jagged shards.

As I pulled the trigger, there was what can only be described as sudden release. An explosion. Not just of a shell and the sharp burn of gunpowder, but of pent-up frustration and whatever swirl of shame, disappointment, and regret had clogged my insides. And as the bottles perched atop those stumps splintered instantly into a million crystals of spraying glass, something inside me broke, too. The woods echoed with the report. I couldn't have told you then what kind of boy I would try to become once we got into Dad's Ford Fairlane and headed for home, or what I'd want to keep of this one wearing mustard-colored boots and taking aim at his past. But maybe if I'd looked far enough down those sights I could have glimpsed the man I'd become—the one who'd someday perform his own brand of taxidermy with the remains.

NERVOUS

I was riding shotgun with my mom. Here she was gripping the wheel of her Chevy Nova, her hands at ten and two, and here I was beside her, grinding my teeth and stewing at the injustice of this arrangement, no doubt, when a car pulled out from a side street and right into our path. Mom stomped the brakes. The tires yowled. My heart plunged to my belly as she threw out her forearm to brace me against colliding with the dash and we slid toward that car's silver paintjob gleaming in the sun like a light beckoning us into the Sweet Hereafter. I caught the faintest glimpse of the other driver, a woman whose panicked expression posed the unmistakable question belonging to us all in that moment: *Am I about to meet my Maker?* The woman only made it halfway across our lane before we plowed into her rear quarter panel. Despite Mom's futile attempt to protect me, I flew forward in my seat, sailing headfirst toward that dazzling light. But first: the windshield.

This was 1983. I was fifteen, with my learner's license in my wallet. By my adolescent reckoning, I should have been driving. I needed practice. I was a boy who wanted the power that came from pressing his foot against the accelerator and feeling the engine surge and the car rise up on its axels as though it's about to take flight. I wanted to lean on the wheel and feel it responding, veering left or right when I directed it there. I had a girlfriend, Beverly, my first of any seriousness, and she made this bone-deep desire seem even more vital and urgent.

I had the feeling Beverly didn't suffer shotgun boys.

But Mom would have none of it. "I'm too Nervous for that sort of thing," she said every time I reached for her keys. But, *Mom*. It was only a short ride to the Kmart, a weekend basketball practice, or my grandmother's house across town. She refused, obstinately. "Who knows what all could happen?" she insisted. "Teaching you to drive is your father's business."

This dubious claim—that she was Nervous—was pure self-diagnosis. No psychiatric professional with a PhD next to his name had deduced as much. But Mom did in fact possess a catalog of symptoms that suggested something off-kilter. An example: Before she left the house for, say, church, she would spend ten minutes checking and rechecking the burners on the stove; then because she couldn't trust her own judgment, she instructed everyone else to do the same, reassuring her our home wouldn't go up in flames while we were away. And there was this random assortment of peculiarities too: She often whispered in a voice so low she must have believed the neighbors possessed superhero powers of hearing. She kept the curtains drawn and our house shadowed in perpetual twilight because some stranger could peek inside and see us. She rarely ate in restaurants because you couldn't be certain the cook washed his hands.

And then there was her disdain for almost all modes of motorized transportation. She never drove on the interstate because cars moved too fast. She refused to ride in a plane because planes fell from the sky. And even if Dad took us on a rare family vacation to the Cherokee Indian Reservation or maybe the Florida Panhandle, it inevitably led to Mom's suddenly declaring, a hundred miles down the road, "I'm not sure we turned the stove burners off!"

After giving birth to my brother in 1954, only once did she hold a job outside the home, and then for only a brief time. She operated the switchboard at the local hospital. She received calls and inserted the plug into the appropriate socket and connected callers to the requested branch of the hospital. Mom found this task confusing. "I'm too Nervous for that kind of work," she declared when she staggered through our door after eight whole hours of employment. She returned the next day for another shift but seemed resigned to a foregone conclusion. She quit after three days. She never earned another paycheck.

So on this particular day Mom ignored my petitions to let me drive and did it her way. She strangled the wheel, puttered along at five miles below the speed limit, and absolutely refused to turn on the radio. She slowed as she approached every intersection, employed her turn signal whenever she changed lanes, and came to a full and complete stop at each red sign. If she and another driver arrived at a four-way at the same time, she always, always deferred to the other guy. I'll give her this: She was a model driver, supremely aware that at any moment, the unpredictable could happen.

Somebody could pull out in front of you and put your life and your son's life in jeopardy.

Which is why I have no rational explanation for this salient fact: when that woman pulled into the roadway and Mom hit the brakes and I flew headlong toward the windshield, I wasn't wearing a seatbelt.

IT WASN'T UNTIL SHE TURNED forty-four that my mother decided the time had come for her to learn to drive. She did not go willingly behind the wheel; she would have been more than content to let someone else chauffeur her to the grocery store, doctor's appointments, and other errands of necessity. But we'd moved to the suburbs, where there was no public transportation, and the elbow room that drew lower middle class white people like us outside I-285, the perimeter that circled the city of Atlanta, had its downside: to get anywhere, you had to drive. Sure, she wouldn't have to fret so much about crime. Her new neighborhood wouldn't be "covered up"—her term for the inescapable presence of black folks. All the "meanness," as she put it, going on inside the city limits wouldn't be her cross to bear anymore. But the fears that made my mother want to flee to suburbia in the first place ironically begat the new concern of navigating its roads.

Two nights per week, Mom took a Driver's Ed course at the local high school. On a couple of occasions, I remember tagging along. I was eight or nine years old. The building was a squat brick structure, abandoned to the outskirts of the campus next to the driving course. A vast expanse of asphalt containing a grid of white lines and orange cones finally petered out in the distance against a plot of woodlands. Inside the building, the cavernous classroom was full of simulated automobile cockpits, each equipped with a standard steering column, turn signal, dashboard, and gas and brake.

The instructor was Mr. Wynn, a bald, hoarse, and cranky old man with a longstanding reputation. Half the people on the roads in our county had learned the finer points of operating an automobile under his tutelage. He was also ex-military, which I recall probably because he taught driving as though it were warfare. You couldn't trust the enemy. That guy in the adjacent lane was dangerous. He was maneuvering a couple thousand pounds of combustible machinery, that guy, without a care in the world for what it could do to you. Every time you pulled out of your driveway, you were executing a treacherous mission, and every safe return was reason enough to thank the good Lord above.

As part of his class, Mr. Wynn would accompany each student in the official Student Driver vehicle on several trips through the various orange cones on the asphalt course. He had high expectations. He made his students nudge their front bumper within eighteen inches of a cone. He required them to parallel park. He demanded that they shift into reverse and back up to a chain-link fence using only their mirrors. And if any of the boys thought they could get away with revving the engine or cranking up the radio or driving one-handed, well, they could just get a refund right now. "I don't have time for nonsense," Mr. Wynn barked repeatedly. "Nonsense gets you killed."

Mom was a fortysomething housewife, but she called him Mr. Wynn. She admired his love of God and country, but mostly she identified with his warnings that the road was a precarious place. She studied her driving manual with the same intensity and commitment I'd seen her study only one other book: the Bible. Perhaps she didn't see operating heavy machinery as a task with eternal ramifications, but her study of that manual can only be described as *devout*.

Almost all of Mom's classmates had one thing in common— they were fifteen year old kids. They were here because they had to be—their parents required them to pass the course in order to keep their insurance premiums as low as possible. During breaks, they gave Mom plenty of elbow room, huddling shoulder-to-shoulder in clusters of four or five, leaving no room for any outsider to infiltrate their space.

And in spite of their youth, they all seemed to grasp the nuances of the road quicker than my mother did. She was a drain on Mr. Wynn. She peppered him with questions, fear-driven inquiries that likely made those fifteen year olds roll their eyes and sigh audibly.

But somehow she passed the course and the subsequent test. The state of Georgia snapped her picture and gave her a driver's license that featured the same unsmiling expression as that of her classmates when they finally turned Sweet Sixteen.

But if you looked close enough, you could probably detect the first strands of gray in her hair, the beginnings of crows feet, and the downright fear in her eyes that this road could lead somewhere terrible.

ABOUT MOM'S FEAR: its origins went back to her youth. As a girl, she never felt safe. "Oh, I could tell you stories about my childhood," Mom often said. To my ears, that statement sounded like both a threat and a promise. She was threatening to shock me with details so sordid, a truth so ugly, I'd wish I hadn't asked. And she was promising that, if she ever did tell me the whole sad story, I'd understand why she was the way she was. It would elicit sympathy from my otherwise callous heart and excuse so many of her behaviors I found embarrassing, annoying, or downright incomprehensible. But in spite of her warning, she never pulled that ace from her sleeve. Too ashamed of the details, the scars too painful still, she never outright disclosed them. Which left me the task of taking the cursory details she did provide and trying to piece them together in such a way that allowed me to tolerate my mom's eccentricities.

I arrived at this: A daughter of the Depression, she grew up in Atlanta's Cabbagetown neighborhood with an alcoholic father and a mother who could do nothing to keep him from his next swig. Some men of his time and place, when they got drunk, they found a stairwell or an underpass or a bed of kudzu and curled into a fetal ball. But others, like my Grandpa Cook, grabbed the globe with their callused hands and shook it with their rage until the whole world felt their vengeance. His profession was house painter. When he couldn't afford a pint of liquor, he resorted to the supplies of his trade and drank paint thinner. The alcohol gave him reprieve from all his demons. He hated the government for milking his wallet, hated the coloreds for taking his jobs, and hated himself for his utter inability to do anything to stop it.

And then the ultimate blow: one day my mother's older brother Ray, ten years old and as mischievous as a stray dog, was riding his bicycle through the streets of Cabbagetown when he zipped into the path of an oncoming truck that struck the boy before either boy or driver could even hit his brakes. The bicycle was a mangled knot of aluminum. The boy was dead.

So by the time she became a teenager, the world must have seemed to my mother like a drunken house painter or a speeding truck.

Which is why it made perfect sense to me when she claimed the highlight of her school career was her election to the school Safety Patrol. As I grew older, Mom told the story with the same pride that fills others when they recall their heroics on the high school gridiron or their straight A's or their prom night escapades. Some adult had decided Norma Fay Cook was capable of protecting others from harm. The details were fuzzy—something about a crosswalk and wearing an orange belt and holding up a sign when the coast was clear—but each telling of those memories made Mom's eyes glassy well into middle age.

Once she graduated high school, she quickly set about trying to find a life for herself that would be more stable than her past. When she was twenty, she got the job at the Sears & Roebuck distribution center on Ponce de Leon. She filled catalog orders. Photos from this time show my mother to be an attractive woman with dark hair and blue eyes, one who could have entertained ideas of rising up the economic ladder through marriage. But Mom lacked fundamental confidence in her manners and social graces, and believed she quickly would be exposed as a fraud. Still, she saw marriage as an escape from her past, and settled on a single, non-negotiable prerequisite for any man proposing matrimony. He could have grease under his fingernails. He could have holes in his socks, his pockets, or maybe even his history. What he could not have was a drink in his hand. "After all I'd seen, I wouldn't have anybody but a teetotaler," she said.

Which is what she got. Dewey Larkin Beaver's only vices were stubbornness and cigarettes. He came by the obstinacy honestly—his old man could impose his will on any mule in his barn—but Dad's nicotine habit was courtesy of Korea, where as a 22-year-old Master Sergeant he had passed his time in frozen foxholes by blowing smoke toward the iron-gray sky. He worked at Sears, too. He stocked supplies.

If there were any romantic tales of soul mates uniting, I never heard them. They married before the justice of the peace on a date only the two of them ever knew. They rented a series of houses, each one slightly less decrepit than the last. Finally they saved enough pennies to build a tiny red brick ranch on Atlanta's east side. In the hallway, my dad hung a plaque on the wall that declared, *As for me and my house, we will serve the Lord*.

And maybe, for the first time in her life, Norma Fay Beaver felt something close to safe.

THE ANTIDOTE TO ALL HER FEAR was religion. The Bible served as her safety belt. Mom seemed to be under the impression that if she swathed our house in God's Word, the devil wouldn't be able to penetrate our bubble-wrapped existence. A sample of her interior decorating: she clipped Bible verses from magazines like *Guidepost, Open Windows*, and Billy Graham's *Decision* and taped them to the refrigerator and the bathroom walls. Her favorites were scriptures from Psalms or Proverbs that offered reassurance and serenity, especially those supplemented with a pastoral photo of a lone sheep grazing in a meadow or a snow-blanketed field shining glassy with afternoon sun. As a Sunday school teacher for many years, she taught children to memorize scripture, and consequently her head brimmed with passages she could call upon at will. While sitting in traffic on Highway 5, she would recite, *He maketh me to lie down in green pastures, he restoreth my soul*. While the story of another homicide on Atlanta's streets filled the newscasts, she'd say, *The fear of man bringeth a snare: but whoso putteth his trust in the Lord shall be safe*.

And never were her fear and faith more visibly on simultaneous display than when bad weather came. A storm was an apocalyptic event—a sure sign the End Times promised by scripture were finally upon us. "I've always believed," Mom regularly declared, "that Jesus is gonna return in my lifetime. All I want is for my family to be ready." And if lightning flashed across the sky and fistfuls of rain splattered against the windows, she'd vow the Four Horsemen were saddling up and the rapture was on its way. Eyes crazed, voice spiked with adrenaline, she'd declare, "The end is nigh." Her vocabulary in these moments echoed King James, as though the occasion required a formal reverence that exceeded her normal Appalachian-inflected dialect.

One night a hailstorm made her insist that the three of us—Dad, Mom, and I—hunker down in a closet. Our late '60s brick ranch contained no walk-in closets, so fitting all of us inside was impossible—especially because Dad was six-two, two hundred pounds. His sheer size prevented him from playing along, even if he'd been inclined to squeeze inside that tight space. But he did his best under the circumstances to indulge Mom. While the white stones pelleted the roof and she and I huddled on the floor of the two-door closet in their bedroom, Dad stood vigil by the window and studied the sky. I'm guessing it looked like God was indeed about to unleash Armageddon on us sad fools below. But Dad gave no such indication. "Things look like they'll be clearing up soon," he said. "Sit tight. It's all gonna pass."

BY THE TIME BEVERLY CLARK entered my life, I'd become convinced Mom's goal was to infantilize me. She claimed her dream was that I'd become a missionary and share the Gospel with natives on the other side of the globe who'd never heard the name of Jesus Christ—but I suspected what she really wanted was for me to become one of those neutered mama's boys who spends his life at the beck and call of the one who brought him into the world.

But Beverly had other designs: on our first date, mere moments after our parents had dropped each of us off at the movie theatre, she possessed the unmitigated gall to kiss me right there on the sidewalk, to slip me the tongue in front of God and every fine citizen of our hometown. She insisted we sneak into an R-rated flick but settled for the PG *Terms of Endearment*, a mother-daughter story that thoroughly stultified me but inexplicably made Beverly nothing short of, well, concupiscent. We sat in the back row, and when she put her hand on my thigh, I couldn't imagine any place I'd rather be than right here, watching Debra Winger die of cancer on the silver screen. Beverly's audacity thrilled me. She acted on every wild and adventurous impulse my mother summarily dismissed as animal behavior. But her blithe attitude also made clear a truth undeniable: she required a guy who could respond in kind. A hard dude. Someone who could grab the wheel and steer.

She regularly worked her ex-boyfriend Mike into our conversations, bitterly complaining about his selfishness, his ego, his unwillingness to talk. From her description, I came to the conclusion that he clearly never would have agreed to pay his hard cash to watch *Terms of Endearment*. And Beverly's biggest competitor seemed to be Mike's '79 Mustang, which received enough of his attention to make her downright jealous of an automobile. Maybe Beverly thought this constant criticism of her ex made me happy. Maybe it should have. But I got hung up on the car. My rival was seventeen. I imagined him cranking up the radio and rolling down the windows and Beverly's hair unfurling and her pulse quickening in her veins. I pictured him finding some desolate road to trundle down, where he parked under a blanket of darkness and cut the engine and listened to it cool as Beverly snuggled close to him and the cicadas hummed in the background.

The more I let my mind wander into this bitter place, the more I began to resent Mom and her overprotectiveness. Nervous. *Please*. I wanted to do something that would prove to Beverly Clark that I was a man to be reckoned with. I waited for her next intrepid idea. Whatever it was, I would oblige unquestionably.

So when she suggested that we should skip school together, I overcame my initial skepticism and shelved the hundred and one reasons why it was a bad proposition.

"We'll spend the day at my house," Beverly said. "My parents will be at work. Nobody will ever know."

But her long-range planning left something to be desired. When the school called Mom to verify my absence, she of course was furious, and knew the only thing that could make me behave so recklessly was a girl. Maybe it was her failure to become a switchboard operator, or perhaps the affront to her religious convictions, or possibly the general conviction the suburbs weren't proving to be the Eden she imagined, but she drove to Beverly's house. (I still have no idea how she knew the address. Maybe she'd done preliminary sleuthing in anticipation of such an event?) She rapped on the door, respectfully at first, but brutally when Beverly did not answer immediately.

Finally Beverly cracked the door. She feigned ignorance. "He didn't show up at school today? Hmm. I have no idea where he is. I haven't heard from him all day."

"You can't tell me you don't know where he is," Mom said.

But Beverly did in fact tell her that very thing; she repeated her claim that she hadn't heard from me, and that she had no clue as to my whereabouts.

I remember standing at the upstairs window of Beverly's bedroom and peering through the blinds, watching Mom pace around the driveway with her hands on her hips; she was down there pondering what to do, deliberating whether to knock again and maybe this time barge inside and pluck her son from the arms of his Jezebel.

Until finally she got in her Chevy Nova, her hands as always at ten and two, and drove away without looking back at the house.

SO THE DRIVER PULLED OUT in front of us, and Mom hit her brakes, and before she was halfway across the road we slammed into the car's rear quarter panel. My head collided with the windshield. I heard a sharp thud, a splintering of glass, and then I rebounded off the windshield and fell back onto my seat. After discovering we were still alive, the other driver, Mom, and I climbed out of our respective vehicles and surveyed the damage. The woman, younger than Mom, seemed relieved we didn't appear to be injured, but not otherwise particularly apologetic.

It was out here, while standing on the roadway, I saw for the first time what I'd done to the windshield. A spider-web crack split the glass. The windshield looked as though someone had tried to throw a baseball through it.

Mom asked me a half-dozen times whether I was okay, and I kept saying yes, even as my own voice sounded to my ears like it was filled with gravel, engine sludge, and stringy wet leaves.

A buggy boy from the nearby Kroger had heard the collision. He abandoned his train of carts and came sprinting up the hill toward us, his blue apron untied and flopping as he ran. Did we need an ambulance? No, we told him. He appeared disappointed, but then his spirits revived when he hit upon the idea of running inside the store and calling the police. He saluted, as though he were proud to assume such a noble mission on minimum wage, and then hurried away.

As we waited for the cruiser to arrive, Mom and the lady talked in low voices while I sat on the curb with my head between my knees. A knot was already swelling high on my forehead. My vision was clear, but passing traffic seemed to be moving through a liquid film. As the drivers gawked at us, the wheels on their vehicles turned so slowly they appeared to be sliding on a sheet of ice. A fog settled over my brain. I did my best to calm the nausea roiling in my belly and hide the fear that ratcheted up one more level every time I took another glance at that windshield.

But my mother could see I was shaken, and by the time the police showed up, she was inconsolable. "I can't believe I didn't make you put on your seatbelt," she kept saying. "Why didn't I make you put it on? What was I thinking? Whywhywhy?" She could hardly put together a coherent sentence as she described to the officer what happened for his accident report.

"Yes, ma'am," the officer kept saying. "But would you go back to the beginning one more time and start from there?"

AFTERWARD, WE WENT TO THE ER. The room was bathed in yellow light and none of the objects had defined edges that I could discern. Even the doctor's head seemed to float detached from his neck. He ordered a CT test. A long delay later, he came into the room with an X-ray. He showed us the outline of my skull. He jabbed his finger at an amorphous blob in the center of the image. "Here's the way a concussion works," he said. "Your brain is like Jell-O, and it floats in liquid." He explained that a jar to your head can bang your brain against your skull. "That's what happened to you when you hit that windshield." He pounded a fist into the palm of his hand. "*Bam*," he said.

That night, Mom woke me every hour on the hour, as the doctor instructed her to do. "Are you feeling okay?" she'd ask. "Son, are you all right?" She flooded the room with lamp light, sat next to me on the mattress, and studied my pupils. She made me tell her my full name and my birthday and what year it was, and when I responded correctly she patted my arm and brushed my hair away from my forehead. Finally the box springs groaned under her weight as she slid off my bed and turned off the lamp on my nightstand.

She turned to leave the room for the next hour, but before she was gone she asked me in a trembling voice, every time, "Why? Why didn't I tell you to put on your seatbelt?"

The truth was, I probably felt too constrained already; the seatbelt was one more extension of my mother's reach, always touching me, never letting me go. Georgia law at the time didn't require you to wear a seatbelt, but I was fifteen and knew well enough that ignoring my seatbelt was nothing short of risky behavior. In my imagination when I pictured Beverly Clark's ex whisking her through the rural zip, the road hugging the natural bend and curve of the land, *he* never wore a seatbelt, so I probably got it in my head that acknowledging your vulnerability with a strap across your chest was a clear sign of weakness.

144

We were just boys, the ex and I. We were indestructible. One day maybe we'd shuck our armor of invincibility and take our place among the mortals. That day was a long way off, though, so likely I simply made the choice not to fasten my seatbelt. Mom probably didn't even know I'd neglected to wear it.

Still, she blamed herself. Over the next few days, while my thinking and vision cleared and the knot on my head sank into my scalp, Mom chided herself for her poor judgment. She was wearing a belt—why hadn't she stopped to make sure I was wearing mine, too? This question, on repeat, into infinity.

It was a long time before she got behind the wheel again. A couple of weeks passed, at least. In the interim, she asked my dad to stop by the grocery store on his way home from his job at the Post Office, and she made sure I was standing at the bus stop in the mornings when the Big Cheese picked up the neighborhood kids.

Eventually, though, all those factors that made it necessary to get her license in the first place beckoned again, and she resumed driving. It would have been impossible to become even more cautious than she already was—so she simply kept up her vigilance and prayed for safe passage. Occasionally she'd be plodding along and see a car idling up ahead, waiting for traffic to clear so it could pull into the intersection. Mom would take one hand from the wheel long enough to aim her finger at the potential offender and say, "Don't even think about it, mister. You just stay right where you are."

YOU PROBABLY SAW THIS COMING: Beverly dumped me. Her old boyfriend rolled up in his Mustang; he was behind the wheel, and his mom was nowhere in sight. Or at least that's the way I imagined it. The news came through a phone call from Beverly, brief and cursory and as cold as her heart. "I've been thinking maybe we should just be friends," she told me. "You're such a nice guy…but, well, you know." I didn't press her for details. Whether she meant it or not, I interpreted "you know" as *you know, your mom dropped you off at the movies when we went to see* Terms of Endearment.

She made no mention of her ex, but it came as no surprise when Mike showed up at our church with her one Sunday night, and sat through the invocation, the hymns, and Pastor Davis' longwinded sermon about some obscure passage in *Malachi*, all the while staring a hole through me. Until finally, before the organist had even finished her postlude, he put his hand in the small of Beverly's back and nudged her toward the exit and whisked her away in his car.

Anyway, Beverly's phone call made me so forlorn I couldn't sleep. I felt worse than when I hit my head because this time my ailment was soul sickness—there existed no such thing as a safety belt for a broken heart. We had pledged ourselves to each other in the way only kids can do when they fail to realize all the different people they'll become. But Beverly changed first—which left me ashamed I was still the same boy who believed all those you're-the-one-for-me clichés we'd whispered together over the phone.

That night, Mom must have heard me tossing and turning. She must have been relying on her maternal sixth sense to know I wasn't well. She got out of her bed and came into my room and lay down next to me. The mattress creaked as she settled near me. Her arm brushed against mine. She didn't ask what happened, but she probably guessed. In short: she didn't say anything much at all. She turned over on her side. In the dim light, she was a lump under the blankets. I thought she was simply waiting for me to fall asleep.

But a moment later, Mom started talking. Her voice was out there somewhere in the darkness, disembodied. I couldn't really see her but I heard clearly when she finally spoke in a voice suspended somewhere between sleeping and waking. "It's okay," she was telling me. "I'm right here. I'll take care of you."

THE BADMOBILE

By now I was sixteen, and adrift in suburbia, so naturally I wanted to be elsewhere, anywhere, to be *someone* else—to roll down the windows, crank up the radio, and squeal away from my life, my only goodbye a nasty skid mark black as a long smear of shit. I wanted to punish the pedal and strangle the wheel until my fists turned white as bone; haul ass away from myself, leaving the boy I was somewhere *back there* in the rearview mirror. I wanted to motor south, toward Florida, stopping only to pick up hitchhikers with sunshine in their eyes, and keep going until we plunged straight into the surf when the road gave out, going and going until my ride took on water and capsized in a beautiful catastrophe. It was a plan. Maybe I could have done it.

But there was an inconvenient fact: my getaway vehicle was a prune-juice colored Camaro that sucked gas, smelled like sulfur, and had a habit of overheating in the drive-through at the Taco Bell. Wherever I was headed and whoever I was to become, I could get there only if the Badmobile could make it.

SHE AND I BECAME acquainted in the usual way: The ad in the local paper read *1974 CAMARO, 350V-8, Good condition, $1500*. It was the fall of 1984. Dad would buy a car, but the gas and insurance would be my responsibility. "I'm not giving away handouts," Dad said—about life in general and cars specifically. "I'll get you a vehicle. It's your job to keep it on the road." Now that I had opened up a savings account and deposited a summer's worth of paychecks, Dad called the seller. They arranged a time for us to come by and take a look. Upon hanging up, Dad offered me some sage advice: "Let me do the talking."

I had spent the summer showing good faith, working ten-hour days at the Warehouse Groceries, stocking milk and eggs and shoving buggy trains across a scorching parking lot bubbling with tar for $3.50 an hour. I had run a million price checks for the register girls, twentysomethings with big hair and no prospects for any future beyond a never-ending conveyer belt of Palmolive, Miller High Life, and broccoli. They had flirted with me shamelessly, those girls, because they were bored out of their skulls and I was a boy. It helped them pass the time. After clocking out at midnight I would pilfer a Snickers bar, climb atop the mile-long buggy train I had rounded up, and wait for my parents in the parking lot. Those register girls would slip into their boyfriends' rumbling vehicles and tear away into the night—but not before they waved goodbye. Sometimes they blew kisses, winked at me. I believed them. I would have chased them down, rescued them from those bad boys with tattoos, criminal records, and ratty mufflers. But, alas, I didn't have any transportation.

When Dad and I went to see the car, we found it sitting among a stand of jack pine. Its hood lay buried beneath a mat of orange needles an inch thick. We spent what seemed an inordinate amount of time debating its color. Maybe it wasn't actually prune juice, but iodine, perhaps, or cough syrup. It was impossible to say with certainty. Black louvers spanned the back windshield. Four bald tires sank into the mushy ground.

The owner had yet to make an appearance. He knew we were coming, and by this time we'd been out here in his yard for a while. But he was apparently waiting us out from inside his low-slung brick ranch, maybe peeking through the curtains, gauging whether our interest was legitimate. He'd likely been burned by false inquiries a few too many times. Which was okay with Dad—if he'd wanted a hard sales pitch, he would have visited the used car lots. Dad did not suffer fools easily.

We peered through the windows. The interior was infested with potato chip crumbs and gum wrappers. A couple of empty beer bottles had rolled to rest in the floorboard. Cigarette stubs crammed the ashtray. When Dad tried the door, the hinges creaked with a long, tomb-opening groan. "Nothing a little WD-40 can't take care of," he said.

Inside, a dank funk lingered. A stale, vanilla-scented deodorizer hung forlornly from the rearview.

It was about at this point in our inspection that the seller finally approached. We heard him before we saw him, when a screen door slammed behind him. He wandered barefoot into the yard wearing cut-off jean-shorts, a shirt unbuttoned to reveal sagging pecs and a beer belly, and a stringy brown mullet. He clutched a can of Pabst Blue Ribbon. After dislodging a ball of phlegm from his throat and spitting in the dirt, he told us his name was Stan. Then he cleared his throat again, producing a sound like a rusty chainsaw, and burped into his fist.

By way of introduction, Stan offered a history of the car, which seemed to tell us much more about him than it. This vehicle, Stan explained, had been good to him, but now he was going through a nasty divorce, and he needed every penny he could get. Stan did not mind telling us the whole sordid story of Teresa and how the love of his life had taken up with another man. "You work every minute of the day," he said, "and she squanders every last dollar, and decides it'll never be enough." Stan studied us to see whether we would offer the sympathy he was clearly soliciting. We nodded as though we understood, though in truth we were a little wary of the consequences of failing to supply the requested compassion. "Saddest part," he continued, "is I'd take her back this minute if she just asked. All she'd have to do is ring me up and say, 'Stan, let's make another run at it' "—and this is where he focused his attention on me for the first time, as though previously he'd been chatting man-to-man with my father—"and you know what I'd do?" By this time Dad was under the hood, probing around somewhere in the dark recesses of the engine. Maybe he knew what he was looking for, but it struck me that what he was really trying to do was duck out of the conversation. Stan regarded me as though he were waiting expectantly—as though he were *depending*—on my answer. "Know what I'd do?" he repeated.

"Take her back?" I ventured.

"Damn straight, boy," he admitted. "In a heartbeat. No questions asked." He took a swig of his beer. He looked down the street that led to the mouth of his subdivision, presumably toward where Teresa was now nesting in the arms of her new beloved. "Just say the word, baby, and we'll wipe the whole slate clean. Me and my Teresa, starting over from scratch." He just stood there for a moment, his belly distended, his shirttails drooping sadly, lost in reverie.

I wasn't sure what Stan wanted from me. I was just a kid, sixteen years old, with a driver's license burning a hole in his pocket but no ride to call his own. I didn't have anything to do with Teresa's callous behavior. I wanted to join my father, climb under the hood of this homely car, pretending to investigate the machinery I knew absolutely nothing about. But Stan kept me fixed in his gaze. "Between you and me, boy, that's highly unlikely—that's a *pipe-dream*, is what it is." I shook my head with shared regret.

Dad emerged from under the hood. He asked Stan a series of questions—something about the mysterious inner workings of the vehicle—and Stan seemed to provide an informed response. Dad crossed his arms, sank into his heels. His lips were working. Stan wouldn't have known it, because Dad was just a stranger to him, but my father was praying over what to do. He wouldn't buy something as pricey as an automobile without firstly taking it to the Lord in prayer.

"Go for a spin," Stan suggested.

Dad's willingness to take a test drive was indeed the first indicator to Stan that he was genuinely interested. Stan disappeared inside his house for what seemed a curiously long time—long enough to make us wonder whether Teresa had run off with the keys—but finally he emerged, a proud grin spreading across his face, jingling the keys above his head as though he'd survived some kind of dangerous mission to retrieve them. He handed them over to Dad, failing to ascertain the man on the receiving end was a Washed-in-the-Blood Christian who was clearly less than impressed by the key ring featuring two stick figures having sex.

"Open her up when you get out on the road," Stan told us. "You'll see what all she can do."

Dad took the wheel; I rode shotgun. He didn't trust me to execute necessary emergency measures, given the dangerous possibilities—an imploding engine, an exploding tire, something vital falling off. When he turned the ignition, the engine sounded like Armageddon, even idling, as though this very instant we'd all better confess our sins to the Blessed Redeemer. Stan stood in the driveway, his potbelly bulging, his hands plunged deep inside his pockets, as we drove away. Dad came to a complete stop at each sign inside the subdivision, trying to calculate the car's disposition. He seemed to be coaxing it along as though he did not trust its temperament. But once we pulled onto the highway, he followed Stan's instructions, and opened her up.

The speedometer hit 80, the wind, hot and dry, billowed through the windows and whistled inside our ears, and I left my stomach somewhere in the middle of the highway a mile back. We rode out Post Road, through the county pastureland, the rural zip, past the strings of rusty barbed wire, the bored cows, the mosquitoes fat as black gumballs. Out here a dog could lie dead for days on the shoulder of the road before the county trucks came by to pry it from the asphalt. The tall and brittle weeds along the roadside rattled as we barreled by. Gnats splattered against the windshield. Dad was getting a sense of what the car could do, all right. It wasn't shy, that much was certain.

Meanwhile I spun the radio dial, which was the car's main attribute I was interested in. All I got was static until I discovered a feeble signal through speakers that sounded as though they were submerged at the bottom of a murky pond. And I was not happy to discover that, in the age of cassette decks, this vehicle sported an eight-track.

When we swung into Stan's subdivision again, a maze of brick ranches almost identical to his, Dad braked. Up the street from Stan's, he veered onto the shoulder and shifted into park. The engine rumbled. The undercarriage seemed to vibrate. "So what do you think?" he asked. "You like it?"

I knew the right answer. My father was a postman, all right, and his forearms were sun-baked a deep red, and he had shouldered a thousand burlap sacks full of junk mail through block after block of Hotlanta heat to save up money to buy a car for his son. In the past few weeks, especially, he'd been working hard, late, overtime. I'd barely seen him. His eyes were rimmed with exhaustion. He knew it wasn't the car a teenage boy dreams of, sleek and shiny and smooth, a model from the *current* decade. But it was a sports car; it was fast, and he seemed to be banking on its speed to compensate for the fact that this heap of metal was all he could afford.

Perhaps he had detected my ambivalence, which might explain why we were having this conversation here, out of Stan's earshot. He wouldn't have wanted to suffer the indignity of pleading with me in Stan's presence to let him buy me a car.

"You like it?" he asked again. "You want it, right?"

The truth was, I didn't like it. I didn't really want it. But I knew that telling him so would be about the most ungrateful thing a boy could say, and it would be a response I could never take back. Dad would think of me as a spoiled brat. He could say *Fine, save up your money and buy your own car,* and he'd be justified. So when Dad asked if I wanted it, I nodded. "Sure," I said. "I guess so."

"You'll take care of it?"

I told him I would.

Stan was waiting for us when we returned. The transaction took the appropriate amount of time. That is, it took approximately as long as it *should* take to buy a crappy car. The cutthroat bargaining unfolded something like this:

Dad: The paper said $1500.

Stan: Uh-huh.

Dad: Give you $1200.

Stan: Okay.

Dad broke out his checkbook. Stan spelled out his last name. When Dad handed the check to him, Stan studied the zeroes to confirm that Dad had included enough of them, then folded the check in half and tucked it into his back pocket.

Before we drove away with his former car, Stan approached me. I was behind the wheel of Dad's Ford Fairlane. Dad was in the Camaro. Dad said I'd have to get insurance before he'd let me drive it, but I knew he was afraid something would go terribly wrong—it was a horse that would have to be broken before a pony-boy like me could saddle up. Stan wedged his hip against my window; he leaned his head inside. I could smell the beer on his breath. His tone was one of confidentiality. "So this is your first car, huh?"

I told him it was.

"You'll treat her right, I reckon?"

"Course I will."

"Cause if you don't, I'll come steal her out of your driveway, sure enough, and bring her back home where she belongs." I waited for a smile to break across his face, but it never came. He gazed toward the Camaro. He *tsked* his tongue. Clearly Stan was experiencing some separation anxiety here. "She's fast, ain't she?" he said.

"Lost my stomach a couple of times," I said.

"She's loud too. You crank her up, *everybody* knows you're coming through."

I nodded. "It's loud all right."

"She's a Badmobile, that's what she is," Stan said. "I'll miss her. Lots of memories caught up in her." Then he shrugged his shoulders. "I hate to practically give her away, but a man's got to make peace with his circumstances."

Moments later, when we pulled away, he was standing in the yard, another Pabst in his fist. But before we were even out of the driveway, he began waving with his free hand—not a grand, sweeping gesture of *Bon voyage* or *Godspeed* but only a feeble wisp of his fingers as if to say, *Goodbye.*

SO NOW I HAD MY FIRST CAR. But instead of coddling her by washing her twice a week, patting the dashboard and calling her *baby*, I immediately commenced running her into the ground. I took every curve on two wheels. I aimed for potholes, mud puddles, low-hanging tree limbs, dead squirrels. I scouted out dirt roads, gravel lots, hairpin curves, rutted paths. The fenders were forever pocked by gravel, the tires rimmed with grime; the hood was always blanketed with pollen, the roof splattered with birdshit. When my mother, who never drove on an interstate in her life because everything moved too fast for her Nervous condition, asked me to drive her to a shopping mall down I-75 on the south side of Atlanta, I scared her such that she refused to ride back home with me. She called my father and told him to pick her up after he got off work. He was not pleased.

Dad had emphasized defensive strategies in lessons in the parking lot at our Baptist church. Keep two hands on the wheel at all times, he told me, at ten and two o'clock, and adjust all the mirrors to work in tandem with one another so that you can see every angle of the road. Check your blind spot. Expect the adjacent car to veer suddenly into your lane with no turn signal. Don't tailgate, he said. Brake gradually as soon as you see red lights in front of you—don't wait till you're eating up the guy's bumper to slam on the brakes. He predicted my first accident would be rear-ending somebody. He said I'd be thinking about some girl and playing the music too loud, and next thing I knew, I'd be picking my teeth out of the dashboard. He said I'd give somebody whiplash and it would go on my permanent record. "Expect the worst," he advised. "You never know what the other guy's gonna do." When I took the driving test, Dad's voice was still ringing in my ears, which probably explained why I forgot to buckle my belt when I took the examiner for a spin. Somehow, maybe because he pitied me, I passed the test anyway.

Maybe he'd been a boy once too.

The few friends who weren't too afraid or embarrassed to ride with me propped their shoes on the dashboard, lounged in the back seat, dangled their bare feet out the windows. They tossed their Coke bottles in the floorboard, chucked bags of Cheetos into the back. They spat out the window, threw snot-rags under the seats, farted on the upholstery. Holly Medford clipped her toenails in the back seat. Brad Austin puked. My buddy Biss just couldn't wait till we made it to the Circle K, so he peed in one of those empty Coke bottles he'd tossed into the back.

I tolerated their foul behavior. I didn't care. I was forever spinning the radio dial in search of some lyric as crude as we were.

One night I rounded up a crowd of five or six boys and headed to the church gym for some hoops. Our last stop was Matt Dawson's house. Once Matt was inside the Badmobile, I shifted into reverse. As I was backing up, I couldn't see around the heads filling the back seat and proceeded to back straight into Matt's mailbox. It was solid brick, four feet high and stout as a boulder—which did not prevent it from breaking at the base and tipping over on its side. It hit the roadway with a thunder like crumbling cinderblocks. We all piled out of the Badmobile and stuck our hands in our back pockets and marveled, speechless, at what I had done. The mailbox lay remarkably intact in the street, with only a couple of bricks split from the rest. "Shit," Biss finally said. "Damn," Matt offered. The lot of us—five or six healthy adolescent males—attempted to lift the mailbox, but it would not budge. Matt's parents weren't home, so we took considerable time pondering how we might resolve this predicament. Someone suggested calling a tow truck. It sounded like a reasonable solution. Inside Matt's house, I thumbed through the Yellow Pages and contacted a local towing service. It took almost ninety minutes, but eventually two burly guys, an assortment of thick, heavy chains, and of course their truck managed to get the mailbox upright again. It was a little shaky on its foundation, but nothing a skilled mason couldn't correct.

The next day, I dropped by Matt's house and offered a sincere apology to his dad. I said I would pay for the damage. He told me I had already paid for the tow truck, which cost a princely sum, no doubt, so he'd take care of the rest. In a futile attempt to rescue some kind of nobility from such an embarrassing situation, I told him I wouldn't hear of it. He shouldn't have to pay a dime. He wasn't even home when it happened, I reminded him. "What's the difference?" he said. "If I'd been there, you'd have still run over my goddamn mailbox."

At stoplights the Badmobile would snarl and lurch forward, like a pit bull straining at its tethered leash. I raced the engine as though itching to burn whatever was inside me through the fuel line and out the muffler. I'd tap the accelerator impatiently until the light blinked green, when I'd peel out and leave behind the stench of burning rubber. I'd clear the city limits and really open it up, splitting the wall of trees crowding the road. Give me a straightaway of a quarter mile or more, and I'd whip those 350 horses snorting under the hood into a galloping lather. The steering column would tremble in my grip and I would glance into the rearview mirror, keeping an eye out for blue lights, sure, but really believing I might see my whole life gradually dwindling to nothing. Somewhere out here, in the thrust of velocity, I could outrun Jesus, my parents, suburbia—and maybe even myself.

All this speed of course depended on somehow managing to keep gas in the tank. The gauge was always buried in red. One night I woke my father at 2 a.m. to tell him I was empty. Predictably, he complained about the boy I was becoming. "When are you gonna grow up?" he wanted to know. "When are you gonna *mature?*" He said it with distaste, the way you say *manure*, probably because he'd decided I was in some deep shit. But he did come fetch me, with a gas can in tow. On nights like those, I began to wonder if the reason my old man bought the car in the first place was to enable me to drive out of his life. It was a *fast* car, after all, capable of topping 100 miles per hour if I could muster the nerve, and it would have been the ideal getaway vehicle from the life I was living. As long as I could keep gas in its tank, it could take me to someplace else, where I could be a new boy—one that wouldn't be such a disappointment to his father. Maybe somewhere on the open road, for example, I could learn to hunt. It would be nice, too, if I could change the oil in the Badmobile. And once I had mastered these fundamental necessities maybe I could get a haircut, pack on a few pounds of muscle, and avoid behavior my father summarized as "timid"—which in his lexicon was a polite way of saying *girly*. If I could acquaint myself with sweat, with grease, with sawdust, maybe, just maybe, we'd be getting somewhere. If I became that boy, perhaps I could come home and try again.

NOW THAT MY FATHER HAD bought my first car, my mission was to get a girl into the backseat. Vehicular *amour* had been a longstanding goal, but the scheme had lain dormant while I puttered around in my father's Ford Fairlane. Dad's ride featured bench seats, front and back, which I would soon learn are more conducive to licentious behavior; but the idea of indulging my carnal desires in my father's vehicle was outside even my moral sphere of conduct. By this point, he was chairman of the Baptist deacons. He kept a pocket-sized New Testament in the glove compartment. Jesus, I was convinced, would have been eyeing me in the rearview mirror.

I had a girlfriend, Tamara, which made the whole plan seem within the realm of possibility. We were fundamentally incompatible, a veritable odd couple, because she was rich and pretty and popular—and I of course was none of the above. But Tamara had this thing about necks, especially hers. She would beg me to find some Prince on the radio, because His Royal Badness made her feel a little naughty, and she would sweep her hair off her shoulders and say *Here, kiss me right here,* on the nape of her neck. I was happy to oblige. It didn't cost a dime. Throughout the relationship I had a sense that Tamara's Rolex was ticking and any day now she would wake up and recognize that I was not like her and she was simply slumming by hanging out with me. But that's probably the way she wanted it. Maybe she was rebelling against her parents. Maybe she thought she was being charitable, offering her affections to the working class for a little while—till she was satisfied she'd done her part to fulfill *noblesse oblige.* A princess who wore her tiara slightly askew, she had a little of the fallen debutante in her anyway. Maybe that's what made me think I had a chance. Whatever. Tamara soon dumped me and took up with a boy with a pool in his backyard, a Mercedes with whitewall tires in his garage, a closetful of T-shirts from various islands he had visited on family vacations, and purebred knowledge of which fork to use. I hardly called it coincidence.

But all that was still to come.

One night in the fall Tamara and I ended up in a cul-de-sac in a deserted construction site for a new subdivision on the desolate outskirts of town. A place called Emerald Lakes. I parked and killed the headlights. It had been raining for three days straight. The sky tonight was ominous, black and bloated. The buildings were in various stages of construction. Concrete slab foundations sat in great pits of mud. The skeletons of three or four houses stood out against the sky.

Foreplay consisted of exploring the building sites. There was a strange feeling of power in walking from room to room, never using the doorways but passing instead through the walls, the dull thud of our footsteps on the plywood the only sound in the

November night. We teetered above the basement on two-by-sixes like high-wire acrobats. We peered up through the rafters at the stars overhead. Soon the promised rain started to fall—a fine mist floating down through the rafters to the rooms. The whole arrangement quickened our blood.

But back in the Badmobile, that hump in the middle of the back seat proved quite the obstacle to fulfilling our lustful ambitions. It was the size of a lumpy pillow, but the solidity of a river boulder. The intention was contour, I'm sure; the back seat was supposed to fit your body with streamlined curves that gave the bench seat as snug a fit as the front bucket seats. And I'm sure it was a good sit. But a good *sit* did not coincide with a good *lay*. Chevrolet, displaying greater moral propriety than I, did not design that back seat to accommodate the pursuit of eros. But Tamara and I persisted. We wrestled as much as we were obliged. It was sauna-like back there. The windows fogged. We made a lot of promises in desperate whispers. There were the requisite histrionics, all that gasping and heaving and bad dialogue.

Until law enforcement showed up.

Tamara and I were still struggling to figure out a way to defy the laws of physics when a set of headlights swung into the cul-de-sac. The patrol car pulled right up behind us, nudged his grille against my bumper. Blue lights swirled through the trees surrounding us. By this time Tamara was down to a lacy bra and purple skivvies. We scrambled into the front seat. She wrapped herself in my jacket. We spent the next thirty seconds trying to brainstorm an explanation.

The officer strolled around to the driver's side window, his belt and gun at eye level. He shone his flashlight in my face. "Evening," he said. He crouched to get a look at Tamara. "You okay in there, miss?"

He didn't ask for identification. He didn't lecture. He just told us that it was dangerous to isolate ourselves out here in the boonies, where any sicko could have us at his mercy, and to move along before he got a mind to pay a visit to our parents. Then, before he returned to his car and waited for us to pull away, he put both hands on the Badmobile's roof, leaned far enough into my window for me to smell his aftershave, and fixed me in his gaze. Then he said something so simple and pure even I couldn't mistake his message: "I got a daughter of my own at home," he said.

SO: TAMARA THOUGHT it might be better if we started taking her car. For her Sweet Sixteenth her father had bestowed upon her a brand new cherry-red Datsun 280-Z. On the morning of her birthday, she had strolled in her pajamas into the driveway to find it wrapped in a big white bow. She took one look at it shimmering like a candied apple and broke into tears. And it really was a sight to behold. Her father washed it every five minutes. Each morning her mother laid a fresh flower from their garden on the dashboard. When Tamara drove me to the Taco Bell I always felt like I was being chauffeured. I was embarrassed by this arrangement and so was she. As we cruised the strip, males were supposed to take the wheel while females leaned out the passenger-side window to holler at friends passing by.

Tamara's car was a stick shift. I did not know how to drive a stick. Tamara was undeterred by such a minor inconvenience. "I'll teach you!" she declared, her voice fluttering. I wasn't sure this was a good idea. I didn't trust her enthusiasm. I felt vaguely embarrassed by the possibility of my girlfriend teaching me anything related to the operation of heavy machinery. Surely some kind of power in the relationship was at stake here. But she insisted. "It'll be fun," she said. She curled her hair around her shoulder, exposed the nape of her neck.

So she drove me to a nearby elementary school, to a big parking lot, where she attempted to instruct me in the finer points of changing gears.

I was a poor student. Under my supervision Tamara's car was making *rrring* sounds it was not supposed to make. The gears were grinding. More than once I thought I had stripped them bare and left her transmission lying in the middle of the parking lot. I would shift from neutral into first but the engine would inexplicably die out, and the car would roll a few feet before shuddering to a halt, wounded. Tamara was patient, but somewhere in it all I got the clear sense that she was thinking I'd never been behind the wheel of such a nice car before, and it would be a long time coming before I ever would again.

This thought did not help. I became flustered. I started getting angry. It was the car's fault that I couldn't drive it. Somehow I got it in my head that I wasn't goddamned rich enough to get it to cooperate. Somewhere in its circuitry it had divined my proletariat status, and had rejected me outright.

I had some harsh words for Tamara's car. I called it names. It did not seem to care. The more I cursed Tamara's vehicle, the more obstinate it became. The *rrring* continued. The engine kept dying out. I slapped the dashboard. I said, *Come on, you fuckin' piece of shit, go!* Tamara did not take kindly to my insults. She took my criticism of her car to be criticism of her. "My *father* gave me this car," she reminded me, her lower lip quivering. It was a good car, she insisted. She said I was hurting her feelings. She was on the verge of tears.

I could give a shit. I called her a poor little debutante. I asked if she wasn't supposed to be sitting on a verandah somewhere with a mint julep in her hand. I couldn't make this girl understand something that was really very obvious.

"Don't take it so personal," I finally told her. "It's not like your car is *you*."

THAT BACKSEAT, IT TURNS OUT, was built for neither screwing nor sleeping. Much to my chagrin and discomfort, I was soon to learn that the back seat of a '74 Camaro was not conducive to *any* type of horizontal activity. By this time I'd settled into my seventeenth year, which meant that nobody told me what to do, so to prove it I got my ear pierced. The girl at the mall who'd performed the procedure warned that the hole would close up if I didn't wear the earring all the time—so keeping it a secret from my father was indeed a challenge. But somehow a couple of days passed before he busted me. "You won't live under my roof with an earring in your ear," Dad informed me.

I told him to deal with it.

He said he'd had enough.

I said I was a *nonconformist.* (Sadly, I'm not making this up.)

He said he was drawing the line.

I said I didn't care about his line.

He told me to get out of his house.

I spent the next two minutes packing a duffle bag and storming out the door. I cranked the Badmobile, tore out of the driveway, ended up in a sanctimonious huff at Tamara's place. Conveniently, her parents were out of town. She took me in, cleaned me up, acted appropriately outraged that a father would boot his own flesh and blood out on the street. "I don't understand how he could *do* that," she said. She even went as far as— and I'm embarrassed to admit this—to wrap me in a blanket. She stopped short of offering a pacifier, but she really did do her best to baby me, which is exactly what I desired.

But, alas, after maybe two hours of blissful domesticity, we had a big fight, which I probably could have predicted, considering that we spent most of our time inventing new ways to push each other's buttons. I have no recollection of what we argued about. We were just fulfilling our duty anyway. There was the obligatory amount of yelling and pouting and threatening. Bottom line: she kicked me out too.

I asked her where I was supposed to go.

"To hell," she suggested.

I played The Homeless Card, shamelessly.

Problem was, she hardly had sympathy for a homeless guy, especially if he was her boyfriend. She told me to take the damn stud out of my ear. "It's infected anyway, you moron," she said. I had thought the round knot the size of a cantaloupe protruding from my lobe was relatively discreet, but apparently it was more conspicuous than I had realized.

So for the second time in a single night, I was slamming the Badmobile into reverse, squealing out of the driveway, this time holding a finger to the wind in search of direction.

I ENDED UP AT THE HOSPITAL. I wasn't *in* the hospital—nothing was hurt but my pride—but outside it, in the parking lot near the emergency room. I had cruised around my claustrophobic little suburban town for a couple of hours, despising the world and everyone in it, searching for a place to sit and ponder and reflect on how dirty the human race was treating me. I was getting *hosed*, man. I was getting jobbed. But the needle was buried in red again and I didn't have any money for gas. So somehow I ended up at the hospital, where I figured the police wouldn't suspect I was loitering, because what kind of reprobate spends all night at the emergency room if he doesn't have to be there?

I'd heard stories of people actually reveling in living in their car—savoring the freedom of the highway, the adventure of it all, the romance of the open road.

What a crock.

I sat inside the Badmobile licking my wounds, watching people file into the emergency room in various states of panic. I briefly savored setting some kind of record—kicked out of two houses in one night!—but no one was present to admire my accomplishment.

I climbed in the back seat to try to sleep. But there was the problem of that hump. I couldn't get comfortable. I shifted, squirmed. Nothing could relieve me. The last time I'd climbed into this back seat, I'd been playing a kind of Twister with the self-same girl who had just come running into her yard holding both middle fingers aloft for my inspection as I drove away. The sheer irony of it all was too much to bear.

It was a bad time for philosophy, because when you're alone in a fugly car in a hospital parking lot at three in the a.m., you want to avoid reflection as much as possible. But, really, there's nothing to do but think. You look at this car and you start remembering Stan and his woman, his whole pathetic story, how he didn't want to sell the car but she had him by the short ones. But you know that was only the sad ending of the tale, and you picture what came before, the two of them in better days, Stan riding high in the captain's chair with his wrist over the wheel, Teresa sitting shotgun with the wind rifling through her hair, singing along with the radio, the two of them set up to take whatever life's got to throw at them. They're Bonnie and Clyde, as long as they're on the road—strung out on love, and bulletproof.

You briefly consider firing up the Badmobile and riding on fumes across town and parking her right under the pine tree where you found her. Leaving the keys and an apology note on the welcome mat. Clearly, Stan had more regard for this vehicle than you ever will. It's a thought, and you've got a heart big enough to do it, but right now this steel shell is the only thing protecting you from the world outside.

The emergency room is packed.

The night is a precarious place to be.

So in the harsh red glow of the hospital, you lock the doors, curl up in that back seat, and wait for the morning light.

TO BE SURE, THIS IS NO Prodigal Son story, but a couple of
days later, I was living under my father's roof again. Apparently
my disappearance had affected him enough to reconsider his
ban on earrings. When he told me I could home, I hung up
the pay phone and drove the Badmobile cautiously, keeping to
the speed limit, locking both hands on the wheel. Upon arriving home, though, I found a pervading sense of concern in the
house. Nobody was quite sure what to do with me. Mom said
people at the church were praying for me. She'd called a prayer
hotline at another church and *they* were praying for me too. It
would be one thing if I didn't know any better, she told me, but
they'd raised me better than this. What kind of payback was
this for all the sacrifices they'd made? Didn't I understand what
a privilege it was to be raised by good Christian parents who
asked nary a thing but for their son to behave himself? Didn't I
know the Bible says, *Train up a child in the way he should go, and
when he is old he will not depart from it?* When her words didn't
seem to create the desired effect, she resorted to other tactics. In
the coming days, she began leaving notes with little handwritten Bible verses in my room.

For his part, Dad took an altogether different tack. I remember him telling me, in maybe the most genuine and respectful conversation we had during my youth, he hated earrings on
boys. "But you're my son," he said, "and if you think you should
wear an earring, well, just wear the thing." Of all the words that
ever would pass between us, those three—*You're my son*—are the
ones I most want to remember.

One Saturday in spring I was running late for my job at
Baskin-Robbins, where I pulled down $3.35 an hour for scooping
ice cream, wearing a shirt with pink, yellow, and orange stripes
and a butterfly collar, and eating my weight in inventory. I was
idling at a stop sign, maybe a hundred yards from my house, the
Badmobile guzzling gas as I waited for traffic to clear so I could

pull out onto the highway and slide under the clock at work about five miles away.

A little ways up the highway, a car was approaching. As it neared the street I would be pulling out from, its turn signal started blinking. It slowed to indicate it would be pulling into my street. It was a nice car, and new—an '85 Trans-Am with black paint and gold trim. I remember thinking it looked vaguely familiar to me, but figured the resemblance was probably only the residue of having lusted many times for just such a machine.

Only seven minutes or so remained until I was scheduled to clock in at the ice cream shop. So when I saw the Trans-Am slow and its turn signal blink, I pulled away from the stop sign and onto the highway. I headed in the direction the Trans-Am had been traveling from. But I was barely in the road before I heard a horn blare and saw the Trans-Am swerve across the middle line trying to avoid me, and then the crash as the Badmobile collided with its passenger-side door, steel and fiberglass converging, and the Trans-Am leaped away as though it were a train jumping the tracks. The Trans-Am's door and the front quarter-panel collapsed like an accordion and we skidded to a stop in the middle of the highway.

Phil Collins' "Sussudio" was blaring through the muffled speakers. I turned off the radio. I got out. I took a quick glance at the Badmobile. Its steel shell was unscathed. I went toward the Trans-Am to see if the other driver was okay. But before I got there, the driver was out in the road, gripping her hair with her fists, panicking at the sight of her car in shambles.

I saw then that the other driver was a classmate of mine, a fellow senior named Lilly Hollowell—a girl I had known since elementary school but had no relationship with whatsoever, because she lived in the nicest subdivision in town, served on the Homecoming committee, led cheers on Friday nights, took only Honors classes, and sang in the school musical.

I asked Lilly if she was okay, but all she could say was *shitshit-shit, I'm gonna be in so much fuckin' trouble, ohshit.*

I reached out to calm her, but she kept circling the wreck with choppy steps. She was still clawing at her hair, clutching at her head as if it were about to explode. The blacktop was littered with debris. A side-view mirror had come to rest in the tall grass skirting the highway.

We had been standing between the cars for quite some time before finally she grew aware I was here. She took a quick survey of my attire. Her face took on an expression of absolute confusion, as though she were pondering the absurdity of standing in the middle of the road with a boy wearing an ice cream uniform while her beautiful new car lay scattered over the asphalt in a thousand pristine pieces. She did not seem to recognize me.

Several cars passed. Each slowed almost to a stop before veering around the wreckage, giving a wide margin, trundling through the rutted unpaved dirt on the roadside. The drivers rubbernecked, their brows knitted with curiosity. Some random piece of fiberglass would crunch under tire as they slid by. Soon, though, a truck came along and pulled over to the side. The driver got out and asked if we were okay.

It was about this time that my father came running up to the crash site. He had heard the collision. I gave a quick summary of what happened. Apprised of the gist and satisfied everyone was safe, he then jogged back to the house and called 911.

Within minutes a police officer was on the scene. He arrived in a blur of sirens and spinning blue lights. The officer took our stories. The positioning of the cars left little doubt about what had happened, and our versions were virtually identical anyway. He was a patient and friendly man, that officer, employing a tone of objectivity when asking us to recount the events. He did not judge us. He seemed genuinely sorry that two good kids like us had been involved in an accident. "Could've happened to anybody," he said. He was apologetic, but nevertheless he cited

Lilly with an improper turn signal violation and nailed me with failure to yield the right of way.

Soon he was standing in the road directing traffic around the collision. Lilly and I were left to wait together on the grassy roadside. I wasn't sure what we could possibly say to one another. The silence was excruciatingly awkward. Other than a couple of scratches, the Badmobile looked the same as it had twenty minutes ago, when I had been idling at the stop sign, waiting for a seam in traffic. But the scattered remains of her vehicle were strewn every which way.

"Sorry about your car," I said.

Lilly didn't respond. She just stared silently at the wreckage of her pretty Trans-Am. Eventually she wandered away—to grieve privately, I guess. She didn't speak to me again. Ever.

From time to time I would see Lilly Hollowell in the hallway between classes. Usually she'd pretend she didn't notice me and strike up a quick conversation with one of her girlfriends, one of her fellow cheerleaders, typically, or just ignore me altogether, her eyes fixed straight ahead. But once, she set aside all decorum and stared directly at me, her pupils lit with venom, regarding me with a kind of blatant disgust. I could read the contempt in her expression. She probably thought it was entirely my fault that her insurance classified her new Trans-Am as totaled; that now it was probably somewhere shrouded in kudzu in a junkyard, salvaged for parts.

Soon enough Lilly showed up in the school parking lot driving another car, shiny and new. I couldn't say I was surprised. Now that we'd collided, there would be no more accidents.

But all this waited in the future. On the afternoon I'm speaking of, she's still stranded on a roadside littered with cigarette butts, aluminum cans, a dirty diaper, a stray hubcap. She's waiting impatiently for the tow truck to arrive and drag away the husk of her new Trans-Am. She's in tears, hugging herself, when they hook up the heavy chains and pull it onto the truck. She clenches her jaw and curses under her breath. It's a thing to see, I'm sure—all that powerful machinery loading up all that dross and carrying it where it needs to go.

But I'm not around to witness it. Dad will have to tell me about it later—because I'm late for work.

The policeman's got my story, and I've issued my apologies. I've climbed back in the Badmobile, fired up the engine and cranked the radio again. Maybe I'm off to Florida, where there's an ocean view and girls with sunshine in their eyes, and you can buy a T-shirt and say you've been there.

But more likely I'm headed to the ice cream shop.

Wherever I'm headed, I'm gunning it, singeing the asphalt with my screeching tires, leaving Lilly Hollowell and her car's lovely corpse in a dense, lingering cloud of exhaust.

ROADKILL

*No cats were harmed during the events related in the
following story, or during the telling of it here. In those
days, as a general rule, we were quite fond of cats.*

D ecember: bitter cold, two in the morning. Stuck in the
suburbs with nothing to do on a Friday night, we cruised
the loop around our town a half-dozen times. We passed
the strip with the bright street lights and neon gas stations that
shone like alien saucers in the night; the Taco Bell where that
greasy night manager slipped cigarettes to the teenage girls who
hung out in the parking lot; the Dunkin' Donuts where the
policemen emptied the racks of Boston Kremes and flirted with
the Mexican women working the night shift. Lap after monot-
onous lap, there it was again: that dead cat lying in the middle of
the road. Each time around, Biss and I stared slack-jawed until
it disappeared from the rearview.

Tonight was not the first time we had seen it; this rug of fur had been lying there in various poses of rigor mortis for at least two weeks. But tonight we were supremely bored. Even more so than usual. We had slipped into a realm of boredom so innately *suburban* that we felt compelled to do something that would distinguish this night from the row of nights streaming vacuously from our discarded past into our infinite future. We were sick of dead cats cluttering up the byways of our town. We were tired of waiting for whoever's job it was to pry animals off the road to come by and get this one. So we took matters into our own hands. We are not to be blamed for cruelty to animals. The cat was, in fact, already dead.

AND WE WON'T APOLOGIZE for making our own entertainment. In those days it was necessary. We had no mall. No organization, league, or mission designed to keep us off the streets. There was an underage dance club called Peppers, but Biss had been told not to return after getting busted for puffing cigarettes behind the Dumpster out back, which ruined the place for both of us because we were a package deal. There was a water tower, too, on the outskirts of the county but we were scared to scale it with spray paint cans in our hands—and we'd have had no love to publicly profess once we climbed up there anyway. Fun was scarce. It was the tail end of 1985, so we had to make-do with an arcade, a skating rink, and a golf course on which we could not afford to play—though in the subversive way of teenagers, we had applauded our friend Matt for sexing up a girl on the fourteenth fairway. Or at least that's the story he told us.

We had one movie theatre rerunning the same three movies for weeks. To while away the time we circled the theatre parking lot, fogging the atmosphere with the exhaust from my rumbling Camaro, waving at the same girls waiting in the same line to see

the same movie they'd seen last weekend when we'd made the same circuit around the lot. If we could pony together the gas money, we'd ride out to a reservoir called Dog River, where we'd dip Skoal until our heads started swimming and break bottles against the rocks until they glittered in the moonlight like tiny fallen stars. We'd fill up the back seat with those girls and bring them with us, all jingly bangles and lip gloss and Bubble Yum breath, if they were tired of the same movies.

ABOUT BISS AND ME: we met as ninth-graders in a class called Research Techniques. And about our stomachs: they were cast iron. We owed a debt of gratitude to Research Techniques both for introducing us and for instilling in us the kind of peptic fortitude that, by the time we were seniors, would now allow us to entertain ourselves with dead cats.

The class roster listed him as William Ward Bissell II; after the teacher alphabetized us in straight rows, and he took his assigned seat directly behind mine, he became Billy, aka Bill the Thrill, aka Bill's Game, aka Game, aka Biss. For the first month of our high school careers, the teacher, Coach Clay, kept confusing us and calling us by each other's names. Sometimes we corrected him; most times we did not. Once, he asked Biss, "Gee, Beave, where's Wally?" and waited for the class to erupt into laughter—which they did, on cue, but not because of his clever reference to old sitcoms.

Coach Clay was one of those men who endured seven hours in the classroom for the reward of coaching football afterward—for the sheer adrenaline rush of barking instructions to his players, butting heads with his helmeted linemen, and riding a blocking sled while his *boys*—he always called them his boys— shoved it across the gridiron. He lived for Friday nights under the sodium lights. Almost daily he boldly predicted that one of his linemen in particular—a three-hundred pound Asian behemoth named William Chan—would one day play in the NFL. He promised us that we'd have William Chan Day in our hometown, and William would sport his Pittsburgh Steeler jersey and flash his Super Bowl ring as he rolled down Campbellton Street in a vintage convertible with a Steeler cheerleader on his arm. Coach Clay vowed that one day we'd all swell our own insubstantial chests with pride because we had known William when he was just a boy; that we had borne witness on Friday nights to his sumo-style blocking skills by which he had pancaked otherwise innocent defensive tackles into submission; that he had walked the same hallways as us; that he ate greasy pepperoni pizza from the same cafeteria as we did. (For the record, William did indeed score a scholarship to UGA but blew out his knee during his freshman year. To my knowledge, our hometown has never celebrated William Chan Day.)

Coach Clay wasn't much interested in science except insofar as teaching it could pay his bills and permit him to coach on Friday nights. But he played the role. He dutifully introduced us to the rigors of the Scientific Method. I vaguely recall his chatter about hypotheses, evidence, conclusions, theory, and law. We spent a lot of time measuring, weighing, and recording what he insisted we call "data." He kept us orderly and on task Monday through Thursday with the promise of rewarding our good behavior on Friday. During one particularly insufferable week he kept us at bay by offering a carrot on a stick: If we behaved ourselves until Friday and kept our mouths shut and measured our data, he would reward us with a screening of what he affectionately called the Maggot Movie. *What's the Maggot Movie?* we asked. *It's legendary*, he said.

Coach Clay commenced his explanation of the Maggot Movie this way: he told us his father had a job videotaping surgical procedures for use in medical schools. Like any good father, he relayed the more gruesome videos to his son. When Coach Clay asked his student assistant, the aforementioned lineman William Chan, to attest to the Maggot Movie's mythical status, William affirmed that he first saw the film as a ninth-grader, and indeed he'd never forgotten it. *You won't be able to get it out of your skull*, William guaranteed. Apparently the recollection sent a chill up William's spine, which he could suppress only by clenching his jaw, balling his hands into fists, and flexing his corded neck muscles. He looked positively nauseous.

It took only one screening for us to realize why the Maggot Movie's reputation was indeed merited: It featured a close-up of a gangrene victim's foot. The toes had become so infected that deep sores developed around the nails. Gaping pools of blood stood where dead skin had rotted and peeled away. Via some sad sequence of events that Coach Clay never bothered to explain, maggots had invaded these sores.

I should note that resorting to shock tactics did not guarantee our interest. After all, it was the 1980s, which meant we youngsters weren't shocked by much of anything. The Cold War was raging in Washington and Moscow (or so we were told), and we had become desensitized to the notion that our lives could be ended with the push of a single button. We'd seen images of mushroom clouds, of Gorbachev's birthmark, and endured dozens of safety drills cowering under desks with our heads buried between our knees.

But when Coach Clay fired up the projector, what we viewed utterly captivated us. In the video, hundreds of maggots crawled around in the sores. They were so numerous, they appeared to be swimming over each other in order to reach some destination known only to them. They resembled nothing more so than a million pieces of white rice puttering through a sea of tomato sauce. As the camera zoomed in on the minute details, the girls in the class shrieked and covered their eyes. They said they wanted to hurl. A couple of them started retching, but it was nothing more than a case of the dry heaves. The boys, most of us anyway, dared not blink. Bearing witness seemed like a way to prove our manhood. William Chan was watching us for signs of weakness.

In those days it was somehow comforting to know the world held things we hadn't yet seen; that it could still startle us. As much as we wanted to turn away, we kept our eyes glued to the screen, following those white maggots as they collided with one another, reversed their directions, and resumed their circuitous treks through all that red blood.

By November, though, the Maggot Movie had lost all its power to shock us. We'd seen it so many times that it failed to seize our attention any longer. We could have eaten all manner of slimy foods—even rice and tomato sauce—while viewing the footage without becoming squeamish or sick to our stomachs. Even the girls found it more entertaining than revolting. As I remember, Biss was among the first to develop a cast-iron belly—which probably had more to do with surviving his parents' divorce that same year than glimpsing the Maggot Movie a dozen times.

Anyway, Coach Clay lost control. He raised his voice when he grew exasperated with us, and issued a series of detention slips to the worst offenders. But he didn't seem overly concerned. He had other, more important matters to tend to. Thanks to William Chan and his other *boys*, the football team put together quite a winning streak, and seemed destined to secure a spot in the regional playoffs.

IT REALLY IS A TESTAMENT to the inertia of our town that somebody didn't do something about that cat sooner. After all, cars had been swerving around the carcass for two weeks now, giving it leeway, because who wants a rotted cat embedded in the grooves of your tires? Not to mention the hair, which by this time had endured enough rainfall and frigid temperatures to cure to the approximate texture of a decade-old welcome mat. But of course some of our townspeople didn't keep a close enough eye on the lookout for carrion. They were on it before they knew it. Already this one had been run over repeatedly and knocked from shoulder to shoulder across two lanes of traffic too many times to count.

Though the government section of our local phone book did not contain a number for anyone officially assigned the task of cleaning up this debris, we were pretty sure somebody was not fulfilling the requirements of his job description. In the best interest of our fellow citizens, then, Biss and I set out to amend the problem, free of charge. We offered our services. We were proud to do our part. We did not expect to be thanked. It was the Christian thing to do.

We pulled over to the shoulder of the road and got out. Preferring to avoid direct contact with the cat—we were bored, okay, but sanitary—I popped the Badmobile's trunk and rummaged through its contents in search of the perfect instrument. A tire iron would have worked splendidly, but alas I was unequipped for changing a flat or, apparently, disposing of roadkill. My algebra book would not be more helpful here than in class; neither would a basketball. We briefly considered the potential of an aluminum baseball bat, but we couldn't decide which end might work best, the barrel or the handle, so we commenced scouring the back seat instead.

The cat was flatter than a frying pan, and in a sense had become part of the road itself—so our method of disposal would require an archeological tool. Lacking a shovel or perhaps a spatula, we settled for the final item on hand in the back seat: a cane. It sat in the floorboard, nestled against a matching top hat. Together they comprised a formal ensemble. The top hat possessed no practical advantages, but Biss plopped it atop his head anyway, because it always pays to look dapper when you are scraping dead cats off cold asphalt at two o'clock in the morning.

THE CURIOUS READER NO DOUBT will wonder why a suburban high school boy would tote around a top hat and cane in the back seat of his car. Was he getting a head start on accumulating prom attire? Was he auditioning to play the role of Abe Lincoln in an upcoming dramatic production? Actually, the hat and cane had been languishing in my back seat since the beginning of the school year.

We were seniors, all right, and a time-honored tradition in our town was to bestow top hats and canes onto all members of the rising group. The message? We were classy. We were leaders in the school and in the larger community. We studied hard, respected our elders, and maintained good posture. And whoever started this annual tradition would be pleased to know that Biss and I now were doing our part to beautify our town. The hats had always been a nuisance, awkward and ill-fitting, the snugness leaving faint red burns on our foreheads; and we had previously used the canes only to duel one another in the Kroger parking lot or swing them at mailboxes. But now we were endeavoring to use them for a purpose commensurate with their noble intention. We were performing our civic duty.

Normally it would have been dangerous to remove roadkill from such a heavily-traveled thoroughfare. Perhaps this explains why the cat had lay unfetched for so long. But fortunately, in the burbs, the wee hours of morning provide a break in the traffic, especially when the temperature lingers somewhere below the freezing point. Because our project was a private enterprise not officially sanctioned by the authorities of our town, we were careful to keep our eyes peeled for a cop car rolling down the straightaway toward us.

Once our chore was underway, it did not take long to complete. Biss went first. He approached the cat skeptically. Keeping a safe distance, creeping up on it, he poked it with the cane. I feel obligated to report that we were a little afraid of the cat, but when prodded, it did not stir. We had expected odor to be an obstacle, too, but by this stage of decay all stench was a thing of the past. We debated whether spearing it would be the best tactic. Finally Biss slid the cane under a portion of the cat that, if questioned, we would be hard-pressed to identify. We were pretty sure it was the anterior parcel—but we would not bet folding money on it. You would think that certain characteristics—the ears, say, or the feet—would be easily distinguishable. But the degree of decomposition was such that we congratulated ourselves for simply recognizing that this lump of fur was, in fact, feline.

Biss was able to get the cat airborne, and to our everlasting surprise it remained in one piece. It was balancing precariously on the tip of his cane when he decided that this should be a duo project. I joined him.

READERS WHO HAVE NEVER HEFTED a dead cat with a cane will be surprised to learn of its bulk, relative to expectations. A dead cat is heavy. Its sheer weight is one thing, but balancing it while maintaining the distribution of that weight is quite another. Anyway, what I'm trying to say: Less committed citizens would have found other means of serving the public good.

Nevertheless, it's much easier for one individual to wield a cane with a dead cat teetering on the end of it. Working in tandem, four hands on the cane, we dropped the cat several times as we maneuvered ourselves under it. But we both recognized the fundamental communal nature of this event. It had to be a mutual experience. One cannot take credit for the noble acts of others. Biss' social consciousness was not automatically going to transfer to me. So together we gripped the cane, hoisted the cat off the pavement, and with one mighty heave, we flung that cat into the tall grass skirting the roadside.

Mission accomplished.

Biss and I high-fived. We pumped fists into the air. We danced in the middle of the road like the heroes we were.

Which is not to say we were content to revel in a job well done, just yet. We were, after all, teenagers. The next thirty minutes consisted of two boys taking turns performing various tricks with our dead cat. Biss tried to hold it suspended in the air directly above his head—until it slipped off the cane and landed with a dull thud on his shoulder. At one point, I remember, I even balanced the cat on the cane, tossed it into the air, and attempted to bat it into someone's yard. I was unsuccessful—only a foul tip, as it were—but perhaps it was that failed attempt and our howling laughter that accounted for why that neighbor's porch light flickered on.

So okay, full disclosure, y'all: we panicked. Scampering to the Badmobile, we left the cat to its own devices. It was now out of the roadway at least. We had done our duty.

A word to our fellow citizens: You're welcome.

WE LOOPED THE TOWN a couple more times that night, but somehow everything else seemed anticlimactic. It was now past three o'clock. I drove Biss home. We were exhausted but still stoked with adrenaline. Sitting in the Badmobile, we told ourselves the story, celebrated our starring roles. We were two boys stranded in the suburbs of Atlanta, Gee-Ay, but tonight epic heroism romped through our veins. We were deserving of a king's feast, something grander than the half-empty bag of stale Doritos and the flat NuGrape rolling around in the floorboard, but we made do with what we had on hand. In truth we felt a little sad that the cat was now off the road, and that tomorrow night our suckhole town would have another chance to swallow us.

It was a night for photos, but we were twenty years ahead of camera phones and YouTube, when even the most trivial moments could be captured and preserved—to serve as reminders years hence of a time when a dead cat was just a dead cat, because you believed you were never going to die.

But in my mind's eye there's still a snapshot. A single distilled image of that night. It's of Biss, straddling the center line of that roadway—the same yellow stripe that in a few short months will lead us out of this town and into the wider world. He's wearing a grin of pride, looking like he's really done something. The cat dangles from his cane. He lifts it toward the sky until it fuses with the streetlights overhead.

He doesn't have occasion to wear a top hat, this high school boy bored out of his mind on a Friday night, but nevertheless there it is, perched atop his head like a crown. He's the king of the world, this kid. He sure looks classy.

IN THE AIR TONIGHT:
PROM '86

I n the photo commemorating that spring night in 1986, my
date is wearing a lavender taffeta dress with a ruffled neckline
and a skirt as big around as a hula hoop, and I'm sporting a
gray tux with matching purple bow tie and cummerbund—and
grinning as if I stole something.

Which in fact I had: Jason Tatum's girlfriend. Truth was,
I didn't know Jason very well, despite the fact we had played
on the same basketball team in eighth grade. We'd somehow
managed to share a locker room, sweat, and a season-long los-
ing streak without exchanging two words. Once high school
began, we proceeded to move in entirely different circles until
he started dating Danielle maybe a year ago—at which time
he transformed from innocuous stranger to sworn enemy. He
seemed oblivious to this arrangement, which made it all the

easier to dislike him. I began observing Jason from afar, scrutinizing his leather Nikes with blue laces and his Members Only jacket, loathing the easy familiarity he seemed to have with Danielle's body when he slid his hand into the back pocket of her blue jeans. I pictured them in all manner of sweaty entanglements. But then came the big blowout, a cutthroat fiasco, a veritable he said/she said slugfest two weeks before prom. A winner was never declared, but one thing was clear to all of us spectators: they were not going to prom together.

Until now my plan had been to avoid prom, this crowning event of adolescence, to dismiss it as yet another in a long list of high school rituals I categorized as *gay*. Prom was a sham, a racket, a subterfuge. By this time I was seventeen, and had been saved and baptized, copped a feel, and heard Run DMC's debut album—so I believed I had attained a plateau of enlightenment that allowed me to transcend the petty concerns associated with anything so insipid and synthetic as prom. I was worldly. I was wise. I'd had enough defining experiences to recognize a ruse when I saw one.

To symbolize my sage status, I cultivated a jaded persona featuring a permanent smirk. You couldn't surprise me. Which is why I worked hard to conceal my excitement when the details of Jason's split from Danielle went public. Upon hearing the news I swooped in, the sympathetic friend, a shoulder to cry on. "It's okay," I told Danielle. "You're too good for him anyway."

She agreed.

"He's not worth the trouble," I offered. "Don't give him another thought."

She nodded.

"You've already wasted too much time," I said, "on something going nowhere."

This incisive comment seemed to cut deeply. Danielle proceeded to cry, at first in shy tears that leaked from her eyes, but soon in great, swelling sobs that smeared her eyeliner and further persuaded me of my own nobility.

I should note this conversation was taking place as we were scraping down tubs of ice cream at the Baskin-Robbins. It was rainy outside that day, as I remember, and unseasonably cold for springtime. Nobody wanted ice cream. I had ample time to work this situation to my advantage.

I hugged Danielle. I felt her considerable breasts mash against me. "I'm here for you," I said. I rubbed her back and buried my face in her hair, inhaling that elixir of cucumber and aloe that was uniquely Danielle.

Somewhere amidst all the tears she told me I was a good friend. "I'm lucky to have you in my life," she said. "You're special." Then came that inexplicable moment—and maybe it was just gratitude that compelled her to do it, or vengeful spite toward her ex—when she slung her arms around my neck and fixed me with those eyes, tawny pools of unfathomable depth, and said this: "I want you to take me to prom." That was part of Danielle Boyd's voodoo, the way she looked you in the eye and outright lied, but you believed her anyway because you figured lips like hers could utter only the truth.

I felt my face flush. My breath came quick.

I believe my exact response was, "Is it too late for me to rent a tux?"

THE SALESMAN TOLD ME THAT, this late in the game, tuxes were indeed in short supply. "The pick of the litter," he said, "is gone. All the black ones anyway. Boys like black, you understand. Prom is in two weeks. But I'll come up with something." He seemed put out by my timing. Annoyed that my suddenly blossoming romantic life didn't correspond to his schedule. For two straight months or longer he'd been outfitting 500 boys in prom attire at the only place in town that rented formal wear. He was past pretending that he cared.

But gradually he loosened up. As he measured my waist, chest, and neck, the salesman queried me about my date. "Tell me about this girl," he said. "She got a name?"

I told him.

"Danielle a looker?"

"Sure."

"Uh-huh, you two going to eat somewhere fancy?"

"We haven't picked a place yet."

"Females love French restaurants," the salesman said. " 'A Night In Paris,' and all that jazz." He paused to make eye contact. "You getting this?"

"French," I said. "Got it."

With three or four straight pins wedged in the corner of his mouth like silver toothpicks, he reminded me of the subtleties of good etiquette. He told me to compliment Danielle's dress, open her car door, make sure she was seated first at the restaurant before I plopped myself down. "And when you're heading out," he said, "and you're leaving the tip on the table—don't forget this—it's very important—when you tip the waiter, put a penny on top of the bills."

"A penny?"

"One penny, that's all. Set it right on top of the greenbacks. Sends a message to the waiter that he gave good service."

"But it's a *penny*. You sure it's not supposed to be a silver dollar or something?"

"Danielle'll be impressed. She'll think you've got class."

When the salesman brought me a sample tux, I carried it into a changing room the size of a coffin. The tux was gray, with tails. I left my jeans in a pile on the floor and wiggled into the shirt, pants, and jacket. Moments later I emerged, spotlighted by the florescent lights overhead, the collar swimming around my Adam's apple like a necklace. My crotch sagged. My knobby kneecaps conveyed the distinct impression I was hoarding golf balls in my pants. The salesman started tugging at the material, jabbing at my pelvis as though trying to pin the pockets on my hipbones. He tugged at my trousers, prodded my chest, and squared my shoulders, shaping me like a particularly stubborn mound of clay. He seemed especially dismayed by my six-two, buck-fifty frame.

"You're a tall drink of water," he explained. "You could stand to eat a chicken leg or two. But we'll get you set up—somehow."

He led me toward a large mirror near the shoe department. There, he stood behind my shoulder and together we inspected my reflection. He turned me around. He knelt beside me to adjust a pant leg, stood back to study me again. Finally, with a wink and a smile, he pronounced me fit for prom. "Danielle won't be able to keep her hands off you," he promised.

I returned to the changing room. But before I stripped off this formal garb, I paused a moment to inspect myself once more in the slender mirror hanging on the back of the door. I examined the stranger staring back at me, scrutinized his countenance. He needed a haircut, that boy, but otherwise he maybe could pass for respectable. He indeed seemed ready.

Minutes later, I'd placed my order and paid the deposit and was headed out the door. But I sensed something was missing— something that might make my sartorial ensemble complete. I turned back toward the salesman. "Sir?" I said. "You got any gloves?"

His tape measure dangling around his neck, he stared at me with a furrowed brow. "C'mon, kid. Who you trying to be— Prince Charming?"

AS AN UNDERCLASSMAN, I had carefully observed the older boys performing a ritual age-old and time-honored. On the Monday after prom, in the student parking lot, they adorned

their rearview mirrors with garters. A trip down just one row
of cars would tally a dozen or more garters of every possible
hue. I don't remember anyone officially explaining the symbol-
ism, but nevertheless it was clear. Hanging a garter from your
rearview sent a message tacit and universal: on prom night *I got
laid*. It implied a story of sliding the lingerie off the girl's leg,
perhaps with your teeth, before getting down to business—and
afterward twirling it around your finger before hanging it with
pomp and circumstance on your mirror. It was ceremony. It was
Americana. It was all we could ever ask of life in the suburbs.
The best we could dream of before graduating and finally getting shut of this place.

I supposed some boys were also telling other, less crude stories with their garters, but nobody much cared to hear those
pedestrian tales.

Now that I was headed to prom with Danielle, I believed my
own story was about to gain some serious momentum. It wasn't
clear whether her mom had already bought her dress when
everybody assumed she was going with Jason, but Danielle
told me it was lavender, which I took to be fortuitous because
purple was my favorite color, and now I had my tux. Over the
next week or so I gradually grew unabashed in my conviction
that prom would be a turning point in my life, and in Danielle's
too—the night when we began our move toward the exits. For
a boy like me—a boy growing up in suburban Atlanta; a boy
whose postman dad delivered mail in *rain, sleet, snow, and dark
of night*; a boy whose mom had officially diagnosed herself as
Nervous; a sensitive and timid boy, one who could recite Bible
verses and Prince lyrics with the same reverence; a punk who
tough-talked loud enough to drown out the beating of his own
heart—for a boy like me, Danielle Boyd represented a by-god
portal to a new life. She wasn't the next rung on the popularity
ladder. She was an around-the-way girl, working class, with a

mother who slogged through two jobs and a father gone, gone. Our conversations weren't like the rare and tedious exchanges I had with some girls, when their stooping to actually speak to me felt like an actress breaking the invisible fourth wall of the theatre and directly acknowledging her audience. She didn't live like those girls either, in a two-story colonial sitting on a hill with rolling lawnscape straight out of a John Hughes movie.

She lived like me—in a boxy brick ranch where honeysuckles intertwined with the kudzu snaking over the chain link fences in our back yards. In my more romantic moments, I imagined the tendrils of the weed creeping between our houses until finally they merged into a single tangled vine.

A LIMO WAS OUT of the question, and the Badmobile was sidelined with moderate to serious transmission troubles, so Danielle's chariot would have to be mom's '79 Chevy Nova: Four-door, vinyl top, AM radio, no cassette deck, bench seats with plaid upholstery, brown. She was hesitant to loan it to me, but my incessant begging—Mom, it's *prom*—finally made enough inroads to guilt her into forking over the keys. "It's against my better judgment," she said when she finally relented. "You're not used to driving it. You could have an accident—and then where would we be?"

With Dad riding shotgun, I took a practice run to the restaurant and the hotel because I feared getting lost on the big night. A wrong turn could ruin everything. To a kid from a suburban town consisting of only two main thoroughfares, Atlanta seemed like a giant maze of one-ways and dead-ends and a thousand streets named Peachtree; but Dad was a postman who knew the city grid the way he knew the blueprints of his own house. As I drove he pointed out landmarks to assure me of my whereabouts.

Once we reached the restaurant and the hotel, I retraced my path and returned to the suburbs. I wanted to guarantee there'd be no chance of running out of gas, so a mile from our subdivision I stopped at the Golden Gallon. While I filled the tank Dad scribbled the directions on a piece of paper and drew a map to accompany them. "A cheat-sheet," he called it. "In case you need it." When we returned to our driveway, he filled my hand with a small stack of twenties. And then, because the moment seemed to call for it, he shook my other hand.

I told him I'd pay him back, but of course I never did. He never asked for it.

AND SO: ON MAY 3, 1986, at six o'clock sharp, I showed up at Danielle Boyd's door dripping sweat and swimming in Polo cologne. Clutching a corsage of purple and white flowers that had sat in our refrigerator between Tupperware bowls until just a few minutes ago, I rang the doorbell. Danielle pushed opened the screen and stepped into the bright sunlight of her front porch, and immediately I saw that all her insistence that I wait until tonight to see her dress was worth it. In a word: luminous. Baby's breath accented her hair. Her lavender taffeta dress seemed crafted especially to fit her body, and even that blooming skirt seemed downright perfect. "Hey, Mark," she said, and I felt stunned by the sound of my own name coming from her mouth.

I slipped the corsage over her wrist, and she invited me inside.

Her stepfather was reclining in a Lay-Z-Boy in the living room. He nodded in my general direction, but did not get up to greet me—he seemed more interested in how the wrestling match on the TV was going to play out than participating in a slice of American adolescence. "That's Craig," Danielle said as she led me past him. In the kitchen, her mother was loading the dishwasher. As she dried her hands on a towel, Ms. Boyd made small talk while Danielle swished in her crinoline and I attempted to act charming. Every movement of Danielle's seemed unbearably precious—leaning against the counter, sweeping a strand of hair from her eyes, tucking it behind her ear. So precious, so unbearably so, that I was already counting her every gesture among the most pure, distilled, and graceful acts I'd ever witnessed.

But soon enough Ms. Boyd shooed us outdoors, where she played shutterbug with a disposable camera while we posed under a sickly magnolia in the front yard. I remember the bald spot of hard red clay circling the tree, and sweat pooling under my rib cage as we endured the snapshots, all that Polo distilling in a slow burn in the heat of springtime.

When the time came to depart, I remembered to open Danielle's door first. I scooped the poofiness of her dress with both hands and shoved it inside long enough to shut the door before it all spilled out again.

On the road I drove methodically, carefully observing the speed limit and coming to a complete halt at every stop sign. I withheld any mention of my practice run, electing instead to offer the distinct impression I was *cosmopolitan* and negotiated these streets all the time. It was Saturday and traffic was light, so within thirty minutes we arrived at the restaurant. A French place, per the tux salesman's advice—despite the fact my exposure to French cuisine heretofore had consisted of eating parfaits and ridiculing the consumption of snails. I'd made reservations, which turned out to be unnecessary because the place was practically empty. A little early for the dinner crowd, I assumed. As the hostess seated us, she told Danielle, *Vouz portez une belle robe*, and the sparse gathering ogled our attire. A waitress clad in all black but for an ivory bow tie welcomed us. We listened carefully to her recommendations and perused the menu. After careful deliberation, I ordered trout amandine; Danielle wanted some kind of steak in a creamy brown sauce.

Our dinner conversation consisted mostly of small talk. School, our boss at Baskin-Robbins, what we expected our classmates to wear tonight. How lame the prom theme was. *In the air tonight? Whatever.*

Toward the end of the meal I recalled the tux salesman telling me that sitting a single penny atop your tip is a gesture complimenting the waiter for excellent service. The service was actually unremarkable—with such a small number of diners the waitress killed most of her time chatting with the hostess—but I didn't want to waste the opportunity to demonstrate to Danielle how worldly and sophisticated I was, to showcase my understanding of the delicate nuances of etiquette and fine dining. After I laid the folding part of the tip on the table, I waited until she was absolutely-for-sure watching, and set a single penny atop the dollar bills.

Then I stood, and offered my elbow. Danielle didn't comment upon my suave and urbane *savoir-faire*, but surely she noted it and was duly impressed. She slid her arm around mine, and together we left the restaurant.

MY PROM LOOKED LIKE YOURS. Balloons and streamers. Punch bowls and plastic champagne flutes. Glitter and glam. They held it in the Grand Ballroom West of the Atlanta Hilton and Towers, a destination that looked very impressive indeed when etched in ornate calligraphy on the invitations. Upon our arrival, teachers greeted us enthusiastically. They told Danielle she was *stunning, gorgeous,* a *knock out.* My math teacher, a demure Southern woman who typically milked a passive aggressive grudge toward me because I was failing her class and seemed generally disinterested in passing it, patted my shoulder and told me I looked dapper.

Inside, the action was in mid-swing, the dance floor crowded. Most of the boys already had shed their coats and ties. Some of them had unbuttoned their shirts to their bellies. Their chests shone with sweat; their hair was pasted to their foreheads. One senior, a pock-faced kid named Scott Baylor, aimlessly meandered his way through the crowd, stopping periodically to ball his fists, summon a growl from the depths of his bowels, and yell, *Hell yeaahh!* By this time my squeaky leather shoes had worn blisters the size of quarters on the knuckles of my big toes, but Danielle and I immediately took to the parquet floor to join the action anyway. I remember trying to close the physical distance between us, using the heat of all these bodies and the pulse of the music to elevate the evening's emotional pitch.

Which didn't really happen until later. Of the rest of prom itself, I remember virtually nothing, as though the blinding flash of the photographer's camera upon our entrance destroyed everything to follow. Except this: at some point during the night Danielle and I separated. She was gone maybe half an hour. I was lingering by the punch bowl, downing yet another Coke, when my buddy Biss sidled up and started tugging on my elbow. "Get a load of *that*," he said. "Are you checking this out?" He pointed toward the dance floor, his finger aiming at some unidentifiable target among all the swaying bodies. I squinted to locate whatever sight was putting the disgust in Biss' voice until, finally, there she was.

Danielle.

And her ex.

They were dancing together. Or to be more accurate: Their bodies were swaying in time to the beat, but they were having a conversation. On first glance I would have deduced they were discussing nothing shy of matrimony. Danielle's eyes were fixed on Jason's with an attentiveness that surpassed any she'd offered me tonight—or ever.

My gut began to curdle.

"Are you down with that *bull*shit?" Biss wanted to know.

I tried very hard to act like I wasn't troubled by the developments. "I don't care," I said. "Really."

"You don't *care?*"

"We're just friends," I explained.

Biss shrugged. "Whatever, man," he said. "Come get me if you need some back-up. I never liked that dude anyway." Then he was off again to the dance floor.

I stayed by the refreshments long enough for the nausea in my stomach to bubble into a cauldron of self-pity, which soon manifested a truth unpretty but undeniable: Danielle had been orchestrating this plan the whole time. It now seemed obvious. How could I have missed it? The absurd gap between the frenetic beat of the music and the sad, lethargic dirge of my inner soundtrack served only to make me ask myself why I was still here. Out there on the parquet, Danielle and Jason's eyes were still locked in an intimacy I could only imagine.

In a feeble attempt at revenge, I danced with a couple other girls—stag-girls, girls who came with boys who were clearly "just friends" and both sides knew it—to see what effect I could create. Danielle seemed unconcerned. If she ever even noticed, she showed no signs. Occasionally she would drop in to ask how I was doing, with no acknowledgement of Jason, before flitting away to join him again on the dance floor. Which is the way it went for the rest of the night.

I'm sure we crowned the king and queen, though I have no recollection of who won the honor. I vaguely recall the deejay announcing the last dance, and everybody squeezing together on the parquet as Phil Collins sang our theme song, *I can feel it coming in the air tonight, O Lord, and I've been waiting for this moment for all my life, O Lord…O Lord.* As if fulfilling an obligation, Danielle joined me for that final soiree. She rested her hands on my shoulders. Despite the plume of her dress, I was able to reach across the taffeta and place my hands on her hips. The whole thing was perfunctory on both our parts. We knew the script. Neither of us liked the song—when it came on the radio during our shift at Baskin-Robbins we usually changed the station—and by the time those drums tumbled down and Phil started screeching *O Lord, O Loo-ord*, one or the both of us—I don't remember which—had headed toward the exit.

AFTERWARD WE WOUND UP at a party in a cheap hotel nearby. As we approached the door at the end of an otherwise vacant corridor, Def Leppard shook through the walls at teeth-rattling decibel levels. Inside, the place smelled like a deep-brewed den of iniquity. Danielle led me on a brief tour of the premises, where we navigated the clumps of groping couples and bypassed the open keg in the middle of the room. The same guy who was yelling *Hell yeaahh* to no one in particular at the prom was now naked but for his tuxedo pants and bow tie, and screaming *Seniors ruuuule!* to an audience consisting of only me. Inexplicably, one of the most beautiful and popular girls in the school, Leigh Conrad, intercepted our circuit of the room and pulled me aside. She was holding a red plastic cup containing some kind of illicit mixture. "You're a ——— ," she garbled above the din of the music. I asked for clarification. "I said you're a *great dancer*," she yelled. "I saw you out there on the floor. I was hoping you'd ask me to dance with you!"

Maybe tomorrow I would regret the choice I was about to make. Maybe I would wish I stayed and pursued this unlikely conversation, or just asked Leigh Conrad to dance with me right then and there among all our drunken classmates in that forlorn hotel room with alcohol-soaked carpet.

But right then, tomorrow seemed very far away. I still wasn't rightly convinced it would ever arrive. Plenty of time remained for me to re-direct where this night was headed.

Whatever Danielle was looking for wasn't found inside the room, so I followed her out of the hotel and we ended up back in Mom's Chevy Nova with a full tank of gas and time on our hands.

IT FELT LIKE WE COULD drive forever, like maybe we could simply skip out on these tedious couple of months separating us from the rest of our lives and just start right now—take I-75 south to Florida where we'd buy matching airbrush T-shirts or to California where we'd snap photos of the Hollywood sign. But instead, as though we were at the mercy of a compass that could only point us toward home, we landed back in our suburban town. Specifically: the Kroger parking lot, where the lights flickered on and off, the air smelled exactly like springtime in Georgia, and I waited for Important Things to say.

"So what do you want to do?" I asked.

"It's up to you," Danielle kept saying. "It's your prom." With those words it suddenly occurred to me that she was a junior—a fact I'd seemingly lost sight of in my plans to exit suburbia together. Her senior prom was next year. Perhaps the rest of her life would consist of a thousand proms. I could have this one. "It's your prom," she said again, her voice full of pity.

I hadn't put much thought into planning where this night would go from here. With the neon lights of suburbia reflecting in the windshield, I pondered the options. I would have climbed with her into the back seat of Mom's Chevy Nova and crawled through miles of taffeta to consummate the beginning of our eternal union. I would have listened to the whole sad story of her father and his adieu and held her when she finished with the telling. I would have cranked the engine and driven toward the outskirts of town, the rural zip, and raced the telephone lines strung alongside the blacktop until all the electricity gathered inside their wires triggered something kinetic inside her heart that would make her forget Jason and seize this moment for all its possibility. I would have done whatever Danielle wanted to do.

Which is why when she yawned and said she was kinda tired, I cranked the car and carried her home.

WHEN WE PULLED INTO her driveway, I killed the ignition and got out. Her mother had left the porch light on. I circled around the hood. The night was humid, the air thick and heavy. Insects sang from somewhere in the darkness. It was late. It *felt* late, finally. As though I were only now comprehending that this night would eventually end.

By the time I got around to the passenger side and opened Danielle's door, a present was awaiting me.

She had slid her garter off her leg and was now offering it to me.

I took it and inspected it. It was frilly and white with a lavender thread running through it. "Thanks for a great prom," she told me. I searched her inflection for irony or outright sarcasm. But what I heard instead was a slight lilt, a sweetness, maybe because tonight really had been a great prom for her. After all, I'd played my bit role in her story perfectly. I'd chauffeured her to the stage where she met her leading man; and one day in the future she and Jason would fondly recall this night and that guy—what was his name again?—and his mom's lame vehicle.

From then on, I behaved in the gentlemanly way. I did my best to conceal my disappointment. I walked Danielle to her door. There, among the thousand moths swarming around the porch bulb, I accepted her obligatory hug. She offered a peck on the cheek. She again said thanks for the evening. I told her I'd see her around. She said goodnight and went inside.

I sat in the car until the porch light died and the house dissolved into shadow before I backed out of the driveway. As I headed out of her subdivision I searched the radio for a song about love gone wrong, something growled by a broken-hearted loner that I could easily identify with. But Mom's Nova only had AM reception, and all I found were newscasts and late-night talk shows.

Driving home, I spent considerable time plotting the demise of that garter. Only something vengeful would do. Destroying it by some ceremonial act maybe would allow me to wrestle the climax of the story away from Danielle and Jason and insert myself as the main character. I saw myself striking up a Bic lighter and burning the garter to ashes. Chucking it out the window as I roared down Post Road at 80 miles per hour. Pissing on it and leaving it to dry on Danielle's front porch. I figured the sight of it going up in flames, disappearing into the night as roadside trash, or soaking in bodily fluids would earn me a kind of recompense.

But in the end, I decided to pass on all that. Revenge wouldn't get me very far. I knew that next week at school, Jason's hand would be in Danielle's back pocket as though he'd never removed it and together they'd be too absorbed in the resumption of their grand romance to care what I did with my souvenirs.

So before I climbed out of Mom's Chevy Nova and headed inside the house, I thought of all the boys who, come Monday morning, would be telling the world they got laid, and the others, like me, who now had other memories worth commemorating. And I did what you're supposed to do when you've been to prom with a pretty girl and you've got a story to tell.

I hung the garter from the rearview mirror.

PRINCE AND APOLLONIA

Tonight Yvette's curfew had come and gone, but still we lunged at each other with the kind of desperation only two teenage virgins could muster. What we lacked in experience we were compensating for with sheer force. Typically we wrestled in my dad's ragged Ford Fairlane in her driveway, throwing ourselves against each other ever more earnestly and intensely as midnight drew near, until finally, at the stroke of the hour, her mom would flip the porch lights and reluctantly we'd pry our lips apart. But tonight, curiously, the lights remained off. The house just sat shrouded in darkness. It was now almost 12:30.

Suspecting Yvette's mom had dozed through curfew, we resumed our groping on borrowed time, knowing any moment

201

now that bulb would ignite and Yvette would have to scurry inside before the moths began congregating. We clutched; we grabbed. We exhaled dramatically, recited all the bad dialogue. As of late our fumbling had taken on new urgency; we had become convinced we were blazing new frontiers of lust, that our blood was running wild in unprecedented ways. But now: the feeling of being watched. Something wasn't right. "Maybe mom's peeking through the blinds," Yvette whispered. We again surveyed the house. No light anywhere. Suspicious, we shushed each other; sat still as thieves, eavesdropping on the darkness. The night was singing its shrill cadence. Somewhere a dog barked. The wind coursed through a stand of pines in the yard.

Soon enough, our tongues dry, stomachs empty, and buzz thoroughly killed, we climbed out of the car. We circled around the back of the house. We followed the flagstones, two skulking shadows passing through the night, toward the back patio, where Yvette's mom and her live-in fiancée often wasted entire Sunday afternoons sitting in chaise lounges and serenading each other with limp and sappy tunes from the Lite-FM station. But as we passed under her mom's bedroom window, we suddenly understood why our arrival had gone unnoticed. We now knew why the lights remained off.

Yvette's mom and her fiancée were upstairs having very serious *relations*.

They had left their window open, as though their ecstasy was too uncontainable, the urge too primal, for them to exercise even a modicum of modesty. As far as we could tell, they were not indulging in behavior resembling the language Yvette and I had used to describe what our relationship had been heading toward. They were not *making love*. This was not *special*. Until now I suppose I had imagined sex to be the way it was in the movies, where a soft instrumental underscores the lovers' furtive whispers; where everything is bathed in golden light and there's a gradual fade to black. It was the mid-80s, after all, and Yvette and I had glimpsed Prince and Apollonia having movie sex in *Purple Rain* a dozen times. In the deep recesses of Yvette's basement, we had curled up on a beat-to-hell sofa and watched a VHS copy of the movie and taken mental notes as His Royal Badness swept his beloved onto the back of his purple motorcycle and stole away to the Minnesota prairie, where vacant barns featuring plush beds of silky hay waited for these young lovers to consummate their carnal desires among slats of sunlight and floating motes of fairy dust. Yvette and I, too, imagined ourselves doing the deed in an abandoned barn somewhere while doves cried softly in the rafters and my dad's pewter-colored Fairlane sat glinting in the dazzling sunlight outside.

But Yvette's mom and the fiancée were tearing at each other with cruel ferocity. A savage, animalistic aggression. From their room up above came a series of eerie moans, long and ghostlike, that suddenly collapsed into a staccato march of gasps building toward an inevitable explosion.

"*That's* my girl!" Yvette exclaimed. She giggled in silent convulsions. It was not the kind of laughter that acknowledged embarrassment and thereby undercut it—it was the kind that seemed to admire her mom's good fortune.

"Are they always like this?" I whispered.

"Pretty much."

"Doesn't it freak you out?"

"Not anymore."

"How can you stand it?"

"No big deal. I mean, my mom has *needs*."

Until this moment it had been rather easy to ignore the fiancée, this fellow who taught music at a local community college and resembled nothing so much as a piece of new furniture—one that required only polite acknowledgment before receding into the background. He rarely spoke, his interaction limited to a few cordial pleasantries, an occasional comment upon the weather. He seemed oblivious to sports, to red meat, to loud music—to any endeavor that triggers testosterone and makes a man spit, curse, fight, or howl at the moon. The fiancée and I had observed a tacit agreement to give one another a wide berth. I took comfort in the knowledge I didn't have to impress him in the same way I would Yvette's actual father, who two years ago abandoned the family and was last heard from somewhere in Texas; and perhaps I could be a little cruel, a bit cocky in my indifference, knowing that he wouldn't dare judge me as he strived to acclimate himself to this pair with whom he'd thrown his lot. After all, he wanted Yvette to like him. Which, despite his innocuous behavior, wasn't a given, because the fiancée commanded no attention: He was simply a bearded and bespectacled gentleman perpetually clad in khakis, a collared oxford, and leather loafers.

It was hard to imagine a man in such attire fulfilling a woman's *needs*. But it's true: Yvette's mom was experiencing something close to rapture. She evinced an exaltation that, thus far in my Bible Belt upbringing, had been reserved only for Jesus. I pictured this fiancée, this guy I'd heard spinning Earl Klugh records in the den, and I couldn't reconcile how such a figure could possibly instigate this kind of euphoria.

We lingered under the window. Yvette's mom was hitting every note on the scale in a tone that, by this time, sounded vaguely soprano. In between, the fiancée also was grunting in an octave that, again, I could not associate with him. In my mind's eye I actually attempted to picture him, sans khakis and collars, rutting with such palpable intensity. But it was inconceivable. It did not occur to me then—but would later that night when I was alone in my own room processing the import of this experience—that I was overhearing another man gratify a woman before I had accomplished the feat myself. Even according to the suspect value system through which I then saw the world, this seemed fundamentally *wrong*.

And then came a finish so jarring that its arrival was unmistakable; and then another, and maybe one more—I couldn't be sure, unfamiliar as I was with expressions of female satisfaction—until finally the volume up there subsided into a few scattered whimpers. A long, stretching yawn. A murmured exchange.

Yvette and I climbed the back deck. Inside the kitchen two empty wine glasses and a half-eaten bar of dark chocolate sat on the table. A corkscrew lay on the counter.

Yvette nonchalantly grabbed a two-liter of Coke from the fridge and a bag of Doritos from the cupboard. She motioned for me to follow her into the living room, where we collapsed onto the vinyl loveseat. Nudging close to me, she squirmed snugly against my chest and swung her legs—tanned a golden bronze from so many afternoons at the neighborhood pool—across my lap. She began nibbling at my neck. Her breath smelled like Bubble Yum and the buttered popcorn we ate at the movies an hour ago. Usually this arrangement led to some heavy petting, maybe some second-base action.

But right now I was a little scared of the extremes of desire— the raw expression of it. The truth was, our petting now seemed tame, childish by comparison with all we'd witnessed tonight. Here I'd been thinking that smashing our tongues together was heavy stuff; that slipping my hand inside Yvette's bra was somehow revolutionary. A few minutes ago I'd been feeling as virile and potent as David on first sight of Bathsheba, but now I felt, well, neutered.

I grabbed the remote, punched up MTV. We had seen all of the videos at least a hundred times. But right now there was comfort in familiarity—security in territory I recognized. Duran Duran was still hungry like the wolf. Corey Hart wore his sunglasses at night. Huey Lewis said the heart of rock and roll was still beating. Martha Quinn smiled her goofy smile and I felt like I'd returned home.

Soon enough there were footsteps on the stairs. Yvette's mom appeared, a little tipsy, saying *Hi kids,* wearing only a satiny gown, its sheen vaguely transparent. One of her breasts was threatening to spill out. She loitered on the final stair, swaying, veritably purring, her face flushed with afterglow and her hair dangling into her eyes. "Want me to microwave you guys a frozen pizza?" she asked.

Sure, whatever, okay.

While the microwave hummed in the background, Yvette's mom tapped the countertop with her fingernails, which—and this was something I'd never noticed before—were painted a deep and abiding red.

A few minutes later the fiancée joined her. He had fastened his wire-rimmed specs behind his ears and meticulously restored the part in his hair. His unwrinkled oxford was tucked perfectly into his khakis, a brown belt completing his sartorial ensemble.

"Mmm, I smell pepperoni," he said. "Any left for me?"

UP TO THIS POINT my cherry had been no great encumbrance. Most of my buddies had been itching to get rid of theirs since the onset of puberty, and many had done so with little difficulty—including one who'd taken somebody's cousin from out of town into his back seat and finished the whole ordeal in under ten minutes despite the inconvenience of the girl's tampon. There was some debate over whether he had in fact consummated the deal, but he insisted he had "crossed the plane of the goal line," which meant his virginity was gone, now and forever more.

I, on the other hand, remained relatively content with what said friends called The Big V. Undoubtedly, religion contributed.

In my parents' world, there was a name for what Yvette and I had been inexorably moving toward: fornication. There was a doctrine too—*Flee fornication. For every sin that a man doeth is without the body; but he that committeth fornication sinneth against his own body*—and a punishment for violating it: *Know ye not that the unrighteous shall not inherit the kingdom of God? Be not deceived: neither fornicators, nor idolaters, nor adulterers, nor effeminate, nor abusers of themselves with mankind.*

As Washed-in-the-Blood Christians, my parents worshipped God with a passion that ran up flush against the carnal, but they displayed no public affection. No hugs, kisses, or fleeting touches. They rarely even sat on the same couch. To them, sex required a ring, a preacher, and a marriage license—and even this holy trinity was subject to the laws of propriety.

For her part, Yvette was saddled with none of the same baggage. Sex did not carry any eternal ramifications that she knew of. Her moral compass seemed uninfluenced by any particular doctrine—only the sweeping conviction that we should be kind to one another in a purely humanist way. Once, I asked her whether she even believed in God. "Of course," she answered, as if I'd asked her whether she believed in puppies. She seemed generally unconcerned with how biblical injunctions might influence her behavior, and particularly disinterested in allowing them to dictate what she did with her body.

For a couple of months now, my car, the Badmobile, had been in and out of the shop with symptoms no trained mechanic could seem to remedy. So I'd been resigned to borrowing my father's ride. And though Dad's Ford Fairlane had been the site of some of our most heated encounters, Yvette and I vowed to stop short of forfeiting the Big V within its confines. Granted, there were those bench seats, front and back, which seemed an open invitation to all manner of vehicular amour. And yes, our corner of suburbia featured a number of dark crevices—vacant, unlit parking lots full of potholes and abandoned grocery carts—that would have been suitable spots. But neither of us wanted our story to be that we had consummated our relationship in the backseat of a car. And besides, Dad kept a pocket-sized New Testament in the glove compartment—out of sight, sure, but like the Holy Ghost, always present.

And so it was that I had adopted the habit of kissing Yvette goodnight, squealing out of her driveway and, once outside the interlocking streets of her subdivision grid, wringing the wheel for speed.

IT'S HARD TO SAY exactly whose idea it was, whether it was Yvette's or mine, but sometime during that summer we began thinking of ourselves as Prince and Apollonia. The whole world, you'll recall, spent the mid-'80s bathing in Purple Rain. The movie ruled the box office, the album the charts. In truth, we were two sad teenagers stranded in the Atlanta suburbs, a thousand miles away from Prince's hometown of Minneapolis. But when His Royal Badness told us a locale called Uptown existed in some as yet unidentified mystical realm, we decided we'd rather pretend we were there. Chances are, Uptown had all the amenities our vacuous setting lacked. There was likely even a mall.

And it's probably fair to say that, had one Prince Rogers Nelson never ascended to the pinnacle of pop culture and commenced his purple reign, Yvette and I never would have exchanged names, much less bodily fluids. Prince acquainted us—in PE class. That spring, I'd been wearing a yellow T-shirt with *Prince* airbrushed across the front and *Rude Boy* across the back. Our class was on the asphalt tennis courts in the shadow of the football stadium, and Ms. Monroe was instructing us in the finer points of the backhand grip, when a girl with reddish-blond hair introduced herself first as a Prince fan and later as Yvette. She said she owned every Prince album—and a couple from his notorious secret vault. She said she knew how to decipher that cryptic backward message at the end of "Darling Nikki." She said her bedroom walls were purple.

Soon we were professing our eternal love for one another.

At first, the effects of this arrangement were minimal, mostly sweet and insubstantial. In the hallways between classes we started exchanging notes mimicking Prince's shorthand in the album's liner notes: *How r u? Can't wait 2 c u 2-night.* Yvette wore lacy scarves, a pound of mascara, and a single red earring just like Apollonia's. I hung purple curtains in my bedroom and plastered posters on my walls. I even gave Yvette my class ring, replete with an amethyst stone. Sometimes she'd drop in while I was scooping ice cream at my afterschool gig at Baskin-Robbins, where between customers I'd serenade her with off-key renditions of "Little Red Corvette" and "Delirious." Which is a hard act to pull off when you're wearing a pink, orange, and brown striped shirt with butterfly collars and using an ice cream scooper for a microphone.

But as time passed, instead of having actual conversations, we began substituting passages of dialogue from the movie. We'd meet up in the parking lot after school:

Yvette: Hey.

Me: We have to go to your place.

Yvette: What for?

Me: 'Cause I wanna show you something.

Yvette: We can't.

Me: Why, is somebody there?

Yvette: Why do you always think there's somebody else?

Me: Let's go.

Yvette: Yeah, but we're not going to my place.

And then instead of climbing aboard my purple motorcycle, we'd take Dad's Fairlane to the local park, where we'd feed bread crumbs to the ducks and pretend the murky pond was Lake Minnetonka. Inevitably I'd tell Yvette that, if our relationship were to go any further, she'd have to "pass the initiation," just like Apollonia had passed Prince's, by stripping to her skivvies and "purifying yourself in the waters of Lake Minnetonka." If she took the bait, she'd jump in, just as I halfheartedly hollered, "Wait— ". Then when she emerged from the water, retching and gasping for breath, I'd of course say, "That ain't Lake Minnetonka." Yvette, however, did not follow this part of the script. She had a smaller rack than Apollonia, but a bigger brain.

And there were other complications to our plan, too. Some inconsistencies needed reconciling. For starters, Prince was black; I was white. He stood five-seven in heels; I was six-two in Converse Chucks. He played wicked guitar and 25 other instruments; I had abandoned baritone in eighth-grade. Onstage Prince wore underwear closely resembling black panties; I sported tighty-whities. There was also the matter of his blatant sexuality: a minister from a nearby congregation conducted an album burning in his church parking lot and commenced the festivities by dousing a vinyl copy of Prince's *Dirty Mind* in lighter fluid. All of which seemed so very cool from a distance as great as ours from Prince.

But these differences became only minor inconveniences when Yvette cued up *Purple Rain* on her boom box, and we'd lie shoulder-to-shoulder on her basement floor and stare up at the ceiling and vibrate to the sheer palpitating intensity of Prince's voice when he broke into those screams at the end of "The Beautiful Ones" and demanded his lover make a decision: *Do you want him? Or do you want me? Cuz I want you.* That kind of bare expression would set our bodies on edge, triggering the release of pheromones or some kind of illicit chemical reaction in our bloodstreams, and we'd curl into each other and be reborn as Prince and Apollonia. The world seemed so small and intimate in those moments, as though all meaning were distilled in the timbre of Prince's voice. We'd been transported to Uptown.

One night, we were listening to *1999* while news of a tornado warning spread across Atlanta's metro area. Outside, the alarms sounded in the distance. The wind was gathering in great gusts of fury and the shrubs in the yard were bending under the force and the whole house seemed to be shaking on its foundations. I should've headed home an hour ago, when the first reports of bad weather had come through the radio; but now it was too late to risk the roads and all we could do was sit tight and wait it out and hope the house stayed on the ground. So we just settled in and began grooving on that opening title track, and Prince was telling us *Everybody's got a bomb / We could all die any day.* Then he was segueing into the chorus—*They say 2000 zero zero party's over, oops out of time / So tonight I'm gonna party like it's 1999.* Of course it was still the '80s, and all this chatter about a purple Armageddon amounted to some sketchy forecasting of the future—but the weather outside was indeed ominous, and we were two suburban kids, seventeen years old and absolutely certain that Prince possessed the gift of prophecy.

We believed him.

APPARENTLY MY FATHER WAS sensing the inevitable. One night, while we watched a Braves game, Dad casually initiated a conversation. Sometime during the middle innings, he said, "You and that girl have been spending a lot of time together." He kept his eyes glued to the TV screen. As though he were just talking out loud to himself.

Throughout my adolescence, there had been no birds 'n bees talk in our house, no rote summary of the biology, and something in Dad's tone made it clear that this conversation would be as close as we would ever come to one. To this point, females had merited no discourse whatsoever between us. Dad was aware, I'm sure, that my voice had deepened some time ago and my body changed, and therefore girls were high on my list of priorities. But sixty-hour workweeks at the Post Office probably had become a blessing of sorts for him, a forgivable ignorance. A convenient excuse for not having to delve too deeply into his son's messy emotional life.

"What's her name again?" he asked.

"Yvette."

We both stared at the screen. We worked hard to convince ourselves what was going down here. We were not having a conversation about females, much less about sex. We were watching a baseball game.

Then, after a long pause, a series of pitches and a couple of batters, came this: "You know a woman's body is a temple of the Holy Spirit, right?" he said.

I was vaguely aware that he was making a reference to scripture, and that he was invoking what my English teacher called a metaphor, though my blue-collared father wouldn't have known to call it that. This was no simile; he was saying a woman's body *is* a temple of the Holy Spirit. But I wasn't sure what he ultimately was getting at—whether he was telling me not to carry a scroll into the temple; or to make sure the scroll was clean if I did enter; or to be sure to wrap the scroll in a sacred cover. It was all a mystery.

I waited for further clarification.

None was forthcoming.

But by this time, thankfully, the question had been sitting there long enough for both of us to reasonably think we could forget it had been asked in the first place. Just in case, though, I let it linger a little longer. I pretended to watch the action until eventually, that's again all we were doing—watching a baseball game.

The next pitch was a slider, low and inside. But with his next offering, a 2-2 pitch, the southpaw tried to sneak a fastball by Dale Murphy, who lined it into left field for a solid base hit.

"Murph could be a decent ballplayer," Dad said, "if he didn't strike out so much."

ONE DAY, WHILE WE WERE alone at her house, Yvette acquainted me with her mother's bedroom. I'd never seen it. It was not unusual in our circle of friends for a parents' bedroom to be sealed off, sacrosanct and inviolable, from our mud-tracked wanderings through each other's houses; and we rarely tested these parameters anyway because our parents' mundane lives never piqued our curiosity. Their bedrooms contained nothing we cared to see. The less we knew, the better. But admittedly there was an allure about her mom's bedroom.

Yvette offered no explanation for why she should introduce it to me now, only a few minutes before her mother was scheduled to arrive home from work. But as she turned the knob and pushed open those French doors, I had clear expectations of what I would encounter.

A den of iniquity.

I'd surely be witnessing all the bells and whistles associated with adult pleasure. A bed, heart-shaped, the sheets in a tangle, sweat-stained and reeking of after-sex. A mirror on the ceiling. A pile of unmarked VHS tapes stacked against the wall. Strobe lights, maybe. Or handcuffs shackled to the bedpost.

But the room surprised me. The sheets weren't silk and crimson; they were coarse—and a neutral beige. Shoes were lined up in orderly pairs under the bed. An alarm clock sat atop a stack of books about World War II on the nightstand. A treadmill, of all things, filled a corner. Minus a Bible, a Sunday school quarterly, and a copy of *Guidepost* magazine on the nightstand, this space looked remarkably similar to my parents' boudoir.

But then Yvette slid open the drawer to her mom's vanity. "Check this out," she whispered. There was an unmistakable impropriety in her voice. I sidled up next to her and peered into the drawer. "Look," she said.

Inside, I detected a spectrum of bright colors—glowing pink, lustrous yellow, sparkling red, pulsing blue, and a metallic, shimmering silver. Then shapes—contoured ovals and long, cylindrical columns.

Initially I had no idea what I was looking at. But then, upon closer investigation, I arrived at a slow but certain conclusion: these objects constituted a rather comprehensive assortment of adult toys.

With my arms crossing my chest, I did my best to act unsurprised, as though viewing her mom's treasure trove of stimulates were simply due course. But truth was, I was shocked. If questioned I would have been hard pressed to identify half the drawer's contents. Yvette stood aside as though giving me space to dig through the drawer with both hands and satisfy every curiosity. But I could only stare, transfixed, stunned silent by all the vibrant colors. I scanned the objects until my eyes lit on an unopened package bearing this titillating inscription: *If she's a moaner, she'll be a screamer...and if she's a screamer, you'll get arrested!*

"I just wanted you to see it," Yvette said. "What do you think?"

When I responded only with what must have been a blank expression, and stood mesmerized by the presence of so many colors and shapes, Yvette reached her hand into the drawer and withdrew a device small enough to hide inside her palm. Like a magician only beginning to showcase the depths of her trickery, she held this little feat of erotic ingenuity near my face, triggered an invisible switch, and proceeded to fill my ear with a tiny, illicit *buzzzzz*.

DURING THIS EPOCH OF MY LIFE, I spent all of my time at school, Yvette's, or the Baskin-Robbins where I worked.

Among my scooping colleagues, a kid named Destry was what our manager called a "provisional employee." Destry was fifteen. His mother drove him to work. Desperate for employees, the manager had hired Destry on a trial basis. If he successfully proved himself he would be hired at full minimum wage: $3.35 per hour. But if the manager had actually paid any attention to Destry, he would have known that his newest worker should be terminated—immediately. Destry's uniform, including his 31 visor, constantly reeked of weed. Anytime a Van Halen song came on the radio—and let's remind ourselves, it's the mid-eighties, so when a Prince song isn't on the radio, a Van Halen song most certainly is—Destry amped up the volume and refused to help the next impatient customer until he'd finished ripping through Eddie Van Halen's solo on his air guitar. Under his breath he frequently mumbled crude and offensive comments about customers, especially old people, whom he universally referred to as "Q-tips." He flirted shamelessly with college coeds who dropped in for low fat yogurt, savoring the skin-to-skin contact when he handed them their change, gaping slack-jawed at their backsides as they exited the store. To summarize: Destry lived with the sincere conviction that at every waking moment he was one second away from getting laid.

Which is exactly what he would have you believe. Destry regularly entertained us with tales of his bawdy escapades. He was dead-set on cataloguing his conquests for us, documenting every in and out of his illustrious career as a lover. If dismal weather outside meant no customers inside, we'd sit around the tubs of Mint Chocolate Chip and listen to Destry weave salacious fantasies. According to Destry, his mom, who was single and worked nights, would push a ten into his hand and tell him to order a pizza as she headed out the door for an eight-hour shift. Immediately he'd be on the phone, importing a veritable harem of heavy metal chicks into his room. He'd recount for us how, under the watchful gaze of Ozzy Osbourne peering down from the poster above his bed, these girls would fulfill their sole desire in life: to sate Destry's insatiable sexual appetite.

It was all cock and jive, of course. Or most of it anyway. The challenge was figuring out which was which—until finally you gave up and willingly suspended your disbelief. We didn't care. Destry made time go faster, God bless him. On a slow night, we'd shake our heads at the realization that we'd just killed a solid hour sitting around listening to Destry make himself out to be a Headbanging Hero at the peak of his carnal powers.

Destry seemed to relish Yvette's visits to the store. He did not attempt to hide his lust. "Damn," he'd say when he saw her crossing the parking lot toward the store. "Lookit that shit." Once she was inside, he'd intercept her, offering a free scoop of Rainbow Sherbet, her favorite, and noting how good her hair looked. With subtle grace, Yvette became practiced at rejecting his overtures, and somehow I took his comments more as a compliment than an affront.

But one slow afternoon, after ogling her departure, Destry turned toward me with that sly and wicked grin and asked, "How does she like it, bro?"

I proceeded to start wiping down the counter, even though it was already clean. Which of course broke the tacit code between boys that all sexual activity was subject to public discourse. I was keenly aware I was violating an agreement, endorsed and longstanding.

Destry eyes grew wide and incredulous. "You mean to tell me you ain't *hitting* that?"

"I didn't say that," I told him. "I didn't say anything."

"You ain't getting any," he declared.

"You don't know what I'm getting."

"Else you'd be telling *everybody*," he said.

"I wouldn't be telling you," I offered.

He shook his head mournfully. "Man, if you ain't getting that poontang, you must be homo."

"I'm not homo."

"Serious queer bait." He tsked his tongue. "What a waste."

"Screw you."

I started drifting away, toward the supply room in the back—anywhere to get some distance. But Destry trailed me, his voice actually veering toward sympathy. There was, dare I say, compassion in his tone. Something that, to my evangelical ears, sounded curiously like *grace*. "Just get you some, bro," he said. "Ain't no reason to be scared of it." He was patting me on the shoulder now. "Do it," he advised. "And if you like it, do it again."

I understood the dangers of giving ear to such an imposter, a boy who had gotten so lost in the maze of his own imagination that even he wasn't sure when a Motley Crue song ended and his real life began. But almost immediately I was ducking inside the walk-in freezer in the supply room to contemplate Destry's statement. The frigid air blasting from the fan served to clear my head, heighten my senses. Surrounded by a hundred tubs of ice cream, I repeated Destry's advice, trying it out on my tongue—*Do it*, I told myself, *and if you like it, do it again*—the visible clouds of frost giving the words concreteness. Saying the words aloud, seeing them form into puffy shapes, made them tangible. Made them real. In their unadorned simplicity, they struck me as the most profound sexual advice I'd ever received.

When I exited the freezer, I had more than a new life philosophy.

I had a plan.

ABOUT THE IMPLEMENTATION of that plan I remember very little. The logistics seemed to involve one of the fiancée's weekend gigs at an Italian restaurant—where he and two other fortysomething men with receding hairlines formed a cocktail jazz trio that sounded like elevator music in a retirement home. The restaurant was in Rome, a hundred miles away. Yvette and I begged off the assignment, lamenting homework, tests, etcetera. *Those teachers are real slave drivers!* we complained with straight faces. I didn't possess the kind of transcript that would make these excuses ring with any authenticity, but Yvette was in fact a stellar student, and sounded convincing when she offered her account of the intellectual evening that lay before us.

After the fiancée's four-door hatchback disappeared from view, we probably spent some time watching television, scrolling through the channels, checking out the latest videos on MTV, assuring ourselves that they hadn't forgotten something and really had vacated the premises for the entire evening. We probably availed ourselves of whatever was in the fridge or the cupboards. We might even have indulged in one last review session by watching a scene or two of *Purple Rain* in search of final reminders.

But at some point we climbed the stairs. There was ceremony, sure—too much of it, in fact. We knew our roles. The spastic, incompetent groping of teenagers was what should have been going on here, but we were *thinking* too much for that. If the sexperts on *Phil Donahue* were right when they claimed sex is as much mental as physical, then we were performing quantum physics here. In our attempt at making it *special*, we began kissing as though obeying meticulous stage directions. There was something very *Days of Our Lives* about removing our clothes. Yvette shut the blinds and slid a cassette into her boom box. She cued up "When Doves Cry." The song, I knew, was five minutes and fifty-two seconds. I hoped I would last that long.

Nothing particularly remarkable happened. There were the requisite whispers that we'd waited so long for this moment. The mechanics to figure out, too, the real life application of the details. All the particulars I still vaguely recollected from eighth grade Sex Ed. But we managed. Biology did its part.

I recall the smell of shampoo in Yvette's hair. Her hands on my back. Maybe the play of shadows on those lavender walls.

The rest seems to have been lost in the fog of memory.

Except this: I do know that what happened in that three-bed-room contemporary on that spring night in the '80s in no way resembled what we'd overheard from Yvette's mom and the fiancée. Or what we'd seen Prince and Apollonia do on the Midwestern prairie.

But it wouldn't be until after I kissed Yvette goodnight and drove home that I started to see the significance of this turn of events. By the time I nudged open the front door of our brown brick on King Arthur Drive and killed the porch light Mom had kept glowing for me, already I was thinking of tonight as a kind of mystical encounter. Inside, the house was silent. Mom and Dad had gone to bed. The fact I was the only one awake in the house, and maybe in the entire world, felt like it mattered. I crept through the kitchen and went into the bathroom and sidled up to the mirror, where I stared at my reflection. I expected to find a stranger there, a new being awaiting proper introduction. I searched my features for signs that I looked different; that somehow people might be able to simply glimpse me and recognize my journey into foreign lands.

But the kid in that mirror looked much the same as he had last time he viewed himself. He seemed, between then and now, to have found no secret knowledge. In a few short months he'd be heading to college—to a school that admitted anyone with a pulse and a high school diploma—and by all appearances he'd be just another kid from suburbia despite what happened tonight. But he was seventeen, and subject to all manner of reinvention from moment to moment, and he was accustomed to assuming a new swagger and pose. So he threw back his shoulders and set his jaw, and waited.

Tomorrow was Sunday, a new day and a new Sabbath, which seemed for all the world right and true. This Baptist boy could vouch for the gospel in his father's words. After all, he had now been inside the temple. He'd felt the Holy Spirit.

BENEDICTION

By the time Dad took sick, I hadn't been inside his church in more than a decade. I was thirtysomething now—with a wife, a mortgage, and a gig teaching in a venerable Atlanta private school—and I'd become what Mom always feared I'd turn into: a Christmas and Easter Christian. One who felt obligated to show up to celebrate Jesus' birth and resurrection, but otherwise didn't darken the church's doors. One who met the news of Dad's illness with a grim certainty: soon he was going to die.

But because my father was a Southern Baptist deacon, my mother a Sunday school teacher, they insisted things could change—God could decide to heal Dad. On Pat Robertson's *The 700 Club*, they'd heard all manner of stories of divine intervention, and of course the Bible was full of bigger miracles than restoring a man's health. "It's in God's hands," they kept telling me. "He's bigger than cancer." Mom was busy enlisting the help of not only their immediate congregation, but also contacting the prayer hotlines at other churches. A whole army of what she called 'prayer warriors' was now tugging on God's ear round the clock. And she told me, too, to do my part. Which I did, often and earnestly, summoning all the faith that, as a boy, had convinced me I could get God's attention.

But I wasn't sure my prayers would take too well. I was still calling myself Christian, but I understood that most of the good church folk who knew me as a boy would label me a backslider at best, or at worst count me among the Lost. Maybe they'd think my prayers did more harm than good.

So I prayed, all right, but in addition to appealing for miracles, my wife Bernadette and I also developed a back-up plan: we decided to have a baby.

Our decision was impulsive and instinctual. A procreative rebellion against death. Dad did not have any grandchildren, and I wanted him to hold his before he died. Casting wishes into the cosmos aside, it seemed like the one good thing I could do for my father.

I suppose our decision to start a family set up a race between our baby and Dad's cancer—to see whether our daughter arrived into this world before Dad departed for the next one.

Unless, of course, all our prayers were answered.

BUT EVENTUALLY WE BEGAN to doubt whether Dad would survive to see his granddaughter. He fell into a precipitous decline, and Bernadette was just starting her third trimester. The cancer had begun in his prostate, which might have allowed him to contain it, but because he was still a hayseed country boy at heart, distrustful of know-it-all doctors and full of stubborn pride, he'd neglected annual check ups and found out too late.

At first Dad hadn't seemed concerned overmuch about the diagnosis. The word didn't strike him so much as a death sentence as it did a curiosity that he couldn't wrap his head around.

In his seventies, he somehow still regarded himself as immortal. The few maladies he'd suffered had only convinced him of his own invulnerability. Once, he tore his retina but quickly rushed back to work at the Post Office against doctor's orders with a patch over his eye. Another time he came down with shingles, which laid him out for two weeks and prompted him to confess he'd never felt so bad in his life, but soon enough he was again striding Peachtree with his mail sack on his shoulder, days before the MDs gave him the okay. Otherwise, he never so much as complained of a headache. As he began piling up a record-setting number of hours of sick leave, the Post Office featured him in a story in their monthly newsletter, wherein they misspelled his surname as Beavers with the plural S and quoted him with this curious anecdote: "One day I came in, and I was feeling bad. I asked the supervisor about getting off. But he asked if I could stay and help out, so I stayed. Later, I felt much better." By the time Dad hand-delivered a retirement note to what he called his "customers" on his mail route, declining gifts but alerting them he was "riding off into the sunset" at age seventy-one, he had accrued over 4,200 hours of unused sick leave.

But now the cancer had spread to his lymph nodes and was feasting on his vital organs. He endured the standard regimens, but every time the urologists gave him news their voices sounded solemn and apologetic. As he underwent steroid treatment, Dad ballooned—as though his belly button was a valve cork and his doctors were inflating him with a needle and pump. His voice, always sonorous and laced with testosterone, increased an octave. He grew unable to complete routine tasks. He couldn't drive, he couldn't change the filter in the furnace, he couldn't fry an egg.

One evening when I was visiting, he asked me, with a look of utter shame, to clip his toenails. It was tough going, those nails. Thick as leather, cracked and yellowed by all those years carrying his mail sack through Atlanta's streets, they stubbornly resisted the clippers—to which I responded by cutting too deeply into the quick, causing Dad to cinch with pain.

It was early March; our daughter wasn't due until late May. We had chosen to call her *Chloe*, but kept the name to ourselves because, in the way of new parents, we wanted to announce it at the birth and speak her into existence. So one night over the phone I told Dad our daughter's name. I explained that it meant new spring life, or, simply, green. I started to tell him it was also Toni Morrison's first name—one of my idols—but he had never heard of Toni Morrison. "That's a good name," he said. "I like it." He promised to keep it a secret.

Neither of us said as much, but we understood: he was making a gentleman's agreement to take it to his grave.

ONE AFTERNOON DAD CALLED and asked if, well, you know, if you don't have too much going on right now—you think maybe you could come over and give the lawn a good cut? The grass was starting to green. By this time of year, Dad usually had scalped it once already, but now he was too weak with chemo and radiation treatments to do it himself. Of course, Dad. Glad to oblige. Listen: When your father is dying and you can do nothing to stop it, you gratefully welcome any assignment that might offer even the slightest assistance. So I climbed into my car and drove the forty-five minutes, north to west, from one point in Atlanta's suburbia to another. Mom met me at the door with an assortment of keys, surely one of which fit the lawn mower's ignition.

But there was this problem: When I climbed onto the seat of Dad's mower and turned the key and stepped on the clutch, the engine clicked a few times but otherwise gave no sign of sparking to life. A ratty, decrepit, and utterly fagged out piece of machinery that Dad no doubt had already resuscitated a dozen times over, the mower had been sitting under a tarp all winter and apparently needed to be jumped off. I climbed down and raised the hood and peered inside. Which led to a bigger dilemma: I couldn't locate the battery. In an increasingly futile search I explored every nook and cranny of the inner workings, but you already know the outcome: I found nothing. Incidents like this one had always humiliated me, because they exposed my failure to master a specific version of masculinity—the main version Dad had raised me to master. I was not presumed to milk the cows and shuck the corn and till the red Georgia clay he had plowed in his youth—but I was expected to accumulate a narrow but vital body of knowledge that in fact defined manhood in suburbia. Surely jumping off a battery—and locating said battery, if necessary—was included in this checklist.

I headed inside the house, where Dad had been spending his days confined to the den of his brick ranch, watching the TV evangelists, reading his Bible, and contemplating the afterlife. He was sitting in his recliner with a shawl draped over his knees. "The mower won't start," I told him. I emptied my voice of all inflection, as though I were merely reporting something over which I had no control, like the weather. "I need to jump it. I've got a set of cables in my trunk, but I can't find the battery."

Dad asked me if I was sure the battery wasn't in a likely place. Somewhere, say, near the engine. "I oughta be able to tell you right off where to look," he said, "but all this medicine is muddling my brain."

To which I declared I had located the engine, okay—that was the easy part—but there was no battery anywhere in the vicinity.

"It's got a battery," Dad said. "Rest assured, them jades at the factory put one on it. Won't go anywhere without a battery."

"I'm not saying it doesn't have a battery. All I'm telling you is I can't find it."

So within a few minutes, I found myself pushing my father's wheelchair into the driveway. As his chair clattered over the uneven cement, Dad's knees fell against each other and his hands sat limply in his lap like a pair of wet mittens. It was an unseasonably warm day for March, but he was dressed for blustery weather—baseball cap, plaid hunting jacket, blue sweat pants, white socks ratcheted up to his knees to stimulate circulation, and house slippers. I nudged Dad close to the lawnmower, then stood back with my arms crossed over my chest to watch him try to locate the elusive battery. He proceeded to survey the machine for about ten seconds. "Raise up that seat," he told me.

Unaware that the seat was in any way mobile, I did as Dad instructed. With a sinking feeling, I lifted it from its horizontal position to a vertical one. There, clearly obvious to anyone with eyes, rested the battery.

"Well, how bout that?" Dad said. "You been sitting on it the whole time."

THEN ONE EVENING IN APRIL, as Bernadette was finishing up her eighth month, Mom called me. "Your daddy's taken to his bed," she said. He was slipping in and out of consciousness, retreating into that tight, insular shell from where the dying shut off this world, buried layers deep. When he communicated at all, he spoke only in monosyllabic responses. He rarely opened his eyes.

A couple days later, on a Saturday morning otherwise splashed with sunshine and possibility, my wife and I made the drive to my father's house. The plan was for me to spend some time with Dad while Bernadette ventured into Atlanta to check on a hospice site, because the doctors now had stopped treatment and decided the important thing now was to keep Dad comfortable. I found Mom in the kitchen, her eyes red-rimmed and bleary, making a cup of coffee and a bowl of instant grits. She asked me to check on him.

Dad was in my old bedroom. When I passed through the door, I saw that the lights were dimmed, the shades drawn. What Mom called his 'death rattle' filled the space. All that saliva clotting up his throat and then a blast of air as he exhaled. Every breath seemed likely as not to be his last.

I took Dad by the hand. When I told him who I was, he said "Yeah," then returned to the death rattle. I told him it was a beautiful day outside, that the dogwoods were blooming, and again he said, "Yeah." Then we sat in silence for a long while. Twice Mom came in to check on him, but after a full night spent at his bedside, she needed to eat her breakfast and maybe steal a few minutes of rest. So it was mostly the two of us, a father and son, his labored breathing the only sound in the room.

Until, completely unexpectedly, Dad began trying to communicate.

He was saying, "For we know in part, and prophesy in part. For we know in part, and prophesy in part…." He was repeating it over and over, as though he had to get a running start on the idea in order to push it all the way through. But he couldn't get enough momentum. His body was too tired, his tongue too sluggish.

Almost immediately I recognized his words as scripture. I remembered them because they had been seared so deeply into my consciousness at some point in my life that now they were encoded there. They came from the thirteenth chapter of First Corinthians—the 'Love Chapter'—the chapter that gets quoted at practically every Christian wedding ceremony.

As Dad kept reciting the opening of the verse, words came to me that had not crossed my mind—much less my tongue—in many years. They'd been lying dormant, but I had the sensation that something deep inside me was being unearthed. Something that had gotten so lost I'd forgotten to even look for it suddenly showed up shiny and new. When he started up again, saying, "For we know in part, and prophesy in part…" I added the rest—"But when what is perfect comes, what is partial disappears." I said the verse aloud, from start to finish. *For we know in part, and prophesy in part. But when what is perfect comes, what is partial disappears.* Dad nodded his chin. "Uh-huh," he said. "Yeah." He began again, and I picked up where he left off. A kind of deathbed call and response.

I understood what Dad was trying to tell me. There was no doubt. He knew death was upon him—and he believed he was about to get a glimpse of perfection. He was convinced he was about to see his mama again, buddies he'd lost in Korea, church members who'd gone on into eternity before him. He was about to see God's face.

He was about to leave behind everything else. Everything *partial*. He would leave behind this disease eating away at his organs. All the mistakes he'd made, too, the things he'd wished he'd done better, the choices he regretted. All the work, the thousands of letters he'd delivered as a postman, the junk mail that had sifted through his fingers, the millions of steps he'd taken on his route, the Hotlanta heat and the sweat and his wishes for the first cool breeze of autumn to finally arrive. He was also about to leave behind his wife and two sons. We were *partial* too. We had to be. We would be staying here.

I was still the only one with him when, maybe an hour later, the moment came when Dad set his jaw and pursed his lips; he shut his eyes even more tightly. He took on what I've ever since thought of as a *rollercoaster face*, as though he were topping a hill and sliding at breakneck speed down a long, dipping track before hitting a ramp and sailing through a sky filled with constellations and finally bursting through whatever veil separates Heaven from us sad mortals.

His doctors called it heart failure. The muscle, now still, literally pressed against his chest. You could see its outline through his V-neck Hanes t-shirt.

OVER THE NEXT WEEK, I trudged around in the same daze every son experiences when his father dies. I wondered how the world seemed to be moving along as always—people idling in gridlock traffic, ordering grilled chicken salads on sidewalk patios, going to Braves games. One day during that dark time I rolled up beside a car at a stoplight, an onyx-colored Cadillac with rims shining like cut diamonds, the stereo system shaking the doors of my vehicle, the guy behind the wheel bobbing his chin in time with the boom. And I remember marveling at the distance between his headspace and mine and wondering aloud, *Man, don't you understand what's happened here?*

I helped make the funeral arrangements and select a headstone for the grave. I wrote a eulogy. I gave it. At the funeral, I stood in the pulpit of my father's church, and told the people what kind of guy he was, filling their heads with clichés. I said he was a servant to others; he had a compassionate heart, especially toward the poor; he never left a task unfinished. At one point I had to pause and regain my composure when I looked out over the congregation and saw that a handful of his fellow postmen had fulfilled one of his dying wishes by showing up at his funeral in their uniforms with the eagle patch on the powder blue shoulder and the navy stripe running down the leg.

When I returned to work, I told my students what I'd experienced in the past week since I'd seen them. I recounted the story, trying to make sense of it as I went along. I made them uncomfortable, no doubt, made them wish we'd talk about the literature they'd read last night, Gatsby's pursuit of his green light, because they were teenagers, and confused about how to respond in the presence of loss. They wanted irony; they wanted clever banter—but all they got from me was blatant emotion that made them squirm in their desks. They were sixteen. Most of them hadn't lost anything of value yet. Nothing that couldn't be replaced. They believed they would live forever. But they kept silent and respectful. They avoided eye contact and fidgeted, but they listened.

To try to shake off my stupor, I drove with Bernadette to a friend's wedding in the mountains of North Carolina. There would be a grand reception, with music and dancing against a backdrop of the Appalachians. On the ride up, rounding yet another in a long series of switchbacks, we came across a home-made sign on the side of the road. Already we'd seen a dozen of these signs, nailed to trees or fence posts, exhorting passersby to *Repent!* or directing them to John 3:16. Sometimes driving the back roads of the South feels like a one-way journey down the Sawdust Trail toward some grand tent revival meeting yonder ahead where all paths converge at a moment of reckoning.

But this particular sign resonated with me in a way they usually do not. For a reason I couldn't name, I pulled over to the shoulder of the road and used my disposable camera to snap a photo. Some devout soul had risked life and limb to scale the steep embankment of the craggy mountainside with a paint-brush in tow and perch himself precariously high above the roadway. In rudimentary letters, this DIY billboarder slapped his paintbrush against a barren patch of stone and scrawled the words that made it clear that tonight's brief respite at a moun-tain wedding wouldn't bring escape from the one question that trumps all others: *R U Saved or Lost?*

It was a question that, like every other in the evangelical cul-ture I was raised in, had a right and wrong answer. A question that reminded you that time is of the essence; a clock was tick-ing and soon—no one knew the hour, but *soon*—the clock and your heart would stop and you'd enter a dimension where there is no time.

All the time in the world would be but one second in eternity.

A COUPLE OF WEEKS after Dad's funeral, I drove to my mother's house to see how she was faring. It was afternoon but as always the boxy interior of the brick ranch was dark, the curtains drawn and pinned to the walls with thumbtacks. It felt as though my father was merely away, outside, maybe tinkering on yet another deadbeat car or pruning the azaleas. I almost expected him to show up in the kitchen, his familiar musty smell of sweat suffusing the house, his jeans flecked with grass clippings or his forearms smeared with axel grease.

Mom was obsessing over whether to upgrade the security system and worrying about an anonymous phone call she had twice received where the caller only held the phone without saying a word. Would the roof last? Would the kudzu snaking over the back fence overtake the yard? And the silence—it was always so quiet in the house. No noise unless she made it. Already she was telling me how a widow's life is a lonely life. "Nobody knows what it's like till they've been through it," she said. "You can't tell them. They have to live it. It's no kind of life, I'm here to tell you."

She said she'd been praying for strength. She told me God never requires us to carry more than we can bear. Life didn't make sense to her right now, she said, but the Lord would reveal his plan for her in time, and it would be for the very best. "All I know is I can't wait to see your daddy again. And I will, by and by."

While we picked over a fried chicken from the grocery deli, we reminisced about the burial. Military honor guards had fired a salute, the shots causing every one of us at graveside to startle, and afterward one of the veterans folded an American flag into a triangle and placed it in Mom's lap. We wondered aloud how long it would take for the grass seeds to sprout atop Dad's grave. He needed six feet of sod. He was a vain man and would not suffer his grave to be barren for too long.

After a while, Mom's sister called. As Mom caught Elaine up on the day's events, the highlight of which seemed to be my visit, I wandered into the den. There, I saw the two deer heads my father had hung on the wood-paneled wall many years ago. Two bucks, ten points and six. Throughout his life, every Opening Day in October had found Dad venturing into the woods at dawn with a thermos of coffee, a tin of Vienna sausages, a pocket-sized New Testament, and his 30.06 in the crook of his arm. Come nightfall, he rode home with a fire and brimstone preacher on the radio and, if he was lucky, a buck in his trunk. By a flashlight and a crescent moon overhead, he strung his prey upside down from my swing set in the backyard, slit it from balls to throat, and let gravity take over.

On two occasions Dad took his prey to the taxidermist, a guy named Russ Fite. Over the next few weeks, Russ Fite removed the natural skin and tanned it and fixed it to a model; he adjusted it, snug, so that it looked like it was ready to spring to life any moment now. And eventually my father fetched his trophy from Russ Fite's shop and brought it home and mounted it on the wall. There it hung throughout my boyhood, a reminder of what happened one fine autumn morning when a low mist was roiling over the ground and a majestic buck stepped into the clearing. He preserved that moment—a prize, sure, but even more so, a memory. In the future, even after Dad was buried in the foothills of the north Georgia mountains where he was raised, I would be able to visit Mom in the house I grew up in and look into the eyes of those deer, those unblinking marbles set deep in their sockets, and see a man's attempt to hold time still.

As I grew older, I held all manner of ambivalence about hunting. The violence, the bloodlust, the cold heart required—all payment for a photo of yourself with Dad's bloody handprints on your face and your hair mussed with gore. But somewhere along the line I would come to see taxidermy for what it is: an art. The taxidermist sculpts, he draws, he paints. His work requires skills of carpentry, woodworking, tanning, molding, and casting—but also imagination. For a deer head, the taxidermist uses only the antlers and the skin; the rest of the mount is entirely man-made. The eyes are glass; the eyelids clay; the nose and mouth wax; the mannequin polyurethane foam. He takes what he has to work with and applies the skills of his trade to bring something dead to the verge of life. He revives a memory. He takes what was once breathing, and animates it again. He achieves a feat we Bible Belters have always wanted to believe in: resurrection.

I possess none of the taxidermist's particular skill set. But I've got a few tools of my own—and plenty of imagination, too. I suppose it was then, gazing into the eyes of those deer, I decided to write some of this down.

THEN, AS NIGHT FELL and I was moving toward the door, Mom told me she had something to give me. "Your daddy wanted you to have it," she said. She disappeared into her bedroom for a moment and when she returned she was handing me a sealed envelope. "Go ahead," she told me. I tore it open and found a letter inside. I unfolded the sheet of college-ruled notebook paper to see that it was from my father. It was in Mom's handwriting and dated April 14, 2003; too ill to write, Dad had dictated it from his deathbed five days before he passed.

It was a letter to Chloe—but true to his promise, Dad did not address her by name.

I am sitting here thinking of a new grandchild and what you will mean to our family as you enter this world to bless us, he began. *We don't know how much longer we have to ponder this question but we*

look forward to the very exciting time of your birth. He told her
he was happy to hear reports that she was healthy. He said he
looked forward to her bringing joy to our lives. Then he included
a couple more brief salutations before closing this mailman's
final letter with a handful of words that summarized the gift
he'd offered to me, and was now offering to this granddaughter
he'd never meet in this lifetime. He ended the letter this way:

*We pray when Jesus Christ speaks personally to your heart you
will make him your Savior and Lord as he has mine.*

  Much love,
  Your Grandpa

THIRTY-TWO DAYS AFTER Dad's death, our daughter was
born. Five pounds and thirteen and a half ounces of life. As
planned, we said her name at her birth and told ourselves the
story that Dad met Chloe before any of the rest of us did—in
passing as she departed Heaven soon after he entered it.

Of course I wished Dad had been here to join us in welcoming his granddaughter to the world. We said, again and
again, that he was watching all of it from Heaven, and we tried
very hard to believe it was true. And when my wife handed our
daughter to me to hold for the first time, I had a hard time
imagining a life any better than this one. All the ruckus and
clamor of the birth had been quieted, the bright lights lowered
to shadows. I had scripted a whole list of things I planned to tell
Chloe when I first held her. I wanted to whisper into her ear and
tell her I'd always known, even when I was just a boy, that she'd
be a girl. I wanted to tell her to use some of her sick leave to go
see the doctor, even if she wasn't feeling ill; to pay attention to
the roadside signs; to look under the seat on the lawnmower to
find the battery. I wanted to tell her that, already, she was living
up to her name.

SUBURBAN GOSPEL

But I'd been raised an evangelical boy, and I knew all about holy experiences and how to recognize them. So when I took my girl into my hands for the first time and cupped her head with my palm, all I could say, over and over under my breath, was *Jesus, Jesus, Jesus...*

ACKNOWLEDGMENTS

Thanks to the fine folks at the following journals and magazines where chapters first appeared in different form: Jameelah Lang and Meggie Monahan at *Gulf Coast*; Claudia Sternbach, Larry Connolly, and Madison Brewer at *Memoir*; Elizabeth Winston at *Tampa Review*; Terry Kennedy at *storySouth*; Jamaica Ritcher at *Fugue*; Susan Fitch at *Southeast Review*; Elisa Cahn at *Third Coast*; Jodee Stanley and Audrey Petty at *Ninth Letter*; H.K. Hummel at *Blood Orange Review*; and Bret Lott at *Crazyhorse*.

Thanks to Betsy Teter, Meg Reid, and all at Hub City; to Michael Parker; to the EDs—Julia Franks, Jonathan Newman, and Bennett Spann; to all at the Lovett School, colleagues and students alike; to my man Bill Bissell; to my big brother David Beaver; and to my mother Fay Beaver.

Thanks to my daughters, Chloe and Leila: You are my heart.

And to Bernadette: *I don't want to bore you with it, Oh, but I love you, I love you, I love you…*

HUB CITY PRESS

HUB CITY PRESS is a non-profit independent press in Spartanburg, SC, that publishes well-crafted, high-quality works by new and established authors, with an emphasis on the Southern experience. We are committed to high-caliber novels, short stories, poetry, plays, memoir, and works emphasizing regional culture and history. We are particularly interested in books with a strong sense of place.

Hub City Press is an imprint of the non-profit Hub City Writers Project, founded in 1995 to foster a sense of community through the literary arts. Our metaphor of organization purposely looks backward to the nineteenth century when Spartanburg was known as the "hub city," a place where railroads converged and departed.

RECENT HUB CITY PRESS TITLES

Minnow • James E. McTeer II

Pasture Art • Marlin Barton

Punch. • Ray McManus

The Whiskey Baron • Jon Sealy

The Only Sounds We Make • Lee Zacharias

In the Garden of Stone • Susan Tekulve

The Iguana Tree • Michel Stone

Patron Saint of Dreams • Philip Gerard

Adobe Caslon Pro 11.54/14.7